# THE UNDERGROUND BASEBALL ENCYCLOPEDIA

# THE UNDERGROUND BASEBALL

# ENCYCLOPEDIA

Baseball Stuff You Never Needed to Know
and Can Certainly Live Without

ROBERT SCHNAKENBERG

TRIUMPH
BOOKS

Library of Congress Cataloging-in-Publication Data

Schnakenberg, Robert.
    The underground baseball encyclopedia : baseball stuff you never
needed to know and can certainly live without / Robert Schnakenberg.
        p. cm.
    ISBN 978-1-60078-331-9
    1. Baseball—Miscellanea. I. Title.
    GV873.S33 2010
    796.357—dc22
                                        2009046108

This book is available in quantity at special discounts for your group or organization. For further information, contact:

**Triumph Books**
542 South Dearborn Street
Suite 750
Chicago, Illinois 60605
(312) 939–3330
Fax (312) 663–3557
www.triumphbooks.com

Printed in U.S.A.
ISBN: 978-1-60078-331-9
Design by Paul Petrowsky
Page production by Patricia Frey
Title page photo courtesy of AP Images
Cover design by Paul Petrowsky; cover photos courtesy of Getty Images, AP Images, TOPPS, and Adam Motin.

# Introduction

Be forewarned: this book contains no entry for Babe Ruth. It contains no entry for Willie Mays. Or Cal Ripken Jr. There *is* an entry for Ty Cobb, but only to illustrate what an abominable cracker he was. And our coverage of Ted Williams is entirely limited to cryonic freezing and the purported severing and monkey-wrenching of Williams' head by overzealous "life extension foundation" employees.

In other words, this is not your grandfather's baseball encyclopedia. It's not even your father's. And it's certainly not Ken Burns', Bob Costas', or Bill James'. This is an attempt to create a baseball encyclopedia out of all the stuff that's typically not covered in other baseball encyclopedias. Many of those volumes are great sources of information and indispensable additions to any true fan's library, but this is the only book that spans the wide world of team mascots and ballpark vendors, ugly uniforms and uglier stadiums, hecklers and superfans, cult icons and infamous rogues, all to bring you the best of baseball-as-pop-cultural-artifact.

So although there's no Babe Ruth, there's plenty on the Baby Ruth candy bar, *The Babe Ruth Story* starring William Bendix, and more than you ever needed to know about Eddie Bennett, the hunchbacked weirdo the Yankees hired to pump Ruth full of bicarbonate of soda when he started farting too much. There's an entry on *Seinfeld*, the sitcom about nothing, and *Mr. Ed*, the sitcom about a talking horse on which Sandy Koufax once appeared. Oh, and Mr. Baseball, Bob Uecker (star of TV's *Mr. Belvedere*), gets a mention or two as well.

As you can see, we here at the Underground Baseball Research Lab work on the principle of free association. As a result, this book is far from comprehensive. No reference book can be. Every effort has been made to include entries on interesting people, events, and ephemera from all eras of baseball history and to ensure that all major league franchises are represented in some way. But due to limitations of space—and the author's own sense of what constitutes "interesting"—some hard choices had to be made. So if you find yourself wondering why the San Francisco Giants' Crazy Crab mascot from the 1980s gets more space than, say, Mark McGwire, remember the words of my favorite Beatle, George Harrison: "He just wrote it like that."

But enough of my yakkin'. Please to enjoy this decidedly unconventional survey of baseball's underground history.

**A note on cross-references:** items in bold are cross-references to other entries in this book.

## Ace

Leigh Mihlrad

Six-foot male "blue jay with attitude" who has been the official mascot of the Toronto Blue Jays since 2000. Ace and his avian gal pal **Diamond** replaced **BJ Birdy**, the original Blue Jay mascot, who had been with the club for 20 years before being unceremoniously grounded shortly before Christmas 1999.

## Adams, John

Brecksville, Ohio, data systems analyst and Cleveland Indians **superfan** who has urged on his beloved Tribe by rhythmically pounding on a large bass drum from his seat in the bleacher section at the team's home ballpark since 1973. According to published reports, Adams has attended more than 2,850 Indians games in that span, moving with the team from Municipal Stadium—also known as the **"Mistake by the Lake"**—to its present home in Progressive Field. A season-ticket holder, Adams began lugging his drum (christened **Big Chief Boom-Boom** by Indians announcer Herb Score) to home games after noticing the bleacher-style seating gave him precious little to pound on during rallies. He now receives two complimentary tickets from the club every season just to accommodate his drum. In 2006, the Indians honored Adams' contribution to their cause with a John Adams "BobbleArms" doll giveaway, in which fans were presented with a toy in Adams' likeness, complete with noisemaking bass drum.

Brad Simpson

# Adams, Margo

Mistress of Hall of Fame third baseman **Wade Boggs**, whose 1988 lawsuit against the mustachioed hit machine made national headlines. The comely California mortgage broker allegedly carried on a four-year-long extramarital affair with the then–Boston Red Sox superstar. According to revelations that emerged from the lawsuit and Adams' subsequent *Penthouse* interview, she also performed personal services for the famously superstitious All-Star, including washing his clothes and giving him financial advice. Adams reportedly turned on Boggs after she found out he was seeing other women. She contended she had sex with **Steve Garvey** to exact revenge and then sued Boggs for $12 million, citing emotional distress and breach of contract. Although the case was eventually settled out of court, Boggs was forced to admit the affair and go on a media apology tour designed to restore his good name.

# Alcor

Scottsdale, Arizona–based "life extension foundation" that serves as the final resting place for the frozen remains of Hall of Famer Ted Williams. According to published reports, the nonprofit facility houses the cryonically suspended corpses of around 60 people at any given time, each of whom paid more than $100,000 for the privilege. In 2003, *Sports Illustrated*

*Forgotten Heroes of the Game*

### Akili the Elephant

Pachyderm enlisted by the Oakland A's to throw out the first pitch with its trunk on Opening Day of the 1989 season. Unfortunately, Akili suffered from a severe case of **the Yips** and could only manage to dribble the ball at its own feet. An Oakland front office official was forced to complete the delivery on the elephant's behalf.

published an exposé on Alcor, including incendiary allegations from former Alcor executive Larry Johnson that holes were drilled into Teddy Ballgame's disembodied head and his DNA misplaced. Even more disturbing were the charges lodged in Johnson's 2009 tell-all *Frozen: My Journey Into the World of Cryonics, Deception and Death*, in which he revealed that Alcor employees routinely used empty tuna fish cans as makeshift pedestals for the severed

heads. At one point, Johnson claimed, "technicians" needed repeated swings of a monkey wrench to dislodge Williams' frosty noggin from the tuna can to which it had become stuck.

## All-Star Baseball

Tabletop baseball game that for more than 50 years was the principal competitor to the more complex—and distinctively branded—**Strat-O-Matic**. Designed by former major league outfielder Ethan Allen and manufactured by board game purveyor Cadaco-Ellis, All-Star Baseball first hit the market in 1941 and remained popular well into the 1990s, when **Rotisserie** and other forms of **fantasy baseball** brought the curtain down on the golden age of tabletop simulations. Game play was fairly rudimentary, even by tabletop standards. Players inserted stats-laden "player cards" for real current and past major leaguers into a circular spinner that spat out the results of each "at-bat" when spun. Tiny plastic pegs were then moved along the baseball diamond to represent each player's path around the bases. Players were not compensated for

the use of their names and statistics—at least not until the game came under the dominion of a Major League Players Association license in 1995. Not to be confused with the popular video game All-Star Baseball, the board game retains a sizable following among tabletop geeks. Old, annually issued editions of player card sets are especially prized by collectors.

## Alomar Spitting Incident

Unpleasant confrontation between All-Star second baseman Roberto Alomar and home-plate umpire John Hirschbeck that took place during a game between the Baltimore Orioles and the Toronto Blue Jays at the SkyDome in Toronto on September 27, 1996. Hirschbeck had just called Alomar out on a called third strike when the slick-fielding second sacker went ballistic, precipitating a nose-to-nose argument that climaxed with Alomar spitting in Hirschbeck's face. The incident made national headlines and severely damaged Alomar's reputation. After the game, Alomar charged that Hirschbeck had uttered a racial slur and that the umpire was still bitter over the 1993 death of his nine-year-old son due to a rare brain disease known as adrenoleukodystrophy (ALD). The next day, Hirschbeck attempted to confront Alomar in the Orioles clubhouse and had to be forcibly restrained by another umpire. Major League Baseball ended up suspending Alomar for the first five games of the 1997 season and fined him $50,000, payable to ALD research. The two men later traded apologies in a pregame ceremony, lending credence to the contention of lip readers that Hirschbeck had in fact maligned Alomar verbally—calling him either a "faggot" or a "fucking spic," depending on whose account you believe.

## Anderson, Greg

Bay Area personal trainer who is alleged to have supplied steroids and other **performance-enhancing drugs** to Major League Baseball players, including home-run king **Barry Bonds**, beginning in the late 1990s.

# Andy the Clown

Unofficial Chicago White Sox mascot who performed without authorization at the club's home games at Comiskey Park from 1960 to 1990, to the delight of fans and the consternation of team management. Outfitted like a traditional circus clown complete with white face paint, polka dot costume, bowler hat, and a light-up red nose, Andy the Clown was the alter ego of South Side resident Andrew Rozdilsky Jr., the scion of a family of Chicago morticians, who had been performing on the children's party circuit for more than 30 years when he first took his act to a White Sox game in 1960. His rallying cry of "Go youuuuuuuuuuuuuuuuuu White Sox!" quickly endeared him to the Comiskey faithful, who chafed when new owners Jerry Reinsdorf and Eddie Einhorn announced plans to evict Andy in 1981 as part of a campaign to "class up" the atmosphere at Sox games. (Although a regular fixture and season-ticket holder, Andy was never an employee of the White Sox organization and was permitted to appear in his clown suit entirely at the pleasure of club management.) Following a public uproar, the cheerleading Punchinello was allowed to remain, although he was ghettoized to a portion of the upper deck and barred from capering in the lower grandstand as had been his custom. Andy's replacements, costumed faux-Muppets **Ribbie and Roobarb**, proved wildly unpopular with fans and provoked an occasionally violent backlash. In the end, Andy would outlast them by two seasons. But when the White Sox moved into their new park in 1991, he too was forcibly "retired" by the team. Ostensibly robbed of his reason for living, Rozdilsky died of a heart attack four years later at age 77.

# Ankiel, Rick

Onetime St. Louis Cardinals pitching phenom who saw his career derailed by a sudden outbreak of **Steve Blass Disease**. After going 11–7 with a 3.50 ERA and 194 strikeouts in his rookie season in 2000, the hard-throwing left-hander inexplicably lost his shit in Game 1 of the National League Division Series, walking six Atlanta Braves and throwing five wild pitches in just $2^2/_3$ innings. His struggles continued in the NLCS against the Mets. Tapped to start Game 2, Ankiel recorded only two outs while walking three and uncorking two more wild pitches in another nationally televised meltdown of epic proportions. Even an off-season away from the mound could not cure Ankiel of his uncontrollable wildness; he returned the following season still incapable of throwing strikes consistently. After several more injury-plagued seasons spent mostly in the minors during which he was unable to isolate the source of his loss of control, Ankiel gave up pitching for the outfield. His slow crawl back to the big leagues culminated in August of 2007, when the Cardinals called him up from Triple A and started him in right field in a game against the San Diego Padres. Ankiel has been a marginally productive, if injury-prone, fourth outfielder for the club ever since.

# Arnie the Peanut Dude

Late, lamented Houston Astros **supervendor** who slung goobers at fans in the Astrodome, and later Minute Maid Park, for more than 15 years. Born Arnold Murphy, Arnie was known for his pinpoint accuracy and control, prompting one national publication to dub him "the Pedro Martinez of peanut

Linda Presson

vendors." He began hawking his nuts as a teenager in Cleveland's Municipal Stadium. In 1993, he offered his services to incoming Astros owner Drayton McClane, who was looking for a way to whip up excitement in the stands. It was

## *Forgotten Heroes of the Game*

### Elaine de Kooning

Who knew Snuffy Stirnweiss could inspire great art? A pioneering abstract expressionist, Elaine de Kooning spent three years in the early 1950s traveling with major league teams, hoping to capture the players' movements on canvas. Her painting *Baseball Players*, which depicts a baserunner sliding safely into home plate, is one of several baseball-themed works to emerge from this period. Others include studies of Cleveland Indians Lou Boudreau and Al Lopez.

said that Murphy could reach 45 miles per hour with his throws. He regularly deputized cancer-stricken "Sunshine Kids" to join him in the stands and learn the tricks of his trade. Murphy's local fame eventually grew so great that he was dispatched to work at All-Star Games by Major League Baseball and was profiled in numerous national periodicals, including *The Wall Street Journal* and *People* magazine. He died in May of 2009 at the age of 61 while recovering from a stem cell transplant intended to help alleviate his heart disease.

## Artificial Turf

Synthetic grass installed in select baseball stadiums beginning in the 1960s and derided by traditionalists as a blight on the game's pastoral purity. The **Astrodome** in Houston boasted the major leagues' first artificial playing surface. Concocted by the agrochemical giant Monsanto at the request of Astros owner Judge Roy Hofheinz—who was tired of watching the grass die in his expensive new domed stadium—**Astroturf**, as this early variety of synthetic grass was called, had its public unveiling at the Astros' April 18, 1966, home opener. (Maury Wills of the Dodgers was the first man to bat on the surface; he singled and was promptly erased trying to steal second.)

Hailed in the press as a marvel akin to sliced bread and the frozen TV dinner, artificial turf rapidly began to proliferate throughout the major leagues during the 1970s. Newfangled **multipurpose stadia** were constructed in several cities using artificial turf as the playing surface, while a number of venerable grass ballparks—including Comiskey Park in Chicago—were rudely retrofitted with the ersatz sod. In 1970, the Cincinnati Reds and the Pittsburgh Pirates played the game's first all–artificial turf playoff series, kicking off an 18-year stretch during which at least one of the four postseason participants played on a non-organic surface. Groundskeepers and team owners loved the stuff because it liberated them from the drudgery (and expense) of having to maintain pristine grass fields. Fans—at least at first—reveled in the novelty of watching baseballs bounce like superballs off of billiard-table-smooth carpets into the gloves (or, in some cases, over the heads) of waiting fielders. Managers and general managers even began to alter the way they built and ran their teams to take advantage of turf's unique attributes. Games at Kansas City's Royals Stadium and St. Louis' Busch Stadium took on an absurd, pinball-like quality, leading to a tremendous spike in the number of triples. By the end of the 1970s, however, the tide had turned, and a number of teams that had switched to turf—including the

## They Said What?

### "If horses can't eat it, I don't want to play on it."

–Philadelphia Phillies first baseman Dick Allen, expressing the widely held disdain for **artificial turf** among major league players

White Sox and Giants—switched back to grass surfaces. Complaints from purists provided part of the reason for the backlash, as did a general trend toward "tradition" as reflected in stadium and uniform design, and the sense among players that the concrete-like artificial surfaces led to a higher incidence of injury. Soon the only new ballparks to be built with artificial turf were domed facilities such as the SkyDome in Toronto. With the advent of **retro ballparks** like Oriole Park at Camden Yards in the 1990s, the pendulum swung back to grass for good. All-grass playoff baseball returned in 1988—and old-line franchises in Cincinnati, Pittsburgh, Philadelphia, and St. Louis opted to go with natural turf in their new parks. See also: **Gores**, **Harold**

# Astrodome

Massive, domed multipurpose stadium, often called "the Eighth Wonder of the World," which served as the home office of the Houston Astros from 1965 to 1999. Originally called the Harris County Domed Stadium, the Astrodome was the brainchild of Judge Roy Hofheinz, the onetime "boy mayor" of Houston who was instrumental in securing the city a major league expansion franchise. Lauded in the press as an architectural marvel akin to the Great Pyramid at Cheops, the self-consciously futuristic facility cost $35 million to build and boasted numerous space-age amenities, including: a central air conditioning system so powerful its engineers claimed they could make it snow inside; an ultraviolet smoke detector; cushioned orange and red theater-style seating; 53 luxury "Sky Boxes" (unheard of in baseball to that point); and a $2 million, 474-foot-long electronic scoreboard, complete with snorting cartoon bull, **dot race**, and a "Tilt" sign that would light up whenever an opposition player hit a home run. Mickey Mantle, in fact, hit the first home run in the new park on April 9, 1965, during an exhibition game between the Astros and the New York Yankees. At that point, the Astrodome had real grass. However, semitransparent tiles installed in the roof—designed to allow grass to grow inside—made fly balls impossible to see. When the ceiling panels were painted over, the grass died, so Hofheinz commissioned the installation of the soon-to-be ubiquitous synthetic sod known as **Astroturf**. Over the years, the Astrodome has played host to a number of strange and noteworthy events, including: New York Mets play-by-play man Lindsey Nelson's bizarre attempt to broadcast an April 1965 game from inside a hanging gondola suspended from the apex of the dome 208 feet above second base; the 1968 and 1986 All-Star Games; the "Battle of the Sexes" tennis match between Bobby Riggs and Billie Jean King on September 20, 1973; baseball's first "indoor rainout," the result of flooding in the Houston area on June 15, 1976; and the 1992 Republican National Convention. Many of the distinct features of the facility are also on display in the final reel of the 1977 baseball comedy *The Bad News Bears in Breaking Training*, which climaxes with a Little League championship game played inside the stadium. Loathed by baseball and football players alike for its poor optics and rock-hard playing surface, the Astrodome was abandoned by the Astros in 2000 when they moved into their new home at Enron Field. The dome still stands, however, and in 2005 it provided temporary shelter for thousands of Gulf Coast residents displaced by Hurricane Katrina. See also: **Domes**; **Multipurpose Stadia**

# Astroturf

Trade name for the **artificial turf** used in the Houston **Astrodome**. Originally called Chemgrass, the synthetic sod was developed by Monsanto Industries in conjunction with the Ford Foundation's Educational Facilities Laboratory, headed by educator and fake grass enthusiast **Dr. Harold Gores**.

Constantly splitting seams were but one of many problems that plagued Astroturf.

AP Images

**B**

## *Babe Ruth Story, The*

Feature film chronicling the life of the legendary slugger that set the standard for hastily made, insufferably reverent baseball biopics. Portly actor William Bendix—who at 42 was both too old and too small to fill Ruth's tent-sized flannels—plays the Bambino. The 1948 film depicts Ruth as a kindly imbecile with near godlike powers. Among its many inaccuracies, Ruth is shown missing a game to rush a small child's injured dog to the hospital (an event that never happened), battling off a pair of evil bookies who try to entice him to throw a game, and healing a crippled child with the might of his bat. Even the story of Ruth's battle with cancer is twisted to suggest that Ruth died testing an experimental serum for the betterment of mankind. To add insult

AP Images

to injury, the film also incorrectly displays Ruth's career home-run total as 725, not 714. The product of a simpler time when sports stars were venerated in popular culture, *The Babe Ruth Story* is appreciated today primarily for its camp value. The prideful Bendix once called it the worst movie he ever made.

# Baby Ruth

Log-shaped chocolate, peanut, caramel, and nougat confection that was named the "official candy bar of Major League Baseball" in 2006. The designation capped off decades of debate over whether the chewy treat was actually named after baseball legend Babe Ruth—as most people have always assumed—or after President Grover Cleveland's daughter Ruth, as the Curtiss Candy Company steadfastly contended. Introduced in 1921 (17 years after Baby Ruth Cleveland died of diphtheria and just as Babe Ruth was enjoying his first blush of nationwide celebrity), the Baby Ruth bar quickly became one of the best-selling candy bars of the Jazz Age. By 1931, sales of Baby Ruths had topped $1 million per month. Ruth himself must have sensed that he was being taken advantage of because he attempted to trademark his own "Babe Ruth Home Run Bar" in 1926. But the Curtiss Candy Company sued for infringement of copyright, and the U.S. Patent Office ruled in the confectioner's favor, decreeing that a second Bambino-inspired chocolate bar "would cause confusion among candy buyers." In 1995, just in time for the centenary of Ruth's birth, Nestlé—which by then owned the Baby Ruth trademark—cut a deal with Babe Ruth's estate to use the Hall of Famer's likeness in its Baby Ruth ad campaign. Whatever the real provenance of the chewy comestible, a strong association with America's pastime persists. In 2006, a survey of candy eaters commissioned by Nestlé found that those who ate Baby Ruth bars were 22 percent more likely to be baseball fans than those who ate any other candy.

## Bad News Bears, The

Popular movie franchise of the late 1970's, resuscitated via remake in 2005. The original *Bad News Bears* starred Walter Matthau as Morris Buttermaker, the curmudgeonly skipper of a ragtag Little League team composed of uncoordinated, potty-mouthed scamps. The surprise hit of 1976, the film spawned two inferior sequels: 1977's *The Bad News Bears in Breaking Training* (featuring real-life major leaguers Bob Watson, Enos Cabell, and the rest of the Houston Astros, complete with their **rainbow uniforms**) and *The Bad News Bears Go to Japan*, a truly execrable finale in which Tony Curtis succeeded Matthau and William Devane as the Bears' beleaguered manager. A fourth sequel was planned in which the team would travel to Cuba, with Matthau returning as Buttermaker and **Fidel Castro** enlisted to play the opposing manager. However, due to *Japan*'s poor box office performance, the project was shelved. A short-lived TV series, starring Jack Warden as Buttermaker and featuring an all-new cast of kids—including Corey Feldman—invaded American homes over 26 weeks from 1979 to 1980. Billy Bob Thornton took the reins as Buttermaker in the scabrous 2005 update.

## BALCO

Acronym for Bay Area Laboratory Co-Operative, the Burlingame, California–based company at the heart of baseball's steroids scandal of the 1990s and 2000s.

## Balk

Intermittently enforced violation of Rule 8.05 of the Official Rules of Major League Baseball, which prohibits a range of actions by a pitcher deemed by the umpire to be deceptive toward a baserunner. The single-season record for balks is 16, set by Dave Stewart of the Oakland A's, in the so-called **Year of the Balk** (1988).

# Ball Four

Incendiary 1970 best seller written by major league pitcher **Jim Bouton**, which ushered in the era of the tell-all baseball memoir and scandalized the sport with its tales of drug- and alcohol-fueled sexcapades involving some of the game's most revered stars, including Mickey Mantle. (The most salacious revelation involved the practice of "beaver shooting," in which players would roam beneath the bleachers during the National Anthem to look up women's skirts.) The tight-knit ballplayers' fraternity, enraged over Bouton's betrayal of confidence, ostracized the pitcher for decades. The San Diego Padres' players burned a copy of the book and left the ashes in Bouton's locker. **Pete Rose** took to screaming "Fuck you, Shakespeare!" whenever Bouton took to the mound. Baseball commissioner Bowie Kuhn himself labeled *Ball Four* "detrimental to baseball" and demanded that Bouton issue a statement disavowing the contents as complete fiction. (Bouton refused.) Controversial at the time, *Ball Four* is considered tame in comparison to subsequent behind-the-scenes accounts of clubhouse misbehavior, such as José Canseco's ***Juiced***. Nevertheless, it was selected by the New York Public Library as one of the "Books of the Century." A watered-down TV sitcom based on the book, developed by and starring Bouton himself, lasted only five episodes in 1976.

# Ballgirls

*See* **Collins, Marla**; **Lawrence, Sheryl**; **Sivyer, Debbi**; **Styles, Mary Sue**

# Balls Deep

Nom-de-column employed by author and baseball blogger "Big Daddy Drew" Magary, whose irreverent commentary on the popular sports blog *Deadspin* so outraged old-school print journalist **Buzz Bissinger** that Bissinger publicly denounced him on an April 2008 episode of the HBO sports show

*Costas Now*. In the infamous rant, Bissinger called Magary "a disgusting voice" whose writing embodied everything that was wrong about the blogosphere. The two men later reconciled.

# Barr, Roseanne

Morbidly obese stand-up comic turned sitcom star whose screeching, off-key rendition of "The Star-Spangled Banner" briefly scandalized the nation in the summer of 1990. Barr, who was then starring on the popular ABC sitcom *Roseanne*, was invited to sing the National Anthem before the second game of a doubleheader between the San Diego Padres and the Cincinnati Reds at Jack Murphy Stadium in San Diego on July 25, 1990, as part of a special "Working Women's Night" promotion. Although Barr was initially greeted with rousing applause, after 53 seconds of her tuneless caterwauling, the crowd of 27,285 turned against her, booing her lustily. Adding insult to injury, the rotund comic then spit on the field and ostentatiously scratched her crotch. (She later claimed she was simply aping the behavior of a typical major league player.) The incident touched off a nationwide furor, with traditionalists charging that Barr had disrespected the flag. President George H.W. Bush called her performance "disgraceful."

## Bartman, Steve

Headphones-wearing yutz whose ill-starred attempt to catch a foul ball is blamed for costing the Chicago Cubs a chance to reach the World Series for the first time in nearly half a century. Bartman, a 26-year-old employee at a human resources consulting firm, was attending Game 6 of the 2003 National League Championship Series between the Cubs and the Florida Marlins at Wrigley Field in Chicago. The Cubs led the series 3–2—and were five outs away from clinching their first National League pennant since 1945—when the Marlins' Luis Castillo lofted a foul pop toward Bartman's seat along the third-base line in short left field (aisle 4, row 8, seat 113, for those keeping score at home). Bartman's clumsy attempt to catch the foul ball denied Cubs left fielder Moises Alou an easy chance at the second out of the inning. Castillo then walked, opening the floodgates for an eight-run Florida outburst

Mark Weyermuller

that effectively turned the tide in the series. The Marlins won the game, and Game 7, to demolish the hopes of Cubs fans for the club's first world championship since 1908. Bartman was vilified in the press and subjected to death threats from enraged Chicago rooters in the wake of the incident, for which he publicly apologized. Detractors focused almost as much on Bartman's schlubby appearance—headphones, glasses, and Little League team sweatshirt—and the fact that he still lived with his parents as on his role in quashing the postseason fortunes of one of the most accursed teams in professional sports. In the aftermath of the incident, Bartman turned down numerous requests for interviews, autograph signings, and personal appearances and concentrated on rebuilding his once quiet life.

# *Baseball* (documentary series)
*See* **Burns, Ken**

# Baseball Annie
Archaic term, once widely used to describe female groupies who await the arrival of road-tripping players to service them sexually. Annie Savoy, the character played by Susan Sarandon in the 1988 film ***Bull Durham***, can be said to be the quintessential fictional Baseball Annie. A more modern term for the same type of person is **Road Beef**.

# *Baseball Bugs*
Bugs Bunny cartoon from 1946 that is considered the *Citizen Kane* of baseball-themed animated shorts. Directed by longtime Looney Tunes stalwart Friz Freling, *Baseball Bugs* features the brash, Brooklyn-born bunny single-handedly taking on a baseball team full of roughnecks known as the **Gas House Gorillas**. Using a variety of feats of deception and chicanery (including his patented "slow ball"), Bugs manages to defeat the Gorillas by a score of 96–95. He records the final out by throwing his glove at a long fly ball from the top of the Umpire State Building.

# Baseball Bunch, The

Syndicated instructional baseball television series, hosted by Hall of Fame catcher Johnny Bench, that aired on various U.S. TV stations from 1982 to 1985 and left an indelible mark on the minds of a generation of children. The 30-minute program featured a cast of real-life Tucson, Arizona–area Little Leaguers who took instruction in baseball fundamentals from Bench and a rotating roster of superstar guests, including **Pete Rose**, Andre Dawson, and Tom Seaver. Tips from the 1980s greats were intercut with highlights and classic game footage featuring the likes of Connie Mack and Mickey Mantle. The **San Diego Chicken** was on hand to disrupt drills and generally create havoc on the sandlot, while then–Los Angeles Dodgers manager Tommy Lasorda appeared regularly in character as "the Dugout Wizard," a benevolent magus who materialized out of a puff of smoke, wearing a turban and a rhinestone-studded tiara, and dispensed nuggets of homespun wisdom such as "Kids, the umpire is *always* right."

*Baseball by the Numbers* | **8**

Number of baseballs Hall of Fame catcher Johnny Bench could hold in one hand at one time

AP Images

## "Baseball's Sad Lexicon"

Full name of a mawkish baseball-themed poem written in 1910 by Chicago newspaperman Franklin Pierce Adams and remembered solely for the famous refrain "Tinker to Evers to Chance." The poem pays homage to the Chicago Cubs' early 20th century double-play combination of shortstop Joe Tinker, second baseman Johnny Evers, and first baseman Frank Chance. It was first published in the *New York Evening Mail* on July 10, 1910, as the Cubs were steaming toward their fourth National League pennant in five years. Oddly enough, none of the three players valorized in "Baseball's Sad Lexicon" was very good; they weren't even especially proficient at turning double plays. Nevertheless, they were elected to the Hall of the Fame *en bloc* in 1946 by the Veterans Committee—a testament to the power of doggerel over common sense.

## Bean, Billy

Marginally talented journeyman out-fielder of the 1980s and 1990s who would be lost to history if he hadn't publicly acknowledged his **homosexuality** in 1999. Bean was the second gay major leaguer to come out of the closet, following **Glenn Burke** of the Los Angeles Dodgers. He published his autobiography, *Going the Other Way: Lessons from a Life in and out of Major League Baseball*, in 2003. He is not to be confused with the presumably straight Oakland Athletics general manager and ***Moneyball*** protagonist **Billy Beane**.

AP Images

# Beane, Billy

Onetime highly touted New York Mets prospect turned whiz kid Oakland A's general manager whose reliance on **Sabermetrics** has made him the messiah of stat geeks everywhere. A toolsy outfielder drafted 23rd overall in 1980, Beane never lived up to his potential on the field, but after taking the reins of a moribund Oakland franchise in 1998 and leading it back into the postseason using **Bill James**–inspired statistical analysis, he was lauded by Sabermetric evangelists in the press as the avatar of a new generation of baseball executives. **Theo Epstein** of the Boston Red Sox and former Toronto Blue Jays GM J.P. Ricciardi are thought to be acolytes of Beane's. His exploits are gushingly chronicled in Michael Lewis' 2003 best seller **Moneyball**. He is not to be confused with gay outfielder **Billy Bean**.

# Beanie Babies

Plush, pellet-filled collectibles, typically fashioned in the likeness of various cuddly animals, that became enormously popular ballpark giveaway items in the 1990s. Originally marketed to children, the stuffed toys exploded onto the scene in 1993 and were keenly sought after by collectors, due mostly to the artificial scarcity created by their Illinois-based manufacturer Ty, Inc. In the aftermath of the 1994 baseball strike, clubs began turning to Beanie Baby promotions to goose attendance at ballparks, with striking success. At some games, attendance spiked by as much as 50 percent on days when the toys were handed out to ticket holders. But there was a downside as well. At the 1998 All-Star Game at Coors Field, a near-riot erupted at one stadium gate as fans clamored to get their mitts on a red-white-and-blue commemorative Beanie Bear named "Glory." Collectors roamed the concourse, cajoling patrons to sell them their patriotic bears with offers of as much as $1,000. At least one box of Beanies was stolen by a ballpark volunteer. Eventually, the police had to be called in to take over the distribution of the bear.

# Belinsky, Bo

Borderline sexual predator who cut an erotic swath through America in the 1960s as a middling left-hander for five major league teams. The first Los Angeles Angel to throw a no-hitter, Belinsky was known for his good looks. ("He's a handsome son of a bitch," declared the Los Angeles Angels' PR director, Irv Kaze. "You can almost feel the animal sex in him. It didn't surprise me that he could turn on the girls.") He also had a rapacious sexual appetite, the details of which he revealed in his authorized biography, *Bo: Pitching and Wooing*, published in 1973. Among the more unsavory revelations: Belinsky had once eluded statutory rape charges in Pensacola, Florida, by fleeing across state lines to Louisiana; he spied on a Miss Universe contestant in her hotel room in Miami by drilling a hole in the wall so he could watch her undress; and he once walked in on the aftermath of a rape perpetrated on a young woman by one of his teammates and failed to report it to the police ("I had a hell of a time soothing that broad that night" was all Belinsky would say). Of the peeping tom incident, Belinsky remarked, "It's harmless and fun, and it sure does help pass the time." In 1965, Belinsky cemented his reputation as the game's greatest playa when he married *Playboy*'s Playmate of the Year, Jo Collins. This capped a long string of celebrity conquests that also included bombshells Ann-Margret, Tina "Ginger from *Gilligan's Island*" Louise, and Mamie Van Doren ("I needed her like Custer needed more Indians," Belinsky lamented). Although undoubtedly promiscuous, Belinsky claimed to have some standards. "I only had one rule about these broads," he said. "They had to come highly recommended. I wouldn't take out a broad without checking her references." In later life, Belinsky became a born-again Christian and alcohol abuse counselor in Las Vegas. He died of a heart attack in 1984 at the age of 64.

# Belle, Albert

Fearsome slugger of the 1990s who was almost as well-known for his anger management problem as his run-producing prowess. A two-fisted drinker and relentless coffee addict with one of the nastiest dispositions in sports history, Belle compiled quite a rap sheet over the course of a 12-year major league career spent mostly with the Cleveland Indians. Among the many items in his voluminous bag of sins: a seven-game suspension for pegging a **heckler** in the chest with a baseball after the man made light of his alcohol problem and called him by his despised childhood nickname, "Joey"; a seven-game ban in 1993 for corking his bat (teammate Omar Vizquel would later reveal that nearly all of Belle's bats were corked); a profanity-laced tirade unleashed without warning or provocation on NBC dugout reporter Hannah Storm before Game 3 of the 1995 World Series; and a fine in 1996 for delivering a vicious forearm shiver to Milwaukee Brewers second baseman Fernando Vina while attempting to break up a double play. Belle was also notorious for trashing clubhouses, upending postgame buffet tables, and even demolishing the personal property of teammates. During one tirade, he took a bat to the boombox of Indians center fielder Kenny Lofton. So obsessed was Belle with keeping the clubhouse well-refrigerated that he once destroyed the thermostat after someone pushed it up above 60 degrees. (Teammates called him "Mr. Freeze.") At the height of his destructive frenzy, the Indians were docking $10,000 per year from his salary to cover the damage he was causing to visiting clubhouses. Belle's high-water mark for antisocial behavior may have come in 1995, when he attempted to run over a group of teenaged trick-or-treaters with his SUV after he caught them trying to egg his mansion on Halloween night. Belle was fined $100 for recklessly operating a vehicle and sued by one of the teens for $850,000. They later settled out of court for an undisclosed amount.

# Bennett, Eddie

Hunchbacked mascot and all-around good-luck charm for several successful Jazz Age major league clubs—including the famed "Murderers' Row" New York Yankees of the 1920s—who is arguably the best-known batboy in baseball history. An orphan who had been permanently disabled in a childhood accident, Bennett established his reputation as a walking rabbit's foot during batboy stints with the infamous 1919 **Black Sox** and the 1920 NL champion Brooklyn Dodgers. In 1921, he signed on with the Yankees. He remained with the club for the next 12 seasons as it won seven pennants and four World Series titles. Duties assigned to "Little Eddie" included bringing baseballs out to the home-plate umpire, fetching bicarbonate of soda for the notoriously gassy Babe Ruth, and serving as the unofficial bench coach to Yankees manager Miller Huggins. Batters would also rub his hump for good luck on their way to the plate. In 1927, the Yankees voted to give Bennett a one-eighth World Series share. After he was seriously injured in a 1932 taxi cab accident, Bennett became too infirm to function as a batboy any longer. He retired to a dingy rented room on the west side of Manhattan and lived off a small stipend provided for him by Yankees management. Depressed and disconsolate, he surrounded himself with baseball memorabilia and descended into an alcoholic stupor. He drank himself to death in 1935 at the age of 31. Yankees owner Colonel Jacob Ruppert paid for the wee mascot's funeral.

# Benson, Anna

Outspoken wife of maddeningly inconsistent big-league right-hander Kris Benson who enjoyed a brief run of demi-celebrity in the mid-2000s. The chesty Atlanta native married Benson while he was a member of the Pittsburgh Pirates in 1999 and posed topless with him in *Penthouse* in 2001,

AP Images

but her real brush with fame began after her husband was traded to the New York Mets in 2004. In short order, Anna Benson was named "Baseball's Hottest Wife" by lad mag *FHM* and made a controversial appearance on the Howard Stern radio show, during which she revealed that she and Benson had engaged in public sex acts in a number of major league ballparks. She also threatened to have sex with all of Benson's New York Mets teammates if she ever caught him cheating on her. In December of 2005, Benson scandalized the Mets' official team Christmas party by showing up in a low-cut Santa suit. She later criticized Mets general manager Omar Minaya for signing too many Latin players. (Her husband was traded to Baltimore less than a month later.) A political conservative, Anna Benson has used her personal website and other platforms to speak out against gun control, animal rights, and opposition to the Iraq War. She once penned an open letter to left-wing documentary filmmaker Michael Moore in which she called him a "selfish, pathetic excuse for an American" and exhorted him to take his "big, fat ass over to Iraq and get your pig head cut off and stuck on a pig pole." She filed for divorce from Kris Benson in March 2006 but later reconsidered.

# Berman, Chris

Burly ESPN personality whose shtick-laden play-by-play has earned him the ire of many baseball purists. Best known as one of the original *SportsCenter* anchors (and as the unlikely Lothario whose pick-up line, "You're with me, Leather" became an Internet-driven catchphrase in 2006), Berman only occasionally broadcasts baseball games, but when he does he grates on the nerves of traditionalists with his promiscuous use of hacky, punny nicknames, such as Bert "Be Home" Blyleven and Albert "Winnie the" Pujols. Berman's other signature baseball call, appropriated from old-school play-by-play legend Red Barber, is to bellow "backbackbackback" at the top of his lungs whenever a batter hits a long fly ball. A perennial target of derision for sports media columnists, Berman belongs in the ranks of polarizing baseball broadcasters that includes **Tim McCarver**, **Joe Morgan**, and local New York Yankees radio man **John Sterling**.

# Bernie Brewer

Since 1973, the official mascot of the Milwaukee Brewers has been this lederhosen-clad beer enthusiast with an enormous, bushy blond mustache. Inspired by the antics of Milt Mason, a rabid 69-year-old Brewers fan who used to sit on top of the County Stadium scoreboard in the early 1970s, Bernie is famous for his home-run slide, during which he emerges from a large barrel-shaped chalet and slides into a frothing mug of beer. At one point, Bernie Brewer generated controversy when Texas Rangers manager Whitey Herzog accused him of stealing his opponents' signs. Exiled from the

Jana M. Hall

park in 1984 when the Brewers rebuilt their bleachers and evicted Bernie from his chalet, the suds-loving character returned by popular demand in 1993. In 2001, in a nod to political correctness, Bernie's beer stein was replaced by a non-alcoholic dugout platform. Traditionalist fans periodically agitate for the return of the beer stein and the rebuilding of the original chalet in recognition of the city of Milwaukee's proud heritage as a beer-making capital. See also: **Bonnie Brewer**

## Big Chief Boom-Boom

Name bestowed by Cleveland Indians broadcaster Herb Score upon the 26-inch-wide bass drum pounded by Indians **superfan John Adams** at the team's home games.

## Big League Chew

Controversial brand of bubble gum co-developed by controversial ex-major leaguer (and **Ball Four** author) **Jim Bouton**. Shredded and packaged in a pouch, the gum is designed to resemble **chewing tobacco**—an addictive and carcinogenic product long beloved by major league players as an alternative to smoking. First introduced in 1980, Big League Chew has been a consistent seller for the Wrigley

Company ever since, though its colorful packaging and association with America's pastime has earned the ire of anti-tobacco advocates for seeming to glamorize chaw. Big League Chew may have reached the height of its cultural salience in 2006, when the American League champion Detroit Tigers engaged in ritualized "rally chews" of the product accompanied by the slogan "It's Gum Time!"

## Billyball

Word coined by *Oakland Tribune* columnist Ralph Wiley to describe the aggressive style of play instituted by Oakland A's manager **Billy Martin** from 1980 to 1982. The former Minnesota Twins, New York Yankees, Texas Rangers, and Detroit Tigers skipper (and Bay Area native) inherited a 54-win club that had drawn fewer than 4,000 fans per game to the cavernous Oakland Coliseum. He encouraged his players to bunt, steal, and take the extra base wherever possible, guiding them to an 83–79 record in 1980. In 1981, the A's reached the American League Championship Series where they were swept by Martin's former team, the New York Yankees. "Billyball" became the club's official marketing slogan and, in 1987, the title of Martin's autobiography. The A's abandoned Billyball (and Billy) after dropping to fifth place in their division in 1982.

# Billy Goat Curse

Malediction purportedly placed on the Chicago Cubs by aggrieved area tavern owner **William Sianis** after he and his pet goat were ejected from Wrigley Field during Game 4 of the 1945 World Series. The story of the Billy Goat Curse is shrouded in media-generated inaccuracies, but this much is true: Sianis was a publicity hound who traveled around the city with his goat, **Sonovia**, to promote his restaurant business. When he showed up at the World Series with a ticket for himself and his goat, he was initially welcomed into the park. But the goat stank so badly it began to irritate the other fans, and ushers asked Sianis to leave. After that, the story gets murky. According to legend, an outraged Sianis put a hex on the Cubs, vowing they would never win another World Series game (or another championship, depending on which version of the tale you believe). However, there is

AP Images

virtually no mention of a "Billy Goat Curse" until the late 1960s, when various Chicago sportswriters began promulgating the notion of an ovine whammy with the support of Sianis and his family. (Sianis was by then running a watering hole called the Billy Goat Tavern and owned a second bar just steps from Wrigley Field.) Although the Cubs cooperated in the dissemination of the legend (by, at various points, inviting goats onto the field for Opening Day ceremonies designed to "reverse the curse"), the tale of Sianis' jinx was virtually unknown outside Chicago until 2003, when Fox announcers relentlessly repeated the story during television coverage of the National League Championship Series. Since that time, there has been renewed interest in the idea of a Billy Goat Curse, promoting several deranged pranksters to engage in gruesome acts of goat mutilation in an effort to expiate the franchise's supposed sins.

## Billy the Marlin

Mischievous eight-foot-tall billfish who has been the official mascot of the Florida Marlins since the team's inception in 1993. Named by Marlins owner Wayne Huizenga in tribute to deceased manager **Billy Martin**, Billy the Marlin has long been one of the game's most popular and active **mascots**. For more than 10 years, the teal marlin suit was inhabited by performer John Routh, who reportedly pulled in more than $80,000 a year and made countless personal appearances away from the baseball diamond. (During one such moonlighting gig at the Sugar Bowl in New Orleans, Routh was grazed in the temple by a stray bullet, prompting him to declare with typical

Carmen Zuniga

mascot braggadocio, "It's going to take more than a bullet hole in the head to keep me out of this game.") Billy was also featured in several humorous TV promos for ESPN's *SportsCenter*. On occasion, Billy the Marlin has been at the center of controversy. The costumed fish's head blew off during an Opening Day skydiving stunt in 1997. It was found two months later hanging from a retaining wall on the Florida Turnpike by two passing motorists. And in 2000, the air cannon–wielding marlin knocked an elderly fan unconscious when he shot him in the face with a wadded-up T-shirt. The man sued for $250,000 but did not prevail. While all this media exposure greatly enhanced the expansion franchise's visibility, it also led to conflict between management and Routh. In 2003, the club fired Routh in a cost-cutting move and replaced him with a less expensive portrayer. Routh later sued the team for its refusal to award him a severance package.

# Bird, The

Cartoonish, black-and-orange, crab cake–loving omnivore who has served as the official mascot of the Baltimore Orioles since 1979. The Bird, who hatched out of a giant egg at Memorial Stadium on Opening Day that year, has been delighting Baltimore crowds ever since with his spirited dugout roof dances and relentless taunting of Orioles opponents. Occasionally, that taunting has provoked a violent response. In May of 1999, the Bird successfully sued a Philadelphia electrician for $59,000 in damages after the man pushed him off the right-field fence at Oriole Park at Camden Yards, breaking his left ankle. See also: **Fidrych, Mark**

# Bissinger, Buzz

Prep school–educated print journalist whose periodic dabblings in sportswriting and outspoken contempt for blogs have earned him lightning-rod status in the online baseball fan community. *Three Nights in August*, Bissinger's hagiographic 2005 chronicle of three games in the dugout with

St. Louis Cardinals manager **Tony La Russa**, was both a national best seller and a significant addition to the corpus of the **Tony La Russa** personality cult founded by **George F. Will** in his 1990 book *Men at Work*. Bissinger further solidified his status as a crotchety tribune of baseball purism with his infamous April 2008 appearance on the HBO sports panel program *Costas Now*, during which the unhinged celebri-journalist railed against the rhetorical excesses of the blogosphere—in particular frequent *Deadspin* contributor Drew "***Balls Deep***" Magary.

# BJ Birdy

Original Toronto Blue Jays mascot who was suddenly and unceremoniously relieved of his duties after more than 20 years of service. A shambling, 6'8" bird who capered in a manner reminiscent of the then-popular **San Diego Chicken**, BJ made his Exhibition Stadium debut on August 31, 1979, and was the brainchild of costume designer Kevin Shanahan. He was released by the club's marketing department shortly before Christmas in 1999. Research conducted by the team supposedly revealed a desire among fans for a younger, hipper mascot. The boyfriend/girlfriend duo of **Ace** and **Diamond** replaced BJ in 2002.

# Black Sox

Derisive nickname for the 1919 Chicago White Sox, eight of whom were implicated in a crooked scheme to fix that season's World Series. Pitchers Eddie Cicotte and Lefty Williams and position players Happy Felsch, Chick Gandil, Buck Weaver, Swede Risberg, Fred McMullin, and Shoeless Joe Jackson were all banned from the game for life for allegedly throwing games to the Cincinnati Reds, with the monetary support of New York gambler **Arnold Rothstein**. Author Eliot Asinof provides the definitive account of the Black Sox Scandal in his 1963 book *Eight Men Out*, adapted for film by director John Sayles in 1988.

# Bleacher Creatures

Media-generated term for the rowdy group of New York Yankees fans who inhabit the right-field bleacher seats in Yankee Stadium. Although the Stadium bleachers have long been home to an especially vocal, exceedingly devoted, and occasionally overserved collection of rooters—known primarily for their battery-flinging antics and profane chants aimed at their enemies in the nearby box seats—they adopted the "Creature" appellation only in the mid-1990s. It was around that time that the group first began issuing its famed "Roll Call," a rhythmic shout-out of each Yankees player's name in succession around the diamond. Antisocial behavior by some of the more inebriated Bleacher Creatures led to a Stadium-imposed beer ban in the section starting in 2000. The ban was lifted in time for the 2009 season.

# Block, Mandy

Milwaukee sausage portrayer who was famously bludgeoned by Pittsburgh Pirates first baseman **Randall Simon** during the seventh-inning **Sausage Race** at Miller Park on July 9, 2003. The 19-year-old college student and part-time Brewers employee received national media attention in the aftermath of the incident and was awarded a certificate of bravery by the National Hot Dog and Sausage Council.

## *They Said What?*

### "It's such a silly little thing. I'm just a sausage, guys."

–Miller Park Italian Sausage portrayer
**Mandy Block**, on the infamous **Randall Simon** beatdown

# Blomberg, Ron

Middling left-handed slugger of the early 1970s who would be lost to history if he weren't the major leagues' first designated hitter. An Atlanta, Georgia, high school phenom who excelled in baseball, football, and basketball, Blomberg turned down a recruiting pitch from John Wooden himself and opted for the diamond over the hardwood. Drafted in the first round by the New York Yankees in 1967, he was touted in the press as a successor to Mickey Mantle. But although he showed early promise at the plate, Blomberg was injury prone and had no facility for playing the field. Those limitations made him a logical choice to step into the new DH role that the American League had instituted before the 1973 season. On Opening Day, Blomberg drew a base on balls in his first plate appearance as a designated hitter. For the year, Blomberg hit .329 and made the covers of *Sports Illustrated*, *Sport*, and *The Sporting News*, but could barely stay on the field for 100 games. He would hit only 52 home runs over the course of his eight-year major league career and would never quite redeem his potential. Blomberg's other distinguishing characteristic was his Jewish heritage, which held him in good stead in polyglot New York City. A folk hero in New York during his mid-'70s heyday, Blomberg at one point had a sandwich named after him at the world famous Stage Deli. After his retirement in 1978, he managed a baseball team in Israel and wrote an anodyne memoir titled, appropriately enough, *Designated Hebrew*.

# Bobblehead Dolls

Popular figurine collectibles, distinguished by their eerily nodding heads, that have been crafted in the likeness of major league players since the early 1960s and are often distributed to fans at ballparks on giveaway days. Also called "nodders" or "bobbers," bobblehead dolls actually date back to 19th century Europe, where they were fashioned from ceramic and often painted to look like woodland animals. After a short-lived collectible craze in the

1920s, the dolls largely disappeared from the market until the late 1950s. That's when Major League Baseball authorized a line of papier-mâché bobbleheads—each with the same angelic face, distinguishable from one another only by their tiny team uniforms. These early dolls were exceedingly fragile and could chip and crack at the drop of a hat. As a result, very few of them survive, and they are quite prized by collectors today. The next great leap forward in bobblehead technology came in the autumn of 1960. In time for the World Series, Major League Baseball rolled out a new line of bobbleheads—the first to feature the likenesses of actual players, in this case Mickey Mantle, Willie Mays, Roberto Clemente, and Roger Maris. Made in Japan and distributed by Bobble Enterprises Inc., the four "superstar" dolls sold for $1 each and were part of a line that included generic bobbleheads representing 20 different major league teams. Thus began the first golden age of bobbleheads, as various Asia-spawned ceramic nodders hit the market throughout the 1960s, often with identical heads and different uniforms, or fashioned in the likeness of various club **mascots**. The popularity of the tremorous tschotskes began to fade in the 1970s, however, and did not pick up again until the late 1990s, when new production methods allowed for the substitution of plastic for ceramic and bobblehead dolls once again became cost efficient to mass-produce. In 1999, the San Francisco Giants ushered in what has become the second golden age of bobblehead dolls when it distributed more than 30,000 Willie Mays bobbleheads to fans at one of the team's home games. The promotion proved so popular that other clubs rushed to schedule bobblehead giveaways of their own. By 2008, there were more than 100 such offerings scattered across the major league calendar, as 27 of the 30 major league clubs elected to cash in on the promotional power of the bobble. The Pittsburgh Pirates led the league with nine bobble giveaways, including dolls forged in the image of seven of the eight starting position players from their 1975 roster. (Only shortstop Frank Taveras was left out.)

# Boggs Lite

Nickname given by beer enthusiasts to Miller Lite in mock recognition of Hall of Fame third baseman **Wade Boggs'** supposed prowess in consuming that beverage. According to legend, Boggs once downed 64 Miller Lites on a cross-country airplane flight. In a 2007 radio interview, former big-league reliever and onetime Boggs teammate Jeff Nelson alleged that it was standard operating procedure for Boggs to consume "between 50 and 60 beers" on *every* cross-country flight.

# Boggs, Wade

Notoriously superstitious Hall of Famer who became a poster child for sex addiction following the revelation of his extramarital affair with California mortgage broker **Margo Adams** in 1988. A 12-time All-Star, Boggs was dubbed "Chicken Man" by Boston Red Sox teammate Jim Rice, apparently for his insistence on eating poultry before every game. Among Boggs' other superstitions: taking precisely 150 ground balls during infield practice; running wind sprints before the game at exactly 7:17 PM; and writing the Hebrew word "chai"—meaning "living"—into the dirt of the batter's box before every at-bat. Besides sex and superstitions, Boggs also earned a reputation as a hard drinker. A persistent, unsubstantiated rumor claims he once drank 64 beers while on a cross-country flight from Boston to Los Angeles. While a member of the New York Yankees in 1996, Boggs was sued by a Continental Airlines flight attendant after he allegedly became enraged when she stopped serving him beer during a charter flight to Milwaukee. In the suit, the flight attendant, Karen Plympton, charged that Boggs jabbed his finger in her face and threatened to "kick your fat lips in." The $6 million lawsuit was eventually settled out of court.

## Bonds, Barry

Surly slugger of the 1980s, 1990s, and 2000s whose prodigious late-career home-run-hitting spree is widely thought to have been aided by his ingestion of various **performance-enhancing drugs**. The son of former All-Star Bobby Bonds (and a distant cousin of Reggie Jackson), Bonds had won three MVP Awards and made three All-Star teams by the time he turned 30, but by the late 1990s he had a reputation as a great regular-season player whose game shriveled in the glare of the postseason. That began to change, along with the circumference of his neck, in the following years as Bonds joined fellow National Leaguers Sammy Sosa and **Mark McGwire** (whom he reportedly fiercely envied) on a long-ball tear that culminated with Bonds setting a new single-season home-run record of 73 in 2001. By the time Bonds clouted career dinger No. 756 to shatter Hank Aaron's all-time home-run record on August 7, 2007, the publication of the best seller *Game of Shadows*, with its documentation of rampant steroid use in major league clubhouses, had already cast a retrospective cloud over the outfielder's offensive accomplishments. The salacious revelations of former Bonds

Barry Bonds OF

mistress Kimberly Bell—including her allegation that the once-buff star developed unsightly back acne and saw his testicles shrink to the size of Le Sueur peas as a consequence of steroid injections—also took its toll on his reputation. Working against Bonds' eventual election to the Hall of Fame is his toxic relationship with the press, toward whom he was invariably churlish, dismissive, and non-communicative. See also: **Anderson, Greg**; **BALCO**; **Conte, Victor**; **Cream and the Clear, The**

# Bonnie Brewer

Presumed wife of **Bernie Brewer**, the longtime mascot of the Milwaukee Brewers. Like Bernie, Bonnie Brewer is outfitted in traditional Bavarian beerhall garb in a nod to Milwaukee's sizable German American community. Bonnie's signature routine involves sweeping the bases clean during the seventh-inning stretch and/or terrorizing the opposing team's third-base coach with her comically large broom. For reasons that remain unclear, Bonnie Brewer was "retired" as an official Brewers team mascot in 1979— reportedly at the behest of then-Brewers owner **Bud Selig**. She was brought back, along with her husband Bernie, in a cartoonish new foam rubber incarnation in 1993.

# Boras, Scott

Powerful player agent, known informally among club executives as "the Antichrist," whose hard-knuckle negotiating tactics disgust purists and occasionally backfire on his clients—the vast majority of whom have grown unspeakably rich as a result of his Mephistophelean machinations. Over the course of a 30-year career representing major and minor leaguers, Boras has negotiated more than $3 billion in player contracts, including the second-biggest deal ever: $252 million over 10 years for Alex Rodriguez with the Texas Rangers. (Rodriguez famously shitcanned Boras while renegotiating the contract with the New York Yankees in 2007.) The Sacramento native is also the keeper of the famed "Boras Binders," elephantine loose-leaf books crammed with statistical and qualitative analysis designed to document the indispensability, value, and historical greatness of each of his clients.

# Bostock, Lyman

Promising major league outfielder who was the tragic victim in one of the most shocking murder cases in baseball history. In 1977, the Birmingham, Alabama, native finished second in batting in the American League as a member of the Minnesota Twins. He signed a lucrative free-agent contract with the California Angels that off-season and at age 27 seemed destined for major league stardom. On the evening of September 23, 1978, just hours after going 2-for-4 in an afternoon game against the Chicago White Sox at Comiskey Park, Bostock was visiting an old family friend in Gary, Indiana, when he was brutally shotgunned to death by a man who wrongly suspected him of having an affair with his wife. The assailant, Leonard Smith, was later found not guilty by reason of insanity and released after seven months in a psychiatric facility.

# Bouton, Jim

Right-handed pitcher whose 10-year major league career was overshadowed by the controversy surrounding the publication of his tell-all book **Ball Four** in 1970. Bouton, who pitched for the Yankees, Seattle Pilots, and Houston Astros from 1962 to 1970 (and made a bizarre, abortive comeback with the Atlanta Braves in 1978 at the age of 39), was primarily known for his whirlwind delivery, which invariably climaxed with his cap flying off his head, until he turned political in the late 1960s. In 1968, he led a delegation of athletes to the Summer Olympics in Mexico City to protest the Apartheid policy in South Africa. Two years later, **Ball Four** scandalized the baseball world by presenting an uncensored look inside the drug-, alcohol-, and sex-fueled world of the major league clubhouse. According to legend, as punishment for the unflattering way he was portrayed in the book, Yankees great Mickey Mantle had Bouton permanently blackballed from Old Timers' Day at Yankee Stadium. Shunned by the baseball fraternity for sharing clubhouse secrets, Bouton turned to sportscasting, and then acting, to make ends meet. He had a supporting role in Robert Altman's private-eye film *The Long Goodbye* in 1973, and also developed and starred in a short-lived adaptation of **Ball Four** for television in 1976. Bouton has also written prolifically, about baseball and other topics, and was reconciled with Mantle and the New York Yankees organization in the 1990s. Most oddly of all, he helped invent and promote **Big League Chew**, a shredded bubble gum product designed to mimic **chewing tobacco** and marketed by the Wrigley Company since 1980.

## Brady Bunch, The

Iconic 1970s TV sitcom set in Southern California and known for its cameos by Los Angeles sports stars of the era. Dodgers Don Drysdale and Wes Parker and Deacon Jones of the Rams (not to mention New York Jets superstar Joe Namath) all found themselves dropping by the Brady household for one reason or another between the show's debut in 1969 and its 1974 demise. In an episode titled "The Dropout" from September 1970, family patriarch Mike Brady calls in the hard-throwing Drysdale in an effort to convince his son Greg not to quit school to pursue a baseball career. Drysdale's cautionary stories of life on the road soon cause Greg to reconsider his rash decision. Parker, the solid first baseman for the Dodgers' 1965 World Series team, had previously turned up on a January 1970 episode called "The Undergraduate," playing the husband of a math teacher on whom Greg Brady has a crush.

# Brito, Mike

Mustachioed, cigar-chomping, Panama hat–wearing Los Angeles Dodgers scout who sat behind home plate at Dodger Stadium for more than 20 years aiming a Stalker radar gun at pitchers. An unmistakable figure in his white sport coat and sunglasses, Brito was actually best known within the organization as the man who brought Fernando Valenzuela to Los Angeles from Mexico. But to millions of TV viewers in the 1970s, '80s, and '90s, he was simply the most recognizable scout in baseball—at least until the advent of the automatic radar gun forced him out of his plush field-level perch. Away from the game, Brito worked part-time as an actor in Mexico. He reportedly owned more than 25 Panama hats and once talked himself out of a speeding ticket by convincing the policeman that his radar gun was wrong.

Getty Images

## Bronx Zoo, The

Catch-all term used to describe the famously dysfunctional New York Yankees clubhouse of the late 1970s and early 1980s. The name derives from the title of ex-Yankee reliever **Sparky Lyle**'s 1979 tell-all best seller, which chronicled the team's squabbling, carousing, and practical joking on the road to two world championships.

## Brown, Mordecai "Three Finger"

Disabled Hall of Famer blessed with one of the game's iconic nicknames. Born Mordecai Peter Centennial Brown, the right-hander lost part of his index finger in a corn-shredder accident when he was a child. He later broke several other fingers in a fall. The middle digit never healed properly and remained twisted and gnarled for the rest of his life (hence "Three Finger"). According to contemporaneous accounts, the deformity enabled Brown to put added topspin on his curveball, which dazzled opposing batters. He retired in 1936 with 239 career wins and a 2.06 ERA, third-best in baseball history. He was elected to the Hall of Fame in 1949. In later years, Brown operated a gas station in Terre Haute, Indiana. He died in 1948.

### They Said What?

"That old paw served me pretty well in its time. It gave me a firmer grip on the ball, so I could spin it over the hump. It gave me a greater dip."

—Mordecai "Three Finger" Brown

# Buccaneer, The

Short-lived Pittsburgh Pirates mascot who revved up crowds at Three Rivers Stadium during the 1995 season. The Buccaneer was decommissioned by the club after his portrayer, Pittsburgh-area actor Tim Beggy, was arrested and charged with public lewdness after being caught having sex with a woman in a public pool. He has since been replaced by a more cartoonish iteration of a stereotypical pirate, **Captain Jolly Roger**.

# Buckner, Bill

Journeyman hit machine whose superb 22-year major league career was overshadowed by a critical error that may have cost the Boston Red Sox the 1986 World Series. "Billy Bucks," as he was known, started out as a fleet-footed outfielder in the Los Angeles Dodgers organization until a serious ankle injury robbed him of his speed and largely limited him to first-base duty. He was an important cog in Boston's drive to the American League pennant in 1986, and at age 36 and despite a near-total lack of mobility had seemingly earned the right to be on the field for the final three outs of what would have been the team's first world championship since 1918. But manager John McNamara's gesture of recognition quickly turned into grist for the greatest second-guess of all time, as Buckner let a dribbler off the bat of New York Met Mookie Wilson roll through his legs, allowing Ray Knight to score the winning run to knot the Series at three games apiece. The Mets disposed of Boston in Game 7 two nights later, setting off an orgy of recrimination in New England that all too often took on an unsavory personal tone. Buckner was vilified by fans, stigmatized in the media as the greatest goat in World Series history, and all but disowned by the Red Sox franchise. After he retired in 1990, he felt compelled to move his family to Boise, Idaho, to escape constant references to his blunder. In 2008, Buckner finally gained some closure on the Buckner Incident when the defending champion Red Sox invited him back to Fenway Park to throw out the ceremonial first pitch at the club's home opener.

## Bull Durham

Baseball-themed romantic comedy that is held in near-totemic esteem by fans who came of age in the 1980s. Written and directed by onetime Baltimore Orioles farmhand Ron Shelton, *Bull Durham* chronicles the athletic and erotic exploits of over-the-hill catcher "Crash" Davis (**Kevin Costner**) and his flamethrowing young batterymate Ebby Calvin "Nuke" LaLoosh (Tim Robbins) as they vie for the attentions of sexy minor league groupie Annie Savoy (Susan Sarandon). The surprise hit of the summer of 1988, the modestly budgeted film charmed critics and audiences to the tune of more than $50 million in box office receipts, empowering Shelton to spend the next decade making less-interesting sports movies, and, together with 1989's *Field of Dreams*, establishing Costner's reputation as Hollywood's unofficial tribune of baseball.

## Bullpen Cars

Once-fashionable means by which relief pitchers were conveyed to the mound from the bullpen. From the early 1950s to the mid-1980s, bullpen cars, carts, and buggies of various kinds were widely used in major league

Richard Lindberg

ballparks until widespread player antipathy, routine beer dousing by drunken fans, and concerns about safety put the kibosh on the vehicles forever. Early bullpen cars were relatively unadorned, but designs grew more baroque beginning in the 1970s. The New York Yankees introduced a pinstriped Datsun as their official bullpen vehicle beginning in 1972; the Philadelphia Phillies painted theirs to look like a fire truck. Many clubs preferred golf carts pimped out with a giant baseball-cap canopy. Oftentimes the home and visiting team each had its own vehicle, complete with a matching hat. The trend may have reached its nadir in 1982 when the Seattle Mariners employed a rolling tugboat on wheels, which the club's pitchers adamantly refused to ride in. By the end of the 1980s, most teams had mothballed their bullpen fleets for good. In 1995, when the Milwaukee Brewers finally garaged their bullpen motorcycle, major league relievers were left with only their own two feet to guide them from their outfield redoubt to the pitcher's mound.

# Burke, Glenn

Budding star who never fulfilled his on-field promise but left his mark on baseball history in another way—as the first openly gay major leaguer. Burke, who came up with the notoriously image-conscious Dodgers organization in the late 1970s, never spoke publicly about his sexual orientation, but his **homosexuality** was acknowledged inside the clubhouse and by the front office—to the point where Dodgers general manager **Al Campanis** once offered to pay for his honeymoon if he took part in a sham marriage. Burke also drew the ire of famously homophobic Dodgers skipper Tommy Lasorda, who resented him for befriending his estranged gay son, Spunky. Shipped off to the Oakland Athletics in a 1978 trade, Burke fared no better in Northern California. In 1980, new A's manager **Billy Martin** publicly declared his opposition to having a gay player on the team. Exiled to the minors, Burke opted to retire from the game entirely at the conclusion of the 1980 season. He came out publicly in 1982 and spent the rest of the decade on a downward slide into drug addiction and aimless drifting. He died of AIDS in 1995. Besides forging a path for other gay athletes, such as major league outfielder **Billy Bean** and NBA center John Amaechi, Burke made one other notable contribution to the world of sports: he is credited with inventing the high-five, the first of which he delivered to Dodgers teammate Dusty Baker at home plate following a Baker home run at Dodger Stadium on October 2, 1977.

## Burns, Ken

Earnest, Beatle-wigged documentary filmmaker who surveyed the history of America's pastime in his Emmy-winning nine-part documentary series *Baseball*. Aired over nine consecutive nights in September of 1994 in the midst of the World Series—killing players' strike that

AP Images

nearly destroyed the game, *Baseball* replicates the stylistic template Burns had previously employed in his acclaimed *Civil War* series from four years earlier. Professional actors speak in the voices of historical figures from baseball's past while a succession of talking heads offer their insights into the game's enduring appeal—all while plaintive instrumental music and stark, haunting renditions of "Take Me Out to the Ballgame" play in the

### GREAT NAMES OF THE GAME

# Burleigh

Nicknamed "Ol' Stubblebeard," Burleigh Arland Grimes was an early practitioner of the **spitball** who won 20 games five times over the course of a 19-year career. Fractious and feisty, Grimes was famous for confronting **umpires**. Burleigh is an Old English name meaning "a field with knotted tree trunks."

background. A general tone of hushed reverence persists throughout. Oddly enough, many of the "experts" interviewed by Burns, such as historian Doris Kearns Goodwin and former New York governor Mario Cuomo, have only a tangential connection to the game and offer little beyond a layperson's perspective.

## Burrell, Stanley "Hammer"

Entrepreneurial-minded African American adolescent who served as the honorary vice president of the Oakland Athletics from 1973 to 1980. He later went on to international superstardom as the baggy-pants rapper MC Hammer. An Oakland native, Burrell was the protégé of A's owner **Charles O. Finley**, who first "discovered" him performing splits for money in the Oakland Coliseum parking lot. (Stanley's brother Louis was the team's batboy at the time.) Finley was so taken with the youth that he hired him on the spot to serve as a special "owner's assistant." He outfitted Burrell in a green-and-gold cap with the initials "VP" stenciled on it and paid him $7 a game to be his West Coast "eyes and ears"—an unusually powerful position since Finley had no front office staff and preferred to spend most of his time in Chicago. Burrell's job was to sit in the owner's box during home games and deliver play-by-play updates to Finley via telephone. He kibitzed openly about managerial strategy, much to the consternation of the club's mid-1970s skippers Alvin Dark and Jack McKeon, who were routinely besieged mid-game by phone calls from Finley issuing orders transmitted to him from Burrell. Burrell was also known to report on clubhouse activity, earning him a reputation among the players as a management spy. They nicknamed him "Pipeline," for his purported role as Finley's informant, and later "Hammer," for his resemblance to slugger Hank Aaron. Burrell at first hoped to parlay his front office experience into a career playing professional baseball but eventually opted for the music business instead. In 1987, he used $20,000 in loans from ex-A's Mike Davis and Dwayne Murphy to start his own record label, Bust-It Productions.

## Campanis, Al

Highly respected Los Angeles Dodgers general manager who detonated his 44-year major league career on live television in April of 1987 when he made a series of racially charged observations about African Americans in baseball. Ironically enough, Campanis was appearing on ABC's *Nightline* on April 6, 1987, to mark the 40th anniversary of Jackie Robinson's breaking of the color barrier. Campanis, who had played with Robinson and later gained notoriety as the scout who discovered **Sandy Koufax**, was known to be one of the more progressive-minded executives in the game, but on this night he answered host Ted Koppel's question about the paucity of African Americans in front office positions with an astoundingly obtuse soliloquy about blacks supposedly lacking "some of the necessities" required for management positions. He also mused that a putative lack of buoyancy affected blacks' ability to swim. After breaking for a commercial, Koppel, sensing that Campanis was in the process of immolating himself in front of a national audience, offered the executive an opportunity to "dig [him]self out" from his ill-considered comments. Instead, Campanis merely dug deeper, cataloging the black athlete's many fine physical features but expressing doubt as to whether they possess the requisite "background" for executive positions. The ensuing public outcry led to Campanis' firing two days later. He never worked in baseball again.

## Captain Black

Brand of pipe tobacco endorsed by manager **Billy Martin** in a series of 1982 TV commercials.

# Captain Earthman

Colorado Rockies **supervendor** and self-described "intergalactic space hippie" who has hawked beer in the outfield bleachers at Coors Field since the park opened in 1995. Known for his **Fu Manchu** mustache, tricked-out beer-bottle space helmet, and jiggling peanut earrings, the beer man formerly known as Brent Doeden experienced a

Jeff Pope

pot- and Budweiser-fueled epiphany in the mid-1970s and became convinced he was a visitor from another planet. Oddly interested in having fans contact him by cell phone when they want a beer, Captain Earthman prowls the bleachers handing out business cards that list his "Planetary Location Number" and claims he's been a "prisoner of Earth since 1956 and at your service since the Rockies landed." ("Selling no beer beneath my dignity" is another one of his taglines.) Every Memorial Day, he throws a party at his house for 200 of his fellow vendors and his most loyal customers.

## They Said What?

"If it's from the earth, man, I'll smoke it."

—**Captain Earthman**'s motto

# Captain Jolly Roger

Costumed buccaneer who has served as the secondary mascot of the Pittsburgh Pirates since 2006. Outfitted in stereotypical pirate garb—complete with a mangy beard, bandanna, eye patch, and tricorn hat—Captain Jolly Roger roams the field at PNC Park rallying fans with his baseball bat–bedecked pirate flag. It's unclear why the Pirates organization felt the

Adam Prince

need to add a pirate commander to its already crowded mascot roster, which features several costumed pierogies in addition to the venerable **Pirate Parrot**. (The club's previous attempt to foist a "human" pirate character on fans, 1995's ill-starred **Buccaneer**, went down in flames after the mascot portrayer was caught having sex in a public swimming pool.) An attempt to appeal to children may have been part of the calculation. "We want our young fans to form that emotional connection with the franchise," the team declared in a press release announcing the Captain's May 2006 unveiling. Indeed, the name Captain Jolly Roger was selected by Pittsburgh-area kids as part of a newspaper-sponsored naming contest.

## Caray, Harry

Stage name of Harry Christopher Carabina, a venerable radio and TV play-by-play man who worked for four major league teams over a 54-year career but is probably best known as the longtime voice of the Chicago Cubs. He began his career in St. Louis in 1945 and lasted nearly a quarter century behind the Cardinals microphone before his high-living lifestyle caught up with him (it was rumored he had an affair with Cardinals owner Gussie Busch's daughter-in-law). After a brief stint with the Oakland A's, Caray spent most of the 1970s in the Chicago White Sox booth, where he teamed with analyst **Jimmy Piersall** for five memorable seasons and introduced the tradition of leading fans in the singing of "Take Me Out to the Ballgame" during the seventh-inning stretch (a crowd-pleasing gimmick he later brought with him to Wrigley Field but which did little to quell rioters on **Disco Demolition Night**). In 1981, he moved to the North Side, joining the Cubs for what would be a 17-year run during which his national profile was heightened thanks to WGN's "superstation" telecasts on cable systems across the country. An unabashed homer, Caray became famous for his comically oversized glasses, inability to pronounce the players' names

## They Said What?

"Booze, broads, and bullshit.
If you got all that, what else do you need?"

—**Harry Caray**

correctly (a deficiency exacerbated by a 1987 stroke), and the catchphrases "Holy cow!" and "It might be...It could be...It is! A home run!" Behind the scenes, he was known to be a two-fisted drinker and inveterate womanizer. "I'm a Cub fan and a Bud man!" he bellowed in a notorious rap music TV promo for Cubs broadcasts in 1985. Stories about his prodigious alcohol consumption abound. Told by his doctor he would have to limit himself to one drink per day, Caray took to consuming his booze out of the largest glass he could find. He once got so plastered during a game that color commentator Steve Stone found him hanging upside down from a metal staircase leading to the broadcast booth. Although most fans found Caray's late-period "old crazy drunk" act endearing, his penchant for blurting out whatever floated into his mind could occasionally get him into trouble. "Well, my eyes are slanty enough, how about yours?" he asked Cubs manager Jim Riggleman on the air before a game against Japanese pitcher Hideo Nomo of the Dodgers in 1995. In the final few years of his life, Caray was well-nigh incoherent, his increasingly aimless rambling providing the inspiration for a spot-on impression by Will Ferrell on *Saturday Night Live*—a skit that lived on after Caray collapsed at a Valentine's Day dinner and died of cardiac arrest on February 18, 1998. The organist at the announcer's funeral played "Take Me Out to the Ballgame" in his honor.

# Carlton, Steve

Idiosyncratic left-hander whose 1994 elevation to the Hall of Fame was tainted by the publication of a rambling interview in *Philadelphia Magazine* that revealed him as an adherent to a stunningly wide variety of crackpot conspiracy theories. The 300-game winner had always marched to the beat of his own drum. He famously refused to speak to the press and followed an unorthodox training regime based on principles developed by the legendary Chinese martial arts master Guan Gong. Before every game he submerged his pitching arm in a garbage pail filled with brown rice and rotated it 49 times—once for each of the 49 years that Guan Gong lived on this planet. He once demanded that the Philadelphia Phillies spend $15,000 to construct a soundproof "mood behavior" chamber into which he would sequester himself before starts. There he would sit for hours in an easy chair staring at the soothing image of a breaking ocean wave while a recorded voice cooed affirmations like "I am courageous, calm, confident and relaxed…. I can control my destiny." For most of his career, Carlton was thought to be nothing but a harmless eccentric. After his retirement, however, a darker portrait began to emerge. The *Philadelphia Magazine* article, which appeared just a few weeks after he had been elected to Cooperstown, used his own words to depict Carlton as an anti-Semitic survivalist who believed a revolution was coming that would release mankind from the grip of various shadowy conspiracies. In a wide-ranging opinion dump, Carlton charged that: the AIDS virus was concocted by government scientists at a top-secret biological warfare laboratory in Maryland "to get rid of gays and blacks"; the previous eight U.S. presidents were guilty of treason; then-President Bill Clinton had fathered a black son and First Lady Hillary Clinton was "a dyke"; and that the world was being enslaved, in various scenarios, by "12 Jewish bankers meeting in Switzerland," the British MI-5 and MI-6 intelligence agencies, "a committee of 300 which meets at a roundtable in Rome," the teachers' unions, Yale University's Skull and Bones Society, the International Monetary

Fund, the World Health Organization, The Elders of Zion, or the Russian and U.S. governments, who "fill the air with low-frequency sound waves meant to control us." Carlton also admitted he lived in a heavily fortified mountainside compound in Colorado atop a 7,000-square-foot survival bunker stocked with canned foods, bottled water, and weapons. The bombshell interview severely damaged Carlton's reputation and put a damper on his Hall of Fame induction later that summer. A number of the left-hander's ex-teammates were forced to defend him in the media, including his former personal catcher, **Tim McCarver**, who called Carlton "a very complicated person" who has "a very difficult time being human."

# Cashman, Terry

Genial former Detroit Tigers farmhand who touched a chord with baseball fans from coast to coast when he composed the ballpark favorite **"Talkin' Baseball"** in 1981.

# Castro, Fidel

Cuban revolutionary turned Communist dictator often erroneously credited with having once tried out for a major league team. The persistent urban legend has Castro being scouted by several different clubs during the late 1940s while he was pitching for the University of Havana. He was then allegedly whisked to the United States for a tryout with either the Washington Senators or the New York Yankees. Unfortunately, there isn't a grain of truth to the story. It's not even clear

AP Images

whether Castro ever pitched anywhere outside of an intramural game. The Marxist strongman's authentic baseball connection is somewhat less romantic. In the late 1970s, Castro was reportedly under consideration to play the manager of a Cuban Little League team in the aborted third **Bad News Bears** sequel.

## "Centerfield"

Title song of a 1985 rock album by former Creedence Clearwater Revival front man John Fogerty that has since become a ballpark and highlight reel staple. Unlike Bruce Springsteen, whose **"Glory Days"** has achieved comparable iconic status among fans of America's pastime, Fogerty manages to get the baseball terminology correct in a song that celebrates the game's history, the arrival of spring, and the appearance of "new grass on the field."

## Chapman, Ben

Racist major league manager who led the campaign to intimidate Jackie Robinson out of baseball in 1947. Among the many big leaguers who opposed Robinson's integration of the game—including **Enos Slaughter** and Robinson's own teammate, **Dixie Walker**—Chapman may have been the most vicious. As manager of the cellar-dwelling Philadelphia Phillies, the bigoted ex-Yankee did everything in his power to terrorize and taunt baseball's first African American player at every opportunity. Among Chapman's more obnoxious tactics: ordering his pitchers to throw at Robinson's head every time the count got to 3–0; wielding a bat like a weapon and making machine gun sounds whenever Robinson walked by; and keeping up a steady stream of verbal abuse from the dugout that included likening Robinson to a monkey. While Chapman's attacks took a personal toll on Robinson—the civil rights legend later admitted they "brought me nearer to cracking up than I had ever been"—they also compelled the other Dodgers to rally around their beleaguered teammate. Public outcry over Chapman's offensive behavior compelled the segregationist skipper to pose for a "let's bury the hatchet" photograph with his nemesis the following season.

## Charlie-O

Five-foot-tall live Missouri mule who served as the official mascot of the Kansas City/Oakland Athletics from 1963 to 1976. Named after A's owner **Charles O. Finley**, Charlie-O was a gift to the club from Missouri governor Warren Hearnes, who was eager to keep Finley from moving the team to California and thought that bestowing him with the state's official animal might do the trick. By all accounts, Finley was quite taken with Hearnes' ass and soon began parading him around the league. Charlie-O was occasionally enlisted to bring the A's lineup card to home plate and even traveled with the club on road trips. He had his own trailer and stayed at the same hotel as the rest of the team. Finley himself once rode Charlie-O through New York's Times Square, waving a white cowboy hat. When the A's did depart Kansas City for Oakland following the 1967 season, Finley took Charlie-O with him. The mule remained a fixture at A's games throughout the club's championship years of 1972–1974. When Charlie-O died in 1977 at the ripe old age of 20, he was cremated and had his ashes scattered in a memorial garden at the Oakland SPCA, near the Oakland Coliseum.

## Chaw

*See* **Chewing Tobacco**

## Chester Charge

Sabre-wielding Confederate cavalryman who served as the original mascot of the Houston Astros until 1990, Chester started out as an animated character who would appear on the enormous **Astrodome** scoreboard whenever the home team started a rally. He was often depicted sounding his bugle while leading the "charge" from atop a boat, rocket, motorcycle, buffalo, or elephant. In 1977, the club introduced a costumed live-action version of Chester— played by a local high school student riding a pantomime horse— who would appear on the field before and after the game and during the seventh-inning stretch.

## Chester, Hilda

Onetime Ebbets Field peanut bagger turned cowbell-ringing Brooklyn Dodgers **superfan**. Zaftig and iron-lunged, Chester was a regular and vocal Dodgers rooter during the 1930s, when the first in a series of heart attacks robbed her of the ability to cheer on her beloved Bums. On the advice of her cardiologist, she turned to banging frying pans instead and later added a cowbell and a Hawaiian hula skirt to her ballpark repertoire. Known for

heckling Dodgers opponents—and the Dodgers themselves—in a thick Brooklyn accent, she occasionally traveled with the team and became something of an unofficial mascot. She was especially fond of longtime Dodgers manager Leo Durocher, even testifying on his behalf at his 1946 assault trial in the brutal beating of a fellow **heckler**. ("This man called me a cocksucker, your honor," Chester told the judge of the alleged victim in the case; Durocher was acquitted.) "Hilda wit da bell," as she preferred to style herself, remained a fixture at Dodgers games until the club moved to Los Angeles in 1958. She died in 1978.

# Chewing Tobacco

Unchopped, unflavored tobacco product, also known as chaw or "chew," that has been consumed in the United States since the founding of the republic and by baseball players since the game was first organized in the 19th century. Once nearly universally preferred by American tobacco users (especially in the South and West, where spittoons were ubiquitous), chaw fell out of favor with the general public around the turn of the 20th century as more and more people started switched to machine-rolled cigarettes to satisfy their tobacco jones. Nevertheless, its popularity among ballplayers held steady into the 1950s. (In addition to being an efficient method of titrating nicotine, expectorated tobacco juice is reportedly very good at tenderizing gloves.) After a relatively fallow few decades when the more fashionable players smoked Chesterfields, chewing enjoyed a resurgence in the 1970s, when the image of the lumbering slugger with a huge wad of tobacco bulging out of his cheek achieved near-iconic status. Bobby Murcer, Catfish Hunter, and **Lenny Dykstra** were just a few of the major league All-Stars of the '70s and '80s readily identifiable by their enormous chaws. **Big League Chew**, a brand of bubble gum promoted by big leaguer **Jim Bouton**, was purposely designed to mimic chaw's stringy, spaghetti-like texture (ironic, since players often combined chaw with bubble gum to enhance

## You Could Look It Up

**Random Baseball Trivia**

An abstemious man, Honus Wagner detested smoking and refused to have his baseball card distributed in tobacco packages.

adhesion to their molars). Players were often recruited to do ads for chaw purveyors such as Skoal and Red Man—long after the link between chewing tobacco and mouth cancer had been conclusively established. Not until the mid-1990s did baseball take action to discourage chewing among the young, even recruiting Dykstra to appear in a series of anti-tobacco PSAs in which he half-heartedly urged Little Leaguers: "Copy my hustle. Copy my desire. But please don't copy my tobacco use." Although they are invariably lumped together under the generic rubric of "smokeless tobacco," chaw is to be distinguished from "dip" or "snuff," which is finely chopped and/or ground and often flavored with mint.

# Chief Noc-A-Homa

Whooping Native American caricature who served as the official mascot of the Milwaukee/Atlanta Braves from the 1950s to 1986. (His name is a pun on the phrase "Knock a Homer.") The screaming Indian (who may have evolved from an earlier Braves mascot, Chief Wildhorse) wore a war bonnet and lived in a teepee in the bleachers at Atlanta Fulton County Stadium. (He once accidentally set his teepee on fire while attempting to send smoke signals, prompting fans to douse the blaze with beer.) He performed a war dance whenever a Braves player hit a home run and was thought by many fans to bring the team good luck. When his wigwam was briefly removed from the stands in 1982, the team fell into a long losing streak. Chief Noc-A-Homa was

AP Images

**Unsurprisingly, Chief Noc-A-Homa fell out of favor in an age of political correctness.**

decommissioned by the club in 1986 after the mascot's portrayer stopped showing up at public appearances and started demanding more than $60 per game. For a brief period during the mid-1980s, the chief had a female consort, **Princess Poc-A-Homa**.

# Chief Wahoo

Grinning Native American caricature who has served as the controversial mascot of the Cleveland Indians since 1947. The current, friendly incarnation of Wahoo—whose name derives presumably from a white person's take on a traditional Indian war whoop—replaced a slightly more sinister hook-nosed version and first started appearing on Cleveland uniform sleeves and caps in 1951. His freakish grin and beet-red skin have outraged many in the Native American community, who liken the Chief to such bygone racist caricatures as Little Black Sambo and the beaming, four-eyed Chinese coolie. Over the years, a number of newspapers and media outlets have called for the decommissioning of Wahoo as the Indians' mascot. (The *Wall Street Journal* labeled him "a symbol of hatred and prejudice.") Partly in recognition of the controversy he generated, the Indians for many years de-emphasized Wahoo as an insignia on their caps, replacing him with a succession of stylized letter C's. In 1986, they returned him to a place of prominence and saw cap and uniform sales soar as a result. But that decision has not come without a price. Native American protestors picketed outside Jacobs Field in Cleveland before the 1997 World Series, and some have even gone so far as to suggest that a karmic "Curse of Wahoo" has prevented the club from winning a world championship since 1948.

# Clemens, Roger

Hard-throwing right-hander whose surefire Hall of Fame career trajectory was called into question by allegations that he habitually used steroids and other **performance-enhancing drugs** in the late 1990s. The barrel-chested Texas native won 354 games over the course of a 24-year major league career with the Red Sox, Blue Jays, Yankees, and Astros but repeatedly courted controversy. He famously begged out of Game 6 of the 1986 World Series, according to manager John McNamara, citing a mysterious blister on his pitching hand. In 1990, he was ejected from Game 3 of the American League Championship Series in the bottom of the second inning after arguing balls and strikes with home-plate umpire Terry Cooney. And in 2000, he hit New York Mets catcher Mike Piazza in the head with a pitch during a regular-season interleague tilt, then weirdly flung the jagged half of a broken bat at the future Hall of Famer during a possibly testosterone-fueled meltdown in Game 2 of the World Series. Clemens likely would have survived these incidents with his reputation as the game's ultimate competitor intact had he not been outed as a steroid user in Senator George Mitchell's report on **performance-enhancing drugs** in baseball, which essentially confirmed allegations made by former teammate José Canseco in his book *Juiced*. Although Clemens has denied all the charges, it is now widely believed that he had Yankees strength coach Brain McNamee inject him in the buttocks with the anabolic horse steroid Winstrol and other substances during the 1998 season. Clemens' good name was further

## You Could Look It Up

### Random Baseball Trivia

Years before he threw a jagged bat shard at Mike Piazza, **Roger Clemens** was showing signs of steroid-induced rage. He once heckled recovering alcoholic Bob Welch during a playoff game by screaming "Drink beer, like a real man!"

besmirched by a 2008 newspaper story alleging that he had carried on a long-term extramarital affair with teenaged country star Mindy McCready and, to a lesser extent, by the revelation in Joe Torre's memoir *The Yankee Years* that he routinely asked Yankees trainer Steve Donahue to rub red-hot liniment onto his testicles before starts.

## Clown Prince of Baseball

Unofficial title claimed at one time or another by professional ballpark buffoon **Max Patkin**, bazooka-wielding shortstop **Jackie Price**, eccentric third-base coach **Al Schacht**, and others.

## Clubhouse Lawyer

Derisive term, often used by front office executives, to single out a player who politicks against management on behalf of himself or other players. Notable examples of clubhouse lawyers include Tom Seaver on the New York Mets teams of the 1970s, who through his incessant bellyaching to the press is credited with engineering his own trade to the Cincinnati Reds in 1977; the triumvirate of **Bill Lee**, Ferguson Jenkins, and Rick Wise, who repeatedly undermined **Don Zimmer** during his late-1970s tenure as Boston Red Sox manager; and Al Leiter and **John Franco** of the early 2000s Mets, who inexplicably acquired the power to dictate trades to ownership—including the ill-advised swap of Scott Kazmir for Victor Zambrano in 2004 (reportedly to punish Kazmir for the crime of playing Eminem instead of Bruce Springsteen on a clubhouse boombox).

*Baseball by the Numbers* | **337**

Number **Bill Lee** wished he could wear on his uniform, enabling him to stand on his head and have it spell out his last name

# Cobb, Ty

Crabby, bigoted Hall of Famer who carved out a well-deserved reputation as one of the game's archetypal bastards. An unreconstructed racist of the old-school Southern variety, the so-called Georgia Peach set a standard for villainy that no player of his magnitude has ever quite matched. His rap sheet of violent outbursts is almost as long as his résumé of offensive accomplishments. In 1908, Cobb knocked down an African American asphalt spreader who had accidentally splattered some tar on his trousers. That same year, the black newspaper *The Chicago Defender* reported that Cobb had kicked a chambermaid down a flight of stairs after she objected to being

Getty Images

## *You Could Look It Up*

### Random Baseball Trivia

**Ty Cobb** was so tough he once had his tonsils removed by a hotel doctor—without anesthesia—to avoid missing a game. He played seven innings the next day.

called "nigger." In 1909, Cobb slapped a black elevator operator without provocation at the Hotel Euclid in Cleveland. When the hotel detective, who was also black, intervened, Cobb pulled a knife and slashed him. Those dustups paled in comparison to the 1907 brawl Cobb got into with an African American groundskeeper who had the nerve to clap him on the shoulder in a gesture of friendship. Already suspecting that the groundskeeper had defiled one of his gloves, Cobb assaulted the man and, when his wife came to his aid, her as well. Cobb's teammates found him with his hands around the woman's neck, choking the life out of her. The savagery of the Peach's attack enraged the team's 240-pound catcher, Charlie Schmidt, who broke up the altercation and challenged Cobb to a formal boxing match to settle things in a more gentlemanly fashion. An ex-boxer, Schmidt subsequently pummeled Cobb, breaking his nose and dealing him the first clear-cut defeat he ever suffered in or out of the ring. "I fight to kill," Cobb once said, and while there's no evidence he ever followed through on that declaration, when he died in 1961 at the age of 74 he left behind a .367 career average, a major league record 4,191 hits, and a legacy of ferocious play, bilious race hatred, and antisocial behavior.

## *They Said What?*

### "**Ty Cobb** is a prick."

–Babe Ruth

# Cocaine Seven

Seven major leaguers who were suspended for the 1986 season by Commissioner Peter Ueberroth in the aftermath of the **Pittsburgh Drug Trials**. They are: **Keith Hernandez**, Dale Berra, Dave Parker, Lonnie Smith, Joaquin Andujar, Enos Cabell, and Jeffrey Leonard. Cited for helping to facilitate the distribution of drugs in baseball clubhouses, the seven had their suspensions lifted by agreeing to perform 100 hours of community service and donating 10 percent of their salaries to drug treatment programs. Four other players—Lee Lacy, Al Holland, Lary Sorensen, and Claudell Washington—received 60-day suspensions that were likewise lifted. See also: **Pirate Parrot**

# Collins, Marla

Comely Chicago Cubs ballgirl who was fired by the club in the middle of the 1986 season after she posed nude for the September issue of *Playboy* magazine. The vivacious college student and aspiring broadcaster spent parts of five seasons trotting baseballs out to **umpires** at Wrigley Field, attracting a national following due to her exposure on WGN telecasts. At one point she had her own sneaker endorsement deal. But Collins angered Cubs officials after she posed naked as well as clad only in a Cubs uniform, accompanied by a leering **Harry Caray**, in an eight-page *Playboy* photo spread titled "The Belle of the Ball Club."

# Collusion

Blanket term used to describe a surreptitious and concerted effort by major league owners to bid down player contracts during the free-agency periods of 1985, 1986, and 1987. Owners secretly agreed not to offer contracts to such prominent free agents of the period as Jack Morris, Kirk Gibson, and Andre Dawson—a clear-cut violation of the terms of their collective

Not content with merely chasing Joe Morgan's fly balls, Marla Collins chased fame by posing for *Playboy* in 1986.

Kasey Ignarski

bargaining agreement with the players union. The union filed a suit and eventually reached a settlement requiring the owners to pay the players $280 million in damages and grant "new look" free agency to a number of aggrieved stars who had reluctantly re-signed with their old clubs.

# Cone, David

Respected big-game pitcher of the 1980s and 1990s who saw his reputation sullied by an accusation of public lewdness in 1989. Cone, who was pitching for the New York Mets at the time, gave new meaning to the term "action in the bullpen" when he reportedly masturbated in full view of a woman identified in various accounts as a ballpark groupie. According to the woman, Cone scolded her after she objected, saying, "You're a big baby. You're not invited to showtime anymore."

# Conte, Victor

Onetime funk bass player turned self-taught pharmacist who emerged as a key figure in baseball's 1990s steroids scandal. A former session man nicknamed "Walkin' Fish," Conte played with the legendary Tower of Power horns and jazz pianist Herbie Hancock, among others, during the 1960s, '70s, and '80s. He gave up playing professionally and founded the Bay Area Laboratory Co-Operative, better known as **BALCO**, in 1984, as a money-making outlet for his longtime interest in chemical nutritional analysis. Suspected of designing and distributing **performance-enhancing drugs to Barry Bonds** and other prominent athletes over a 10-year period, Conte plead guilty in July 2005 to one count of conspiracy to distribute steroids and was sentenced to four months in prison and another four under house arrest.

# Cooper, Joseph

Lincolnshire, Illinois, marshmallow salesman who famously brawled with New York Yankees manager **Billy Martin** outside the Hotel de France hotel bar near Minneapolis on October 23, 1979. Cooper went into the bar to grab a drink with a friend and struck up a conversation with Martin, who was bending the elbow with his longtime drinking buddy Howard Wong. According to Cooper, Martin grew belligerent after Cooper commented favorably on Dick Williams of the Expos and Earl Weaver of the Orioles winning the Manager of the Year Awards. "They're both assholes and so are you for saying it," thundered an apparently inebriated Martin, who then challenged Cooper to a fight. "Here's five hundred to your penny I can knock you on your ass," the Yankee skipper bragged, slapping a roll of bills down on the bar. On their way outside, according to Cooper's account, Martin sucker punched him, opening up a cut on his upper lip that required 15 stitches to repair. (Martin would later claim that Cooper "fell" and cut his lip on the floor of the hotel lobby.) The public relations fallout from the incident—which was curiously heightened by the fact that the other man involved was a marshmallow salesman—led to Martin's being fired from the Yankees for the second time.

## *They Said What?*

**"The marshmallow man I hit was saying bad things about New York and the Yankees."**

—**Billy Martin**, commenting on his altercation with marshmallow salesman **Joseph Cooper**

## Corked Bats

Inventive method of cheating whereby hitters attempt to enhance bat speed and increase the distances traveled by batted balls by filling the interior of their bats with cork or other substances. **Albert Belle** and Sammy Sosa are the most famous recent practitioners of the corked bat scam. In Belle's case, his bat was confiscated by the home-plate umpire after suspicions were raised by the opposing manager. A postgame examination revealed the cork, although Belle futilely dispatched reliever Jason Grimsley to the **umpires'** locker room during the game to try to replace the corked bat with a legal one. He was suspended for seven games for his actions. Sosa received an eight-game suspension for a 2003 incident in which his corked bat literally shattered on contact, sending cork flying all over the field. On rare occasions, a bat is said to be "corked" with a substance other than cork proper. In a game against the Detroit Tigers in September 1974, New York Yankees third baseman Graig Nettles was caught corking the hollowed-out barrel of his bat with superballs, the high-bouncing vulcanized rubber balls manufactured by Wham-O.

## Costner, Kevin

Popular matinee idol of the 1980s and '90s who gained sports-icon status as the star of two of the most beloved baseball movies ever made—*Field of Dreams* and ***Bull Durham*** (as well as a third, *For Love of the Game*, that nobody has ever seen). Costner's ability to portray wizened, worn-out, washed-up jocks who get a belated chance at redemption appealed to male moviegoers of a certain age who could identify with his predicament, while his dreamy blue eyes lured in female fans who otherwise would have no interest in a baseball picture. With his association with the game came increased proximity to its stars, which caused Costner adverse publicity on at least one occasion. According to a widely circulated urban legend, Costner nearly caused the premature termination of Cal Ripken Jr.'s consecutive-games streak by sleeping with Ripken's wife before a game in August of 1997. The rumor contends that Ripken caught his wife Kelly and Costner—who did have a burgeoning friendship—in bed together at the couple's Maryland home just hours before a scheduled tilt between the Orioles and the Seattle Mariners. Ripken was so distraught over the incident, according to the story, that he failed to show up for the game, prompting Orioles management to stage a bogus "power outage" and cancel the contest in order to keep "the Streak" intact. As it turns out, there was a game cancelled due to lighting problems at Camden Yards on August 14, 1997, but no evidence to suggest the electrical failure was deliberately staged by the club—or that Kelly Ripken and Kevin Costner were anything but friends. All sides have denied the incident ever took place.

## "Cotton-Eyed Joe"

Pre–Civil War traditional American folk song that has been a sing-along staple at Texas Rangers home games since 1972. "If it hadn't been for Cotton-Eyed Joe," go the lyrics of the irresistibly catchy hoedown starter, "I'd been married a long time ago." (The meaning of the song's somewhat obscure lyrics are the subject of much debate. One theory holds that Cotton-Eyed Joe was a slave who had imbibed an unhealthy quantity of wood alcohol that turned his eyeballs abnormally white.) The version played during the seventh-inning stretch at Rangers games is by Al Dean and the All-Stars. In the mid-1990s, a novelty rendition by Swedish "techno-country" band Rednex became a worldwide dance-club hit. That version has been regularly played at Yankee Stadium, and a number of other professional sports venues, ever since.

## Cowbell Lady

*See* **Chester, Hilda**

## "Cowboy Up!"

Longtime rodeo rallying cry adopted by the 2003 Boston Red Sox as their team motto. First baseman/designated hitter Kevin Millar is credited with introducing the club to the catchphrase, which translated from rodeospeak means "Suck it up" or "Get it together." Its currency in popular culture can be traced to the 1994 film *8 Seconds*, in which a legendary bull rider played by *Beverly Hills 90210* hunk Luke Perry is exhorted by a fellow rider to "cowboy up" after a particularly nasty spill.

## Cracker Jack

Caramel corn and peanut snack food, often erroneously called "Cracker Jacks," that has become a ballpark food staple based largely on a single mention in the lyrics to "Take Me Out to the Ballgame"—which some have called the greatest product placement in history. In fact, Cracker Jack was being eaten at ballgames long before the song was first copyrighted in 1908, and the term "cracker jack" was often used to refer to an especially talented player.

### *They Said What?*

**"I don't know what the big deal about Cracker Jack is."**

—**Harry Caray**

# Crazy Crab

Widely reviled crustacean "anti-mascot" introduced by the San Francisco Giants during the 1984 season. Inspired by the city of San Francisco's reputation for excellent seafood—and variously likened to a blob of rancid meat and a "hamburger with arms"—Crazy Crab was the brainchild of Giants marketing director Pat Gallagher and a local advertising copywriter, John Crawford, who provided the character's distinctively irritating nasal voice for a preseason TV commercial rolling out the anti-mascot concept. The idea was to  provide jaded Bay Area residents with an alternative to the warm and cuddly **mascots** then proliferating throughout the major leagues. When a poll commissioned by the club indicated that 62 percent of Giants fans would boo a fan-friendly mascot on sight, the front office decided that a rude, annoying parody of a traditional mascot was the way to go. Originally, there was to be no costumed incarnation of the character at Candlestick Park. But the TV spot, which featured a catchy Crazy Crab jingle and depicted Giants manager Frank Robinson having to be restrained from physically assaulting the creature, proved so popular that the club decided to hire a local actor named Wayne Doba to appear inside a foam rubber crab costume for $75 a game. During his first day on the job, Doba mooned the crowd at Candlestick, prompting a rain of boos and abuse that would be repeated at every home game during the Giants' dismal 96-loss season. In fact, the obnoxious mascot became the focal point of fan ire at the team's performance, as angry Candlestick patrons routinely pelted Crazy Crab with food, beer, batteries, golf balls, and even urine-filled balloons. Eventually the sickmaking torrent got so bad the club had to

THE UNDERGROUND BASEBALL ENCYCLOPEDIA

reinforce Doba's costume with a fiberglass shell for his own protection. By the end of the season, Doba feared a sniper might take a shot at him from the stands. Even the Giants' own players got in on the act. They dumped beer into his suit, poured red-hot ointment into his armpit holes, hit him across the shins with a fungo bat, turned fire hoses on him, pegged him with resin bags and baseballs, and dropped lighted firecrackers in his path. Pitcher Greg Minton once spit tobacco juice into Crazy Crab's eyehole. Outfielder Chili Davis doused Doba with Gatorade while he was inside the costume. During the last game of the season, as he circled the field hoisting a rubber torch aloft to the strains of the theme from *Chariots of Fire*, Crazy Crab was tackled by a member of the visiting San Diego Padres. Doba sustained back injuries in the assault and sued for damages. He eventually settled out of court for $2,000. The actor briefly entertained the thought of ritually killing off the Crazy Crab character by tossing the costume out of an airplane over Candlestick Park but ultimately opted not to "because I thought it might send the wrong message to kids." In any case, Crazy Crab was not long for this world. The club "retired" him before the start of the 1985 season. The character has since been resurrected for the occasional retro-themed promotional evening—including a 2008 **bobble-head** giveaway—but without Doba in the crab suit. An entire website, rehabthecrab.com, devotes itself to lobbying for the mascot's permanent reinstatement.

## They Said What?

"All those fans in Giants land, love that **Crazy Crab.** Down by the bay, the folks all say, love that **Crazy Crab.**"

–lyrics to the **Crazy Crab** theme song

# Cream and the Clear, The

Mysterious, performance-enhancing ointments reportedly supplied to **Barry Bonds** and other players by the **BALCO** nutrition center during the steroid era of the early 2000s. Bonds has long maintained that the Cream and the Clear were arthritis balm and flaxseed oil, respectively, though most experts dispute that assertion. The Cream is thought to be a mixture of testosterone and epitestosterone; the Clear is an anabolic steroid called Tetrahydrogestrinone, also known as THG. Both were engineered to be undetectable in traditional drug tests. The slang terms were the brainchild of **BALCO** founder **Victor Conte**.

# Crystal, Billy

Comedian, actor, and onetime *Saturday Night Live* regular who rebranded himself in the mid-1990s as America's unofficial Yankees fan-in-chief to the consternation of many of the team's longtime fans and some of its players. A native New Yorker, Crystal grew up rooting for the Mantle/Maris Yankees of the early 1960s but rarely spoke about his fandom during the club's lean years of the late '60s, 1980s, and early 1990s. He seemed to emerge publicly only after the team returned to dynastic status in the late 1990s under manager Joe Torre, in whose office the comic increasingly tarried to schmooze with coaches and Yankees legends such as Yogi Berra. According to published accounts, Crystal often irritated players with his penchant for hogging the massage table at the team's spring training complex in Tampa. Many traditionalists were also put off by the front office's decision to sign Crystal to a one-day contract and allow him to play in an exhibition game in 2008 as part of his 61st birthday celebration—an apparent reference to *61**, Crystal's reverent chronicle of the 1961 home-run race between Mickey Mantle and Roger Maris. For the record, Crystal struck out in his only plate appearance.

# "Curly Shuffle, The"

Novelty song by Chicago pop septet Jump 'N the Saddle Band that briefly and incongruously became a ballpark sing-along during New York Mets games at Shea Stadium in the mid-1980s. The song, which somehow reached No. 15 on the *Billboard* singles chart, celebrates the antics of The Three Stooges—with special emphasis on bald, witless Stooge Jerome "Curly Howard" Horwitz—and has nothing whatsoever to do with baseball. The accompanying music video was often displayed on the Shea Stadium Diamond Vision screen between innings of Mets home games, promoting the crowd to descend into a sing-along frenzy.

# Curse of the Bambino

Supposed hex that prevented the Boston Red Sox from winning any world championships between 1918 and 2004, said to have arisen as a consequence of Sox owner Harry Frazee's sale of Babe Ruth to the New York Yankees in 1920. The term "Curse of the Bambino" may have been coined, and was certainly popularized, by *Boston Globe* sports columnist Dan Shaughnessy, who used it as the title of a 1990 book. But the general concept of a curse on the Red Sox franchise related to the Ruth sale had been spoken about for years in Boston. At various points, the Red Sox even hired professional exorcists—as well as comic priest Don "Father Guido Sarducci" Novello—to perform rituals designed to expel the Bambino juju from Fenway Park. There was also talk of excavating a mysterious upright piano, supposedly hurled by Ruth into a Sudbury, Massachusetts, pond during a fit of drunken rage in the winter of 1918, as a means of "reversing the curse." True reversal was not achieved until the fall of 2004, however, when the Red Sox roared back from a 3–0 deficit to take the American League Championship Series from their archrivals from New York, then went on to sweep the St. Louis Cardinals to capture their first World Series title in 86 years.

# Curses

*See* **Billy Goat Curse**; **Curse of the Bambino**

# Dandy

Short-lived costumed mascot of the early 1980s New York Yankees. A mustachioed, pinstriped bird named in honor of "Yankee Doodle Dandy" George M. Cohan, Dandy prowled the nosebleed seats at Yankee Stadium from 1982 to 1985. The character was developed at the behest of Yankees management by the husband-and-wife design team of Bonnie Erickson and Wayde Harrison, creators of the popular **Phillie Phanatic** and the somewhat less popular **Youppi**. Sadly, Yankees fans never quite cottoned to Dandy. (According to a widely disseminated rumor, the mascot was once beaten into submission by an irate mob at Yankee Stadium.) The character was confined to the far reaches of the upper deck and barred by club officials from doing any outside appearances. To date, Dandy is still the only officially sanctioned mascot in Yankees history.

# D. Baxter the Bobcat

Costumed predator who has been the official mascot of the Arizona Diamondbacks since 2000. The mascot's somewhat awkward-sounding name came from Brantley Bell, the five-year-old son of Diamondbacks infielder Jay Bell, and is an amalgam of D-Backs (the club's nickname) and BOB, the widely used

Alex Sommers

acronym for Bank One Ballpark, the former name of the team's home stadium. Routinely rated one of the worst **mascots** in the major leagues, D. Baxter the Bobcat has also been a source of controversy. In January of 2009, the Diamondbacks fired D. Baxter's human portrayer, David Hamilton, after club officials learned that he had been busted for "extreme D.U.I." the previous September. According to published reports, Hamilton was stopped by police driving 95 miles per hour on Loop 101 in Phoenix in a Toyota Scion festooned with the Diamondbacks' team logo, with his bobcat costume stowed in the back of the car. He had a blood alcohol level of 0.155—nearly twice the legal limit—and boasted of having smoked marijuana earlier in the day.

## Delahanty, Big Ed

Lumbering slugger of the Dead Ball Era who earned an immortal place in baseball lore due to the mysterious circumstances surrounding his death in 1903. The hard-living home-run king was kicked off a Chicago-to–New York

### *Forgotten Heroes of the Game*

#### Nelson "Mahow" de la Rosa

Twenty-nine-inch-tall Dominican movie actor who served as traveling companion/lucky charm to Boston Red Sox hurler Pedro Martinez during the team's 2004 world championship season. Often incorrectly referred to as "Pedro's midget," de la Rosa was actually a dwarf, certified at one point by the Guinness Book of World Records as the shortest man on Earth. After the 2004 season, when Martinez signed a free-agent contract with the New York Mets, the temperamental pitcher publicly disavowed de la Rosa, calling him "a palm-sized pipsqueak." De la Rosa died of heart failure in 2006.

train one night for being drunk and disorderly. He then either jumped, fell, or was pushed—depending on whose story you believe—off the International Bridge connecting the U.S. and Canada and into Niagara Falls. His mangled corpse was fished out of the water a week later. Over the years, some have speculated that Delahanty was murdered for the diamonds he was carrying or that he staged his suicide to look like an accident so that his daughter could recover on his life insurance policy. In 2008, Delahanty's demise was immortalized in song by the indie supergroup The Baseball Project on a track called "The Death of Big Ed Delahanty."

# Denkinger, Don

Respected major league umpire whose blown call at first base in Game 6 of the 1985 World Series in all likelihood cost the St. Louis Cardinals their 10th world championship. The Cardinals led the Series 3–2 and were ahead 1–0 in the bottom of the ninth when Denkinger called Kansas City Royals pinch hitter Jorge Orta safe at first base on a slow roller fielded by Jack Clark. Replays clearly showed that Orta was out, and Denkinger himself later admitted that he was out of position on the play. The Royals went on to score two runs to win the game and knot the Series at 3–3. They blew out the Cardinals the next night to take the championship in a game that saw Cardinals manager Whitey Herzog ejected in the bottom of the fifth inning for continuing to badger Denkinger about his Game 6 mistake. For years afterward, Denkinger was subjected to angry letters and death threats from aggrieved Cardinals fans—including one who promised to "blow him away" with a .357 Magnum. He eventually had to call the FBI in for his own protection.

# Diamond

Female half of the boyfriend/girlfriend duo **Ace**
and Diamond, avian **mascots** of the Toronto Blue
Jays. While still listed as one of the club's official
**mascots**, Diamond has not been seen publicly
since 2004, leading some to speculate about the
status of her relationship with **Ace**.

# Dinger

Purple-horned dinosaur who has served as the official mascot of the Colorado
Rockies since 1994. An anthropomorphized triceratops, Dinger was designed
to commemorate the long-standing link between that herbivorous creature
and the city of Denver. The very first triceratops specimen ever discovered
was found near Denver in the spring of 1887. In January of 1994, construction crews working on the Rockies' new home ballpark, Coors Field, uncov-
ered fragments of a dinosaur rib during
excavation of the area that would become
home plate. By way of homage, Dinger
was developed and "hatched" from a
dinosaur egg during the Rockies' season-
opening homestand three months later.
The Barneyesque beastie (whose purple
hue derives from the Rockies' team colors
and not from the then-popular TV dinosaur) began to court controversy from the
very beginning. In August of 1994, just a
few months after his debut, Dinger got
into a physical altercation with Rockies
radio announcer Jeff Kingery after
bumping into the broadcaster during a

Paul Dineen

game at Coors Field. In 1997, the mascot was reportedly assaulted by a fan while playing with a child in the stands. That same year, a poll conducted by a Denver newspaper found that nine out of 10 Rockies fans wanted the irritating dinosaur to be declared extinct in time for the 1998 season. Yet still Dinger lived on. In 2007, a group of exasperated Rockies fans even started an online petition campaign to "kill" Dinger, calling the mascot a "carpet-covered, shit-and-Febreze-smelling, sorry excuse for a cheerleading, anthropomorphized cartoon fossil."

## Dip

Finely ground smokeless tobacco product, also known as "snuff," that is not to be confused with **chewing tobacco**.

## Disco Demolition Night

Ill-starred ballpark promotion that sparked a riot at Chicago's Comiskey Park on July 12, 1979. Organized by local deejay Steve Dahl and approved by White Sox executive Mike Veeck, the pyrotechnic spectacle was designed to capitalize on the anti-disco backlash then sweeping the country after five years of nonstop boogie. The idea was to encourage fans to bring their disco records to a doubleheader between the White Sox and Tigers—thereby qualifying them for discounted admission. Between games, a controlled explosion would result in the "demolition" of the offending LPs in an enormous purgative bonfire. The event began to go awry almost immediately, as club officials seriously underestimated the appeal of their promotion. Instead of the few thousand extra fans they had expected, more than 75,000 people showed up. For ballpark staff used to dealing with crowds that averaged 16,000 that summer, that was way over capacity. Many patrons were turned away at the gates. Others found their way into the park without paying. A sizable contingent got drunk and stoned before, during, and after the first game of the doubleheader. A raucous party atmosphere prevailed

Richard Lindberg

throughout the contest, marked by the setting off of firecrackers, the wanton flinging of vinyl records like Frisbees, and repeated chants of "Disco sucks!" The Tigers won the game 4–1. Between games, LPs were collected into enormous crates in center field and rigged with dynamite. The portly Dahl then strolled onto the field wearing an army helmet and full military regalia and proceeded to set off the promised explosion. The ensuing conflagration tore a huge hole in the outfield grass and precipitated a general melee, which saw wasted fans spill onto the field en masse. As the disco bonfire burned, some lit small secondary fires. Others simply milled about like zombies. The batting cage was pulled down and the bases ripped off their moorings. Attempts by White Sox announcer **Harry Caray** to persuade the mob to get off the field proved fruitless. Only the arrival of Chicago police in full riot gear restored order. Thirty-nine people were arrested and charged with disorderly conduct. The White Sox were forced to forfeit the second game. The incident made international headlines and was interpreted in the media as a sign of the demise of disco as a musical genre. It was the worst ballpark riot since the **Ten-Cent Beer Night** fiasco in Cleveland five years earlier. Oddly enough, outfielder **Rusty Torres** was on the field both times. See also: **Duncan, Michael Clarke**

## Dodger Dog

Familiar name for the large, plump frankfurters served at Dodger Stadium since 1962. Introduced at the old Los Angeles Coliseum to coincide with the club's move west in 1958, the wieners were the brainchild of longtime

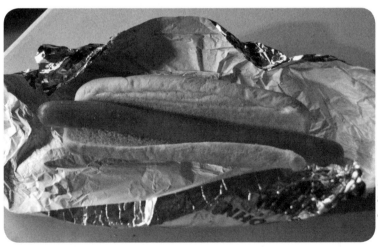

Bryce Edwards

Dodgers concessions director Thomas G. Arthur. Arthur originally dubbed them Foot-long Dogs, but he changed the name after some patrons pointed out (correctly) that they were actually 10 inches long. Offered in grilled or steamed varieties and served on a super-sized bun, the 240-calorie franks are considered an integral part of the Dodger Stadium experience. Dodger Dogs are also sold in many supermarkets across Southern California.

# Doeden, Brent
*See* **Captain Earthman**

# Domes
Covered, climate-controlled sports facilities that came into vogue in the 1960s and '70s, maddening baseball purists who saw them as inimical to the game's outdoorsy, pastoral ambience. The Houston **Astrodome**, which opened in 1965, was the first domed stadium used for baseball. In all, there would be five such facilities built (not counting Montreal's **Olympic Stadium**, which featured a retractable Kevlar roof that almost never functioned properly), most of them multipurpose monstrosities shared with the local football team and occasionally used to host non-sports events as well. The **Astrodome**, Minnesota's cavernous Metrodome, and Seattle's much-despised Kingdome are no longer in use, leaving only two extant domed stadia: the Rogers Centre in Toronto (formerly known as SkyDome) and St. Petersburg's Tropicana Field, home of the Tampa Bay Rays. See also: **Hubert H. Humphrey Metrodome**; **Multipurpose Stadia**

# Dot Race
Between-innings diversion at Texas Rangers home games that has migrated in subtly altered form to other ballparks around the country over the decades. The ingeniously simple scoreboard exhibition invites fans to cheer on various brightly colored dots as they engage in a "race" around an animated track.

## They Said What?

### "The dots are in the gate!"

–Texas Rangers public address announcer **Chuck Morgan**'s call to arms at the beginning of each **Dot Race**

**Chuck Morgan**, the Rangers' longtime public address announcer and director of in-game entertainment, is widely regarded as the granddaddy of major league dot racing. He reportedly refined the concept after hearing about a similar event being staged at a minor league park in Oklahoma City. Dot racing proved such a hit with the Arlington crowds that other clubs began adapting the idea, often with a local twist. Hence there are subway cars at Yankee Stadium, cable cars in San Francisco, and racing friars in San Diego. Scoreboard dot racing also begat live-action dot racing in all its forms, including the popular **Sausage Race** and **Pierogie Race** in Milwaukee and Pittsburgh, respectively.

# Doubleday, Abner

Mediocre Civil War general who had nothing to do with baseball but is nonetheless widely credited in the public mind with inventing the game. Nicknamed "Old Forty-Eight Hours" for his chronic indecisiveness on the battlefield, Doubleday saw action at Fort Sumter, Chancellorsville, and Gettysburg but made a pest of himself by bickering with other Union generals. His marginal martial career would be his only claim to fame had 20th century sporting goods magnate Albert Spalding not spearheaded a campaign to consecrate Doubleday as the man who codified the rules of baseball near Cooperstown, New York, in 1839. Spalding's creation of the

"Doubleday myth" had more to do with selling bats and balls (and promoting the idea that baseball was an all-American game and not descended from British pastimes such as cricket and rounders) than historical accuracy. In his own letters and diary entries, Doubleday never once mentions baseball or claims to have played any role in its development.

## Double Knit Uniforms

Aesthetically dubious sartorial innovation that metastasized throughout the major leagues in the 1970s and '80s. In 1970, the Pittsburgh Pirates became the first club to wear 100 percent polyester, pullover double knit uniforms, eschewing the stultifying wool/cotton blends that had dominated the game since the 19th century. Holding the form-fitting tops in place, instead of the customary belt, was a newfangled elastic waistband. Traditionalists objected to the use of synthetic fabric, while futurists argued that the new uniforms were lighter, airier, and easier to clean than the flannels of yore. As the 1970s progressed, nearly every team in the majors began to adopt the double knit look. Not until the late 1980s did the style pendulum swing back toward baggier, button-fronted tops and belted bottoms.

## Doyle, Harry

Buffoonish play-by-play man portrayed by **Bob Uecker** in the 1989 baseball comedy *Major League*. A jaded alcoholic, Doyle punctuates his call of a wildly overthrown pitch with the catchphrase "Ju-ust a bit outside."

## Dr. Feelgood

*See* **Jacobson, Max**

# Drinkwater, Dennis

Massachusetts glass magnate and Fenway Park season-ticket holder, known for his striking resemblance to actor Robert Redford, who has been a behind-the-plate fixture at Boston Red Sox home games since 2005. Drinkwater, the president of New England's largest glass replacement company, Giant Glass, actually attended a game at Fenway with his Hollywood doppelganger in October of 2005. While not quite a **superfan**, and certainly not a **heckler** (he doesn't believe in booing), Drinkwater (whom others have likened in appearance to tabloid talk show ringmaster Jerry Springer) falls into the nebulous category of recognizable ballpark fixtures that includes the likes of radar gun–toting Los Angeles Dodgers scout **Mike Brito**.

# Duncan, Michael Clarke

Hulking 6'5" African American actor, Oscar-nominated for his role as a doomed death row inmate in *The Green Mile*, whose previous claim to fame was his participation in the infamous **Disco Demolition Night** riot at Chicago's Comiskey Park on July 12, 1979. A native South Sider and lifelong White Sox fan, Duncan was 21 years old and working in the stock room of a local department store at the time of the ill-fated ballpark promotion. He was also a huge disco music fan, which didn't stop him from jumping the outfield wall and joining the general melee that ensued after several crates of disco records were detonated between games of a doubleheader. By his own admission, Duncan slid into third base and stole several bats from White Sox players before departing the field ahead of the arrival of Chicago police. He was not among those arrested or caught on film during the incident.

# Dwarf

*See* **Van Zelst, Louis**

# Dykstra, Lenny

**Chewing tobacco**—chomping, hard-nosed outfielder of the 1980s and '90s—nicknamed "Nails" for his belligerent style of play—who had devolved into a muscle-bound monstrosity by the time of his retirement in 1998 and then spent most of the 2000s building up and then squandering an enormous personal fortune. One of the rare players beloved in both New York and Philadelphia, Dykstra won a World Series with the high-living 1986 Mets and led a ragtag Phillies squad to the 1993 National League pennant. He consistently denied allegations of steroid use, although a check of his neck size through the years seemed to indicate otherwise. After his playing days were over, Dykstra reportedly made a killing as a car wash mogul—although there is so much self-promotion and media-enabled mythmaking surrounding his supposed financial genius that it's hard to tell where the truth ends and the hype begins. At one time or another, Dykstra's business ventures included real estate development, publishing a high-end magazine for wealthy athletes and other "players," renting out time-shares on luxury jets, and touting stocks. This last "talent" won him the endorsement of both hyperactive CNBC investment guru Jim Cramer and ultraconservative telejournalist Bernard Goldberg, who shamelessly trumpeted Dykstra's purported mastery of Wall Street on a 2008 segment of HBO's *Real Sports with Bryant Gumbel*. Soon after that piece aired, Dykstra's financial house of cards began to collapse. He was sued by dozens of unpaid creditors and outed in a magazine article by a former employee as a deadbeat boss and

*Baseball by the Numbers* | **56,762**

Amount in dollars for which **Lenny Dykstra** sold his 1986 World Series ring to pay off numerous creditors in 2009

## *Forgotten Heroes of the Game*

**Don Daglow**

Computer-gaming legend who designed the first baseball video game in 1971. Titled, appropriately enough, Baseball, the game was developed as a lark out of Daglow's dorm room at Pomona College in Claremont, California, and could be played only on an enormous mainframe. Daglow went on to co-create the seminal Earl Weaver Baseball for Electronic Arts in 1987.

credit card fraudster who had once tried to bilk his own mother out of $13,000. It was unclear whether Dykstra had ever in fact made a killing in the stock market or had merely parlayed his celebrity into a web of loans and credit lines on which he'd serially defaulted. Whatever the case, by mid-2009 he had filed for bankruptcy (listing among his assets a German shepherd valued at $10,000) and was reportedly living out of his car. His wife left him, and he was accused of stealing a $40,000 French stove from his own foreclosed mansion.

**E**

# Earl Weaver Baseball

Highly popular baseball video game of the late 1980s that helped establish Electronic Arts, or EA Sports, as the dominant brand in sports gaming. Developed by pioneering game designers Don Daglow and Eddie Dombrower, EWB was the first video game to utilize the artificial intelligence ("AI") of a real-life major league manager—in this case former Baltimore Orioles skipper Earl Weaver. Originally "published" in 1987, the game combined Weaver's actual game strategy—collected through hours of in-person interviews—with detailed statistics, sophisticated graphics, and TV-style "camera angle" presentation. In 1996, *Computer Gaming World* magazine named Earl Weaver Baseball one of the top 25 video games of all time.

## Eephus Pitch

Tantalizingly slow, high-arcing **trick pitch** first invented by Truett "Rip" Sewell of the Pittsburgh Pirates sometime in the 1930s, so named by Sewell's teammate Maurice Van Robays, who told inquiring reporters the pitch was called Eephus because "eephus don't mean nothin', and that's what that pitch is—nothin'." Sewell rode his Eephus to back-to-back 21-win seasons in 1943 and 1944. His most famous use of the pitch came in the 1946 All-Star Game, when he lobbed three straight Eephi at Ted Williams, the last of which the Splendid Splinter deposited into the right-field stands for a home run. Copycat versions of the Eephus include **Bill Lee**'s Leephus Ball, Steve Hamilton's **Folly Floater**, and Dave LaRoche's **La Lob**.

## Ehrhardt, Karl

*See* **Sign Man**

## Elia's Tirade

Profanity-laced jeremiad directed at Chicago Cubs fans by the team's manager, Lee Elia, after a heartbreaking home loss to the Los Angeles Dodgers on April 29, 1983. The tirade, which was captured on tape by WLS radio man Les Grobstein, has circulated widely thanks to its inclusion on a *Celebrities Gone Wild* CD compilation in the 1990s and the subsequent advent of audio file–sharing and the Internet. (An entire website, leeelia.com, remains devoted to the episode more than a quarter century after it occurred.) Elia's rant took place in the manager's office at Wrigley Field, where reporters had gathered to get his impression on the Cubs' 4–3 loss—an especially crushing affair, punctuated by the dousing by beer of Cubs Keith Moreland

and Larry Bowa as they exited the field of play. At the time, the club was 5–14 and playing before crowds of fewer than 10,000 fans, many of whom drank heavily and heckled the hometown nine without mercy on a daily basis. Clearly, Elia had reached his breaking point, and in a three-minute-long, 448-word philippic, he vented his frustration at the fickle nature of Chicago fans, as well as their purported laziness and alcoholism. Calling the daytime patrons at Wrigley Field "fuckin' nickel-dime people" who "don't even work" and failed to appreciate the progress being made by the team, Elia questioned the loyalty of the club's rooters and challenged disappointed Wrigleyville denizens to "kiss my fuckin' ass right downtown." It's unclear whether Elia was aware he was being taped, although he later expressed consternation at Grobstein for his efforts to publicize the diatribe. Cubs general manager Dallas Green was eventually forced to fire Elia later that season, more for the team's poor play than the tirade itself.

## They Said What?

**"Eighty-five percent of the fuckin' world is working. The other 15 percent come out here."**

–Cubs manager Lee Elia, on the fans at Wrigley Field

# Ellis, Dock

Free-spirited, substance-abusing Pittsburgh Pirates right-hander who famously threw a no-hitter under the influence of LSD. Ellis, who admitted to interviewers that he spent nearly his entire 12-year major league career high on drugs, dropped Purple Haze acid with his girlfriend in his Los Angeles

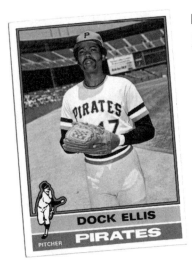

**DOCK ELLIS**

PITCHER **PIRATES**

home on the night of June 11, 1970, just hours before he was scheduled to start the first game of a doubleheader against the Padres in San Diego. At about 1:00 PM on the day of the game, his girlfriend helpfully reminded him that he was pitching that day. Ellis hustled out to the airport and arrived at the park 90 minutes before game time, still feeling the drug's effects. He took a handful of amphetamines in an attempt to bring himself down off his high and proceeded to no-hit the opposition in a 2–0 victory. An uncommonly wild Ellis walked eight batters and hit another, hallucinated throughout the game, and experienced an overall feeling of euphoria. At various points, he later claimed, he became convinced home-plate umpire Tony Venzon was Richard Nixon, or that he was pitching to Jimi Hendrix. Crowned "the most intimidating pitcher of his era" by no less an authority than Dave Parker, Ellis continued to court controversy in non-drug-related ways throughout the 1970s. In May of 1972, he was maced by a security guard at Riverfront Stadium in Cincinnati after

## They Said What?

"The ball was small sometimes. The ball was large sometimes. Sometimes I saw the catcher. Sometimes I didn't."

—**Dock Ellis**, describing the experience of pitching a no-hitter while tripping on LSD

failing to show proper ID. (Ellis brandished his 1971 World Series ring in an attempt to gain admittance to the visiting clubhouse.) In another game against the Reds on May 1, 1974, Ellis intentionally beaned the first three batters in the Cincinnati order—**Pete Rose**, **Joe Morgan**, and Dan Driessen—and attempted to hit another before being pulled from the game by manager Danny Murtaugh. (He had vowed before the game to "do the do" on the Big Red Machine for allegedly disrespecting the Pirates.) And Ellis routinely ground the gears of baseball's fashion police for his habit of wearing curlers during pregame workouts. Under pressure from the league office, the Pirates eventually ordered Ellis to remove his curlers before stepping onto the field. "They didn't put any orders about **Joe Pepitone** when he wore a hairpiece down to his shoulders," Ellis fumed.

## Epstein, Theo

Guitar-playing, gorilla suit–wearing boy genius general manager widely credited with single-handedly transforming the seemingly accursed Boston Red Sox into the major leagues' model franchise in the mid-2000s. Awarded the stewardship of one of baseball's prestige teams at the tender age of 28, the Brookline, Massachusetts, resident (who was actually born in New York City, home of the archrival Yankees) immediately set about remaking the Red Sox in accordance with the principles of *Moneyball* icon **Billy Beane** and **Sabermetrics** stats guru **Bill James** (whom Epstein would later hire as a senior advisor to the front office). Consecutive playoff appearances in his first two years on the job helped fuel Epstein's burgeoning cult of personality in Boston, although his wunderkind reputation likely would have taken a major hit had the club not rallied from a 3–0 deficit to vanquish the Yankees in the 2004 American League Championship Series and capture its first world championship since 1918. A year later, Epstein stunned fans by walking out on his dream job—oddly enough, while wearing a gorilla suit on Halloween night. He subsequently reconciled with ownership and was elevated to general manager and executive vice president in time for the 2006 season. The Red Sox added a second World Series trophy to their mantel in 2007, solidifying Epstein's status as one of the game's most able executives.

# Error Cards

Collector-approved term for baseball trading cards marred by misprints, misspellings, incorrect information, or other flaws that, according to the perverse economics of the hobby, actually render them more valuable. Some of the more noteworthy error cards of the past half century include the famous Bump Wills card of 1979 (on which the mediocre Texas Rangers second baseman was erroneously identified as playing for the Toronto Blue Jays), a 2007 Derek Jeter card that preposterously shows President George W. Bush in the stands and Mickey Mantle watching from the dugout, and the so-called **Fuck Face Card** of 1989, featuring Orioles infielder Billy Ripken and his profanity-inscribed bat.

# Everett, Carl

Highly touted prospect turned journeyman outfielder of the 1990s and 2000s who is best known for his controversial opinions on paleontology, space exploration, and other topics. In a 2000 interview with Tom Verducci of *Sports Illustrated*, Everett—an Evangelical Christian—disputed the consensus opinion of the scientific community regarding the origins of the human species. "God created the sun, the stars, the heavens and the earth, and then made Adam and Eve," he charged, before explicitly disavowing the existence of dinosaurs. "The Bible never says anything about dinosaurs. You can't say there were dinosaurs when you never saw them. Someone actually saw Adam and Eve. No one ever saw a Tyrannosaurus Rex." The fossil record, he contended, has been fabricated by humans. Everett also expressed doubts about whether the 1969 Apollo moon landing actually occurred, although he offered no Biblical justification for that contention. In 2005, Everett added **homosexuality** to the list of things he didn't believe in. "Gays being gay is wrong," he told *Maxim* magazine. "Two women can't produce a baby, two men can't produce a baby, so it's not how it's supposed to be.... I don't believe in gay marriages. I don't believe in being gay."

## Exploding Scoreboard

Ballpark innovation introduced by Chicago White Sox owner **Bill Veeck** to Comiskey Park in 1960. Technically speaking, the scoreboard did not explode. The 130-foot-high screen merely served as a focal point for a loud, ostentatious pyrotechnic display—marked by fireworks detonation, spinning pinwheels, and blinking strobe lights—that would erupt every time a White Sox player hit a home run. Veeck got the idea for the exploding scoreboard from an exploding pinball machine he saw in the play *The Time of Your Life* by William Saroyan.

Getty Images

# Famous Chicken
*See* **San Diego Chicken**

# Fancy Clancy

Genial African American **supervendor** (born Clarence Haskett) who has peddled beer in the home park of the Baltimore Orioles for more than 30 years. A favorite among season-ticket holders, Fancy Clancy is known for two signature moves: doing a backbend over the stadium handrail while doling out bottles of beer, and allowing his regular customers to run tabs. Greasing Haskett's palm is a good way to get on the beer man's good side and earn yourself the privilege of not having to pay up front. The onetime traffic engineer for the Maryland State Highway Administration claims to rake in $100 per hour in tips—not that he needs the extra money. When he's not working the aisles at Oriole Park at Camden Yards, Haskett is the vice president of All Pro Vending, the company that holds the vending contracts at several local sports venues, including M&T Bank Stadium, home of the NFL's Baltimore Ravens. His tagline is "If you want it served fancy, get it from Clancy."

John Fabrizio

# Fantasy Baseball

Popular pastime in which baseball fans with extra time on their hands build and manage imaginary teams composed of real-life major league players, typically using a scoring system pegged to the current season's statistics. Tabletop games such as **Strat-O-Matic** and **All-Star Baseball** can be seen as early forms of Fantasy Baseball, although the game did not take on its present-day form until the advent of **Rotisserie** leagues in the 1980s.

# Fantasy Camp

Popular pastime in which baseball fans with extra time on their hands and a lot of disposable income pay enormous sums and travel great distances to participate in "training" sessions with current and former major leaguers. Typical fantasy camp activities include taking infield practice, running wind sprints, and playing exhibition games alongside highly compensated baseball legends. Attendees often get to socialize with players after-hours and are sometimes sent home with a personalized baseball card featuring their likeness. Most camps have a minimum age requirement, which is largely unnecessary since it's doubtful anyone under the age of 40 would want to take part in such an exercise. The fantasy camp experience is often bestowed by wives to husbands as a 40th or 50th birthday present. One of the most noteworthy fantasy camp participants in recent years was U.S. Supreme Court Justice Samuel Alito, who attended a Philadelphia Phillies fantasy camp in 1994 as a gift from his wife.

# Faust, Charles "Victory"

Eccentric hayseed who served as the unofficial mascot and good-luck charm of the New York Giants during their pennant-winning seasons from 1911 through 1913. The Kansas-born son of illiterate German immigrants, Faust bamboozled Giants manager John McGraw into letting him try out for the team by claiming that a fortune teller had informed him he would lead the

Giants to a championship. Although the gangly Faust proved supremely inept on the pitcher's mound (one reporter commented that he "plays ball as if he were a mass of mucilage"), he was right about bringing the club good fortune. From the day Faust first started suiting up for the Giants, the team won more than 80 percent of its games. His dim-witted capering also entertained the crowd before games, making him the rare triple threat as player/mascot/human rabbit's foot. Over time, however, Faust's insistence that he be allowed to pitch began to grate on McGraw's nerves. He grew increasingly unhinged and was dispatched back to his native Kansas without so much as a severance check. He was eventually confined to a mental hospital, where he died of tuberculosis in 1915. None of the Giants showed up at his funeral.

## Faust, Nancy

Longtime ballpark organist for the Chicago White Sox who initiated the tradition of playing the 1969 Steam song **"Na Na Hey Hey Kiss Him Goodbye"** at major league stadiums. In October 2009, Faust announced that she would retire following the 2010 season.

## *Fear Strikes Out*

Flawed 1957 biopic that chronicles the life and career of bipolar major leaguer **Jimmy Piersall**. Anthony Perkins, who later gained fame as Norman Bates in Alfred Hitchcock's *Psycho*, plays Piersall in the film, which was based on the ballplayer's 1955 autobiography of the same name. Well-regarded upon its initial release, the film has not aged well, due in part to its outdated, overtly Freudian interpretation of Piersall's struggle with mental illness. The outfielder's instability is almost entirely laid at the feet of his father, portrayed as a pushy stage parent by hulking actor Karl Malden. (In reality, Piersall's father was a small, gregarious man who had little or nothing to do with his son's subsequent breakdown.) An even bigger handicap is Perkins' complete lack of athletic ability. His laughable attempts at swinging a bat and throwing a ball seriously undermine the film's credibility. Piersall himself hated the picture, citing Perkins' spastic gyrations and the liberties screenwriters took with the facts. "The book was the truth," he once said. "The movie was not my story."

# Felton, Happy
*See **Happy Felton's Knothole Gang***

# Fernandomania
Term coined by the national media to describe the frenzy that gripped Southern California during the 1981 Rookie of the Year campaign of left-hander Fernando Valenzuela. The morbidly obese, Mexican-born screwballer with the elaborate windup went 13–7 with a 2.48 ERA in the strike-shortened season to wrest the Cy Young Award away from the more deserving Tom Seaver. The fact that Valenzuela faded after a torrid 8–0 start did not stop huge crowds from showing up at Dodger Stadium every time he pitched, creating what was invariably described in press accounts of the time as a "fiesta-like" atmosphere (read: many Mexican Americans

## *They Said What?*

**"It went beyond a normal fan love of a player. It became, I believe, a religious experience."**

–Dodgers broadcaster Vin Scully, on **Fernandomania**

attended). Valenzuela's cherubic face graced the covers of numerous national magazines over the course of the summer, his supposed precocity providing a feel-good story for sports fans dispirited by the midseason work stoppage. "He may be 20, but he pitches 30," observed Astros manager Bill Virdon. In fact, he may have indeed been closer to 30; rumors abounded that Valenzuela's stated age of 20 may have been off by as much as half a decade.

## Fidrych, Mark

Scrawny, curly-haired Detroit Tigers pitching prodigy—nicknamed "the Bird" for his resemblance to *Sesame Street*'s shambling canary, Big Bird—who became a national sensation for his bizarre on-the-field antics in the summer of 1976. A 21-year-old phenom from Worcester, Massachusetts, Fidrych seemingly came out of nowhere to win 19 games that year, capturing Rookie of the Year honors. But it was his behavior *on* the mound, not his contributions to the won-loss ledger, that endeared him to fans from coast to coast. The Bird was a natural showman whose ritualized shtick included talking to the ball before each pitch, getting down on his hands and knees to clean the pitching rubber, and running around the diamond shaking hands with his teammates after a victory. Fidrych later denied that he actually conversed with the baseball ("What I'm really doing is talking out loud to myself, not the ball," he said. "I'll tell myself to bring my arm down, things like that."). However, the very fact that he was talking at all, out there on the mound by himself in front of 30,000 people, was enough to pique the interest

## You Could Look It Up

**Random Baseball Trivia**

At the height of "Birdmania," the Michigan State legislature passed a resolution decreeing that **Mark Fidrych** should receive a raise in salary.

of baseball audiences looking for a distraction after years of Vietnam, Watergate, and waning interest in the national pastime. And talking wasn't all Fidrych did on the pitcher's mound. Upon getting the news that he had made the Tigers' big-league roster for 1976, the Bird and his girlfriend reportedly celebrated by having sex on the mound at the team's spring training complex in Lakeland, Florida. On another occasion, Fidrych realized during warm-ups that he had forgotten to don his protective cup. Unfazed, he simply pulled down his uniform pants and put it in place right there on the mound. Sadly, 1976 proved to be Fidrych's only year in the national limelight. He blew out his knee in spring training of the following season and was plagued by multiple arm problems thereafter. He made numerous attempts to return to the game, but years of surgery and painful rehab slowly sapped the Bird's magic wing of all its power.

## They Said What?

**"Tell that guy that if he pulls that shit in New York we'll blow his ass off the field."**

–New York Yankees catcher Thurman Munson, on **Mark Fidrych**

Fidrych retired in 1982 and settled down on a pig farm in his native Massachusetts, where he earned a living paving driveways and playing semipro ball until his untimely death in April of 2009. Coroners concluded that Fidrych suffocated when his shirt got caught in the gears of a crankshaft as he worked on one of his trucks.

## Finch, Sidd

Preposterously hard-throwing right-hander invented out of whole cloth by author and bon vivant George Plimpton for a feature in the April 1, 1985, edition of *Sports Illustrated.* "The Curious Case of Sidd Finch" heralded the arrival of a New York Mets pitching prospect who could throw a ball 168 miles per hour thanks to his yogic training in "siddhi," the ancient art of mind-body mastery. The elaborately drawn hoax actually fooled many readers, despite the fact that the first letter of the words in the article's subheadline clearly spell out the words "Happy April Fool's Day." Plimpton later capitalized on the publicity surrounding the prank by expanding his mildly amusing 14-page piece into an unnecessary and unreadable 300-page novel.

## Fingers, Rollie

Hall of Fame relief pitcher of the 1970s and '80s, widely regarded as possessing the greatest mustache in baseball history. Fingers (born Roland Glen Fingers) recorded 341 saves over a 17-year career spent with the A's, Padres, and Brewers. He appeared in 16 World Series games and won both the American League MVP and the Cy Young Award in 1981. But he is known to the general public principally for his heavily waxed handlebar mustache, which he initially adopted before the 1972 season on a challenge from A's owner **Charles O. Finley**, who offered a $300 bounty to any player willing to grow his facial hair out by Opening Day. Many players did, resulting in the team being nicknamed the "**Mustache Gang**." Before long, other short relievers—including **Sparky Lyle**, Goose Gossage, and **Al Hrabosky**—

began to imitate Fingers, donning distinctive upper-lip hair configurations designed to intimidate or amuse opposing hitters. Fingers, to his credit, has never seen fit to shave off his mustache—even if it meant retiring prematurely. In 1986, Reds owner **Marge Schott** was willing to take a flier on the 39-year-old hurler—provided he adhere to club rules and remove his soup strainer.

Getty Images

Fingers refused. "Tell her to shave her St. Bernard and I'll shave my mustache," he said, then promptly retired.

# Finley, Charles O.

Eccentric health insurance magnate who served as principal owner of the Kansas City/Oakland Athletics from 1960 to 1981. A flamboyant maverick with a nose for headline-grabbing gimmicks, Finley is rivaled only by **Bill Veeck** for the unabashed showmanship he brought to the task of running his franchise. Unlike Veeck, Finley was also something of a martinet, universally loathed by his players and a regular source of embarrassment for the Major League Baseball office. Among the numerous brainstorms Finley brought to the A's over the course of his 20-plus years at the helm: outfitting his players in garish green-and-gold uniforms; offering a $300 bounty to any player willing to grow an outlandish mustache in time for Opening Day; personally bestowing colorful, marketable nicknames such as "Catfish" and "Blue Moon" on several star players (once refusing to sign pitcher Don Sutton because he didn't have one); and hiring a break-dancing Bay Area teenager named **Stanley "Hammer" Burrell** to serve as his de facto general manager. Finley also had a well-documented fondness for farm animals. He built a petting zoo behind the bleachers at Kansas City Memorial Stadium; made his namesake mule, **Charlie-O**, the A's team mascot; brought in a sheep to graze on the outfield grass to save him the expense of hiring mowers; and installed a mechanical rabbit named Harvey in an underground warren behind home plate to supply the umpire with fresh baseballs. Although Finley's introduction of **ballgirls** to the game in the early 1970s started a league-wide trend, most of his other ideas for improving the game failed to catch on. He unsuccessfully lobbied for the replacement of the traditional white baseball with a day-glo orange alternative, talked about instituting a two-strike strikeout and three-ball walk, and argued for the addition of a "designated runner," to no avail. Many of these "innovations" seem endearing in retrospect, and the club's run of three consecutive championships from 1972 to 1974 ensures him a place above P.T. Barnum status, but Finley also had a destructive side. His players staged a near-mutiny after Finley "fired" infielder Mike Andrews for making two critical errors in Game 2 of the 1973 World Series. And Commissioner Bowie Kuhn grew enraged at Finley's repeated and brazen attempts to dismantle the A's

## Forgotten Heroes of the Game

### Bob Dylan

When it comes to writing elegiac pop songs that name check ex-Yankees legends, Paul Simon may get all the glory, but Bob Dylan's contribution should not be underestimated. His song "Catfish," a bluesy ode to 1974 Cy Young Award winner Catfish Hunter recorded at the height of Hunter's fame, circulated as a bootleg for many years before its official release in 1991. The real Catfish Hunter was said to be none too pleased about the song, which depicts his contract quarrel with Oakland A's owner **Charles O. Finley** and subsequent defection to the Yankees on a million-dollar free-agent contract.

by selling off star players during the 1976 season. Barred by Kuhn from purposely denuding his roster, Finley eventually sued the league and lost. His last few years before selling the team were consumed with efforts to move the franchise to New Orleans. He died in retirement in Chicago in 1996, three days shy of his 78th birthday.

# Finger, The

Obscene gesture occasionally offered by ballplayers (and managers) to show their contempt for fans, opponents, and photographers. The use of the middle finger is almost as old as the game itself. Some of the more noteworthy bird-flipping incidents include:

- In 1886, future Hall of Fame pitcher Charles "Old Hoss" Radbourn of the Boston Beaneaters flashes the finger in a team photo. It is thought to be one of the earliest existing photographs of this particular obscene gesture.
- In 1972, Tigers manager **Billy Martin** poses for his Topps baseball card with his left middle finger subtly extended down the handle of a bat.
- In 1981, St. Louis Cardinals shortstop Garry Templeton flips off Busch Stadium fans after they boo him for not running out a ground ball. He is traded in the off-season for Ozzie Smith, whose patented "Ozzie Flip" offends no one.
- In 1995, Jack McDowell "salutes" angry fans at Yankee Stadium after getting shellacked in a July game against the White Sox. He is fined $5,000. New York tabloids brand him "the Yankee Flipper."
- Before a 2003 playoff game against the A's, embattled Red Sox pitcher Byung-Hyun Kim flips off the crowd at Fenway Park during the player introductions. He will later apologize "to the fans of the Red Sox, the people of New England, and baseball fans throughout the world."

- In 2005, Cincinnati Reds pitcher Danny Graves offers a double-barreled bird to a **heckler** taunting him after a poor outing. He is released by the team the following day.
- In August of 2006, Baltimore Orioles shortstop Miguel Tejada takes the bait from a taunter in Toronto. His gesture nearly earns him a suspension that would have curtailed his consecutive-games-played streak at 1,033.
- During a 2008 game at Yankee Stadium, Yankees first baseman Jason Giambi flips the bird at the visiting Baltimore Orioles after their severe overshift fails to prevent him from getting a base hit.

## Folly Floater

Proprietary **Eephus Pitch** developed by New York Yankees left-hander Steve Hamilton in 1969. Like most high-arcing slow pitches, Hamilton's had the effect of infuriating opposing hitters. In his most famous use of the pitch, Hamilton induced Cleveland Indians slugger Tony Horton to pop out to the catcher after throwing him two consecutive Folly Floaters during a game at Yankee Stadium on June 24, 1970. The emotionally volatile Horton suffered a nervous breakdown and retired after the season—a development presumably unrelated to his humiliation at the hands of Hamilton.

## Ford, "Disco" Dan

Dependable if unspectacular American League outfielder of the 1970s and '80s (real name: Darnell Ford) who earned cult fame for his distinctive nickname (he was part-owner of a discotheque), for hitting the first home run in the remodeled Yankee Stadium, and for posing nude for a centerfold in the July 1981 issue of *Playgirl* magazine.

## Forkball

Tumbling, dipping off-speed pitch, often classified as a **trick pitch**, that combines elements of a **knuckleball** and a changeup and is considered the precursor to the modern split-fingered fastball. Although it's often associated with Dave Stewart, Jack Morris, and other mound mavens of the 1980s, the forkball actually dates back to the early 20th century. Its invention is often credited to Bullet Joe Bush of the Boston Red Sox, although Ernie "Tiny" Bonham and Elroy Face were early masters who helped popularize the pitch around the majors. With the advent of the harder, more swing-and-miss-inducing splitter in the 1980s, the forkball fell out of fashion, although it remains nearly ubiquitous in Japan.

## Foshball

Proprietary **trick pitch** developed by Baltimore Orioles right-hander Mike Boddicker in the early 1980s. Variously described as a "glorified changeup" and a "fastball with a little slosh thrown in," the foshball (originally called a "forkscrew") was in fact a cross between a **forkball** and a change, or "dead fish," in pitchers' vernacular. In 1983, Boddicker, a 26-year-old junkballer who only months before had been working in a Norway, Iowa, grain elevator, used the pitch to shut out the Chicago White Sox in Game 2 of the American League Championship Series and help lead the Orioles to their first world championship in 13 years.

### *They Said What?*

**"It doesn't really break. It just kind of dies."**

–Philadelphia Phillies third baseman
Mike Schmidt, on Mike Boddicker's foshball

# Franco, John

Successful major league closer who became a lightning rod for controversy because of his alleged Mafia ties, his reputation as a **clubhouse lawyer**, and his propensity for making indelicate comments. In 1995, the mustachioed, Brooklyn-born Franco outraged members of the Asian American community by referring to Japanese-born right-hander Hideo Nomo as "Ho Chi Minh." (He later apologized.) According to FBI documents released in 2004, the lefty reliever was a known associate of several high-ranking members of the Bonanno crime family—including caporegime Frank "Curly" Lino and consigliere Anthony Spero—and regularly provided them with free tickets to New York Mets games throughout the 1990s. In a statement released through his agent, Franco refused to discuss the allegations, saying only "I am proud to be an Italian American, and have lived my life in a respectable fashion."

## *They Said What?*

### "What's his name? Nomo? Homo?"

—**Marge Schott,** on Los Angeles Dodgers pitcher Hideo Nomo

# Fredbird

Anthropomorphized passeriform bird who has served as the official mascot of the St. Louis Cardinals since 1979. Fredbird wears a Cardinals home uniform and engages in typical mascot antics such as dancing on the dugout roof,

Barbara Moore

playfully pecking his beak on fans' heads, and shooting T-shirts into the crowd with the aid of "Team Fredbird," a cadre of comely female cheerleader assistants.

# Freddy "Sez"
*See* **Schuman, Freddy**

# Frisch, Frankie
Scrappy second baseman of the 1920s and '30s who later became chairman of the Hall of Fame's powerful Veterans Committee and is reviled by stat geeks for packing the Hall with cronies from his playing days. Among the numerous purportedly unqualified candidates whom Frisch had enshrined in Cooperstown were pitchers Jesse Haines and Rube Marquard, outfielder Chick Hafey, and George Kelly, a slick-fielding first baseman of the 1920s whom statistician emeritus **Bill James** once dubbed "the worst player in the Hall of Fame."

# Fuck Face Card
Notorious **error card** issued by Fleer in 1989, which featured Baltimore Orioles infielder Billy Ripken posing with a bat that had the words "Fuck Face" inscribed on the knob. Discovery of the obscenity-bedecked collectible set off a feeding frenzy among baseball card hobbyists which saw its price rise to nearly $500. Fleer was forced to blot or white out the phrase on subsequent printings. When confronted about the card, Ripken denied having written the obscene inscription, blaming the entire kerfuffle on an unidentified clubhouse prankster. Finally, in 2008, after 20 years of denials, he came clean, admitting that he had scrawled "Fuck Face" on the knob to distinguish his regular batting practice bat from the others in the bat rack. He denied knowingly posing for the photo with the offending lumber, although he did intimate that officials at Fleer may have actually *enhanced*

the inscription in order to generate publicity for their cards. In any case, the company later sent Ripken a box of pristine Fuck Face cards for his personal use. He elected to sign them and give them out to the groomsmen at his wedding. Billy Ripken Fuck Face cards remain in high demand among baseball card collectors, although there are a wide variety of bootleg cards floating around of questionable authenticity—many of which feature black boxes or scribbles over the offending phrase. An entire website, billripken.com, is devoted to weeding out the fake cards from the originals.

# Fu Manchu

Intimidating style of mustache adopted by pitchers **Al Hrabosky**, Goose Gossage, and Dave Stewart, among many others, in an attempt to gain a psychological edge on their opponents. Colorado Rockies **supervendor** Brent "**Captain Earthman**" Doeden also sports a Fu Manchu.

# Gaedel, Eddie

Three-and-a-half-foot-tall midget hired by St. Louis Browns owner **Bill Veeck** to lead off the second game of a doubleheader between the Browns and the Detroit Tigers on August 19, 1951. The publicity stunt garnered national headlines and briefly made the semi-employed circus performer a celebrity. Hastily signed to a contract and sprung from a papier-mâché cake as part of a "festival of surprises" promotional event pegged to the 50th anniversary of the American League, Gaedel was sent up to the plate to pinch hit for the Browns' announced leadoff man, Frank Saucier. He carried a toy bat and was on orders from Veeck—under penalty of death—to refrain from swinging at any pitch. Sure enough, Gaedel drew a walk, and was promptly removed for a pinch runner. Even in an age before political correctness, the crass exploitation of a little person outraged the league office. American League president Will Harridge issued a formal condemnation of Veeck's action and voided Gaedel's contract. Major League Baseball expunged the wee man's plate appearance from its official records. (It was later reinstated.) Gaedel died of a heart attack after being mugged on a Chicago street in 1961.

## *Forgotten Heroes of the Game*

### Donald Davidson

Four-foot-tall dwarf batboy who rose through the ranks to fill several key front office positions with the Boston, Milwaukee, and Atlanta Braves. As a 13-year-old batboy for the Red Sox, Davidson was once sent in to pinch hit for Moe Berg, though the home-plate umpire nixed the substitution, depriving Davidson of a distinction that would later go to fellow little person **Eddie Gaedel**. Players used to delight in stuffing Davidson inside clubhouse trash cans. His autobiography, *Caught Short*, was published in 1972.

# Gamble, Oscar

Lefty-swinging outfielder/DH known as much for his enormous Afro as his sweet stroke at the plate. Like the works of the French artist Christo, who famously wrapped the Pont Neuf bridge in 450,000 square feet of plastic, Gamble's righteous mid-1970's 'fro was monumental in its conception and awe-inspiring in its achievement. So luxuriant was Gamble's hairdo that it added four inches to his height and routinely made his batting helmet pop off when he ran the bases. Sad to say, Yankees owner **George Steinbrenner**, obviously no fan of body art, ordered Gamble to tone down his unique look during spring training in 1976. Especially prized by Gamble

Afro-ficionados is the 1975 Sports Stars Publishing Company trading card of the outfielder as a member of the Cleveland Indians. The sheer physics involved will astound you.

# Gamboa, Tom

Kansas City Royals first-base coach who was savagely beaten by a pair of deranged White Sox fans at Comiskey Park in Chicago on September 19, 2002. Gamboa was minding his own business in the first-base coaching box when a father-and-son team of **heckler**s—who had been razzing him all game from the seats behind the White Sox dugout—abruptly leapt onto the field and began pummeling him into submission. The tattooed miscreants were identified as 34-year-old ne'er-do-well William Ligue Jr. and his 15-year-old son. The elder Ligue, who was unapologetic about the assault and actually claimed that Gamboa "got what he deserved," later pleaded guilty to two counts of aggravated battery and was sentenced to 30 months probation. Gamboa escaped with minor cuts and bruises and went on to become a spokesman for an organization that advocates on behalf of victims of violent attacks.

## *Game of Shadows*

Best-selling book by *San Francisco Chronicle* reporters Mark Fainaru-Wada and Lance Williams that blew the lid off baseball's steroids scandal of the 1990s and 2000s. **Barry Bonds** is a major focus of the 2006 release, which relies heavily on leaked grand jury testimony from a federal investigation into the Bay Area Laboratory Co-Operative, better known as **BALCO**.

# Gammons, Peter

Stentorian baseball wise man best known to younger fans as a TV talking head—and to older ones as the longtime *Boston Globe* and *Sports Illustrated* columnist who invented what has come to be known as the "Notes" column.

AP Images

A Hall of Famer and three-time National Sportswriter of the Year, Gammons has been a near-ubiquitous figure on basic cable baseball telecasts since 1988. His career was briefly derailed by a brain aneurysm in 2006, but he made a rapid and seemingly complete recovery. A quietly authoritative figure of presidential mien (he bears a striking resemblance to America's seventh commander-in-chief, Andrew Jackson), Gammons prefers to save his rug cutting for his second life as a rock 'n' roll animal. In 2006, the sixtysomething diamond maven released his debut album, *Never Slow Down, Never Grow Old*, which featured a wince-inducing cover of "Death or Glory" by The Clash.

# Sounds of the Lame

**Five must-have CDs for your major league music collection.**

*Denny McLain at the Organ* by **Denny McLain** (1968)
When he wasn't dealing drugs or gambling away his career, one-time Tigers ace **Denny McLain** was an accomplished jazz organist. This LP, released the year McLain won 30 games, features a picture of the pitcher in uniform on the front sleeve and the following inscription on the back: "He has the erupting, violent temper of the Irish and it frequently flares." And how!
VERDICT: Totally listenable

*Just a Thought* by Stickfigure (1995)
The debut album from 1993 AL Cy Young Award winner Jack McDowell, best known for giving **the finger** to fans at Yankee Stadium, appropriately enough features a song called "Forgive Me."
VERDICT: Surprisingly listenable

*Covering the Bases* by Bronson Arroyo (2005)
The onetime Red Sox wunderkind parlayed his brief brush with fame into an abortive recording career. The obligatory covers include "Everlong" by the Foo Fighters and Pearl Jam's "Black."
VERDICT: Moderately unlistenable

*Never Slow Down, Never Grow Old* by **Peter Gammons** (2006)
The baseball maven rocks out to "Promised Land" by Bruce Springsteen among other classic and self-penned tracks, with a pickup band that includes George Thorogood and **Theo Epstein**. Right after he released this, Gammons had a brain aneurysm. I'm just sayin'.
VERDICT: Totally unlistenable

*Tim McCarver Sings Selections from The Great American Songbook* by **Tim McCarver** (2009)
Oh baby, I love it! America's favorite color commentator channels his inner Sinatra as he croons his way through chestnuts such as "Two for the Road" and "I Wish I Didn't Love You So."
VERDICT: You have to ask?

Paul F. Lori

## Gapper

Fuzzy red mascot introduced by the Cincinnati Reds in 2002 as a plush-toy-adaptable alternative to the team's traditional mascot, **Mr. Red**. The child-friendly monster, who belongs in the family of new-school Muppet-like **mascots** that includes the Red Sox's **Wally the Green Monster** and the White Sox's **Southpaw**, was created by a character-branding firm founded by the designers of the original **Phillie Phanatic** and named by the winner of a "Name the Mascot" contest.

## Garvey, Steve

Clean-cut All-Star first baseman of the 1970s and '80s who became a national joke in 1989 when it was revealed that he had fathered children with two women—neither of whom was his wife. The shocking details of Garvey's extramarital affairs, aired in his ex-wife Cyndy's tell-all memoir, *The Secret Life of Cyndy Garvey*, helped torpedo the retired major leaguer's burgeoning career as a television personality and inspired two separate palimony lawsuits. A popular bumper sticker of the period read: "Honk If

You're Carrying Steve Garvey's Baby." Another dubbed him "Steve Garvey: Father of Our Nation." Bob Hope quipped "I haven't seen so many gorgeous girls since I spent Father's Day with Steve Garvey," while T-shirts began cropping up across Southern California bearing the legend: "Steve Garvey Is Not My Padre."

AP Images

## Gashouse Gang

Colorful team nickname given to the 1934 World Series champion St. Louis Cardinals—a team known for its unkempt, ungainly looking players and roughneck style of play. Although many people assume the term "gashouse" refers to the place where death row inmates go to die, it actually refers to the so-called Gashouse Districts of several major Depression-era cities, rough-and-tumble neighborhoods where gas tanks were housed and vagrants often gathered. It's unclear who exactly hung the unflattering moniker on the Cardinals of Pepper Martin, Dizzy Dean, and Leo Durocher, but it could not

*You Could Look It Up*

### Random Baseball Trivia

Pepper Martin, the pugnacious shortstop of the **Gashouse Gang**, was notorious for "going commando" on the diamond. He refused to wear a jockstrap, a cup, or even a pair of sweat socks.

have been more apt. On their way to winning 95 games and a world title, the Cardinals developed a reputation as the grimiest, smelliest, most uncouth club in the National League. Players were known to abjure shaving and washing their uniforms. Their aim was so poor they routinely spit tobacco juice all over their hands, then wiped the expectorate on their white flannel uniforms. In the 1946 cartoon *Baseball Bugs*, the Warner Brothers animation shop parodied the Gang as a bunch of quasi-simian galoots known as the **Gashouse Gorillas**.

## Gashouse Gorillas

Fictional baseball team featured in the 1946 Bugs Bunny cartoon *Baseball Bugs*. The team is made up of cigar-chomping roughnecks—an obvious reference to the St. Louis Cardinals **Gashouse Gang** of the previous decade.

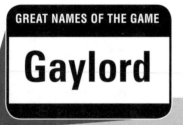

GREAT NAMES OF THE GAME

# Gaylord

Baseball's "splendid spitter" Gaylord Perry bewildered major league batters with his array of doctored baseballs for 22 years, during which he accumulated 314 career victories. The first pitcher to earn the Cy Young Award in both leagues, Perry was ejected for throwing the **spitball** only once, in August of 1982, when **umpires** caught him smearing **Vaseline** on a ball in a game against Boston. The name Gaylord derives from the Old French "gailard," meaning "brave."

# General Admission

Fictional United States cavalryman who supplanted the more overtly Confederate **Chester Charge** to become the principal mascot of the Houston Astros in the 1990s. Named after the unreserved $4 seating section in the old **Astrodome**, General Admission (or "G.A." as he was popularly known) led the cheers from an outfield platform, where he would fire off a toy cannon and pin a gold star on his uniform every time an Astro hit a home run. At the close of the 1999 season, General Admission was ritually murdered with a ray gun by a green space alien named **Orbit**, his successor as Astros mascot.

# George Michael Sports Machine, The

Syndicated sports highlight TV program, hosted by Washington, D.C., sports anchor George Michael, that predated ESPN's *Baseball Tonight* and served as the non-cable-ready fan's only source of national baseball highlights for most of the 1980s. With its frenetic pace and faux-futuristic set (Michael pushed a button on a "machine" to cue up the highlight packages), *TGMSM* was both a product of its time and a taste of things to come in the dawning age of interactivity. Originally called *George Michael's Sports Final*, the *Machine* chugged on for more than 20 years before the plug was finally pulled in 2007. At its peak, the show was syndicated to more than 200 stations nationwide. After the *Machine* powered down, host Michael covered local sports in Washington, D.C., until his untimely death from leukemia in 2009 at the age of 70.

# Gerbil, The

Nickname pinned on chubby-cheeked Boston Red Sox manager **Don Zimmer** by his personal bête noir **Bill Lee**.

## "Glory Days"

Hit single by Bruce Springsteen from his multiplatinum 1984 album *Born in the U.S.A.* Along with **"Centerfield"** by John Fogerty, it is one of the iconic baseball songs of the 1980s. (Unlike Fogerty's classic, it doesn't quite get the baseball terminology down pat; the Boss sings "speedball" where he presumably means "fastball.") A rueful tale of faded youth sung in the voice of a man looking back on the "glory days" of himself and his friends—including a high school pitching phenom—the song reached No. 5 on the pop charts and is still regularly played at ballparks nationwide.

## Gomez, Chuy

Onetime Kansas City Royals **supervendor** turned self-employed concessions magnate. Renowned for his good looks, his thick accent, and his distinctive shouts of "Leemon-ay! Lee-mon-ay! Leemon-ay! Wooooo!" (and popularly known, appropriately enough, as "the Lemonade Guy"), Gomez peddled his juice at Kansas City's Kauffman Stadium for six seasons, winning a vocal fan following. But when new subcontractors took over lemonade sales at the park in 2004, he opted to start his own company, Gomez Concessions, which now sells snow cones, cotton candy, popcorn, funnel cakes—and lemonade—at golf events, Little League tournaments, and Independent League games in the greater Kansas City area. For a time, the Royals tried to trade off Gomez's popularity by playing his trademark "Wooooo!" call over the loudspeakers during home games.

## Gores, Dr. Harold

Educator who played a pivotal role in the development of Chemgrass, a precursor to **Astroturf**, the earliest variety of **artificial turf** used in major league stadiums. In the late 1950s, Gores collaborated with Monsanto

Industries on a springy synthetic grass he hoped could be installed on inner city playgrounds, thereby saving municipalities the cost and labor of maintaining real sod. As it turned out, installing Chemgrass on playgrounds turned out to be cost prohibitive, but when the Houston Astros needed to address the problem of dying grass in their new multimillion-dollar **Astrodome**, Gores' carpet provided the perfect solution.

## Gorilla Suit

*See* **Epstein, Theo**

## Grand Hatching, The

Epic pregame ceremony held on June 29, 1979, at a sold-out San Diego Stadium to herald the return of the **San Diego Chicken** to Padres games following a two-year absence. Original Chicken Ted Giannoulas had been fired in 1977 in a dispute with radio station KGB-FM, sponsors of the unofficial Padres mascot. In 1979, he successfully sued to get his costume back and with it the right to entertain fans at Padres home games. Giannoulas staged the Grand Hatching prior to a midseason game between the Padres and the Houston Astros. More than 47,000 fans showed up for the festivities, at a time when the moribund San Diego franchise was averaging fewer than 14,000 per game. The game itself was delayed half an hour to accommodate the Chicken's spectacular unveiling, which involved the transportation into the stadium of a 10-foot Styrofoam egg carried atop an armored truck and escorted by California Highway Patrol motorcycles. Giannoulas, inside a newly redesigned Chicken costume, then "hatched" from the egg to the strains of Richard Strauss' "Also sprach Zarathustra," the theme to *2001: A Space Odyssey.* Raising his wings in triumph, the reborn mascot was paraded around the field on the shoulders of Padres players John D'Acquisto and Kurt Bevacqua. Whatever vindication Giannoulas may have felt about his return, his euphoria also had a financial incentive. Before agreeing to appear, he had shrewdly negotiated a deal whereby he got a percentage of the gate receipts for the event. When all was said and done, he ended up pocketing a cool $40,000 on the day.

## Gray, Pete

Talented minor league outfielder who became baseball's first one-armed player in 1945. Gray (born Peter Wyshner) had lost his right arm in a gruesome childhood wagon accident. After batting .333 and winning the Southern League Most Valuable Player Award in 1944, he was promoted to the big leagues by the St. Louis Browns—as a consequence of the wartime talent shortage. Although Gray's story was inspirational—providing a path to the majors for future disabled players such as Jim Abbott—his performance on the field was pedestrian. He hit only

AP Images

.218 during his short stint with the big club and spent the rest of his career beating the bushes. He died a penniless alcoholic in 2002.

# Graziosa, Rocco

Yonkers, New York, ne'er-do-well who earned national attention in 2002 when he assaulted Yankees pitcher **David Wells** inside a New York City diner at 3:00 AM, knocking out two of the lefty's teeth. In the wee hours of September 6, 2002, Wells was enjoying a late-night, high-protein dinner with a small group of friends at Gracie's Corner on Manhattan's Upper East Side when he first encountered Graziosa, a 27-year-old bartender who lived with his mother. Described by Wells in his 911 call reporting the incident as "a

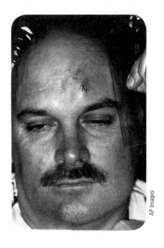

AP Images

fucking Italian, little squatty-body motherfucker," Graziosa reportedly teased the heavyset southpaw about his egg white omelet order before their confrontation turned violent. "Why don't you order a fucking cheeseburger?" Graziosa taunted, according to Wells' account. Graziosa would later claim that Wells became enraged because Graziosa and his party showed no interest in talking to him. Whatever the cause of the enmity, the two men at some point began exchanging insults, and Graziosa may or may not have brandished a butter knife in Wells' general direction. Wells claims that Graziosa made fun of his deceased mother, sucker punched him, and threw him to the ground. Graziosa and his dining companions were seen outside the establishment high-fiving each other after the incident. Graziosa was arrested and charged with assault and menacing. He telephoned his boss from his jail cell to tell him, "I'm not going to be able to make it to work tomorrow. I beat up **David Wells** from the Yankees." He was tried and convicted of misdemeanor assault two months later. Graziosa briefly returned to the headlines in 2004 when he plead guilty to misdemeanor charges of fondling a 21-year-old woman who fell asleep during a New Year's Eve party in Yonkers.

# Great Dodger in the Sky, The

Fictitious deity often invoked by longtime Los Angeles Dodgers manager Tommy Lasorda.

# Great Pierogie Race, The

Polish-themed mascot-racing competition, modeled on Milwaukee's **Sausage Race**, which has taken place in the home ballpark of the Pittsburgh Pirates since 1999. The Great Pierogie Race, devised to pay homage to the city of Pittsburgh's Slavic heritage, pits four costumed dumplings— Jalapeño Hanna, Cheese Chester, Sauerkraut Saul, and Oliver Onion—against one another in a frenzied dash from the outfield to the visiting dugout. (Oliver Onion replaced the forcibly retired Potato Pete in 2002.) Once per season, the four pierogies travel to Miller Park, home of the Brewers, for a highly anticipated grudge match against Milwaukee's formidable costumed sausages. The prize is the coveted Golden Skillet trophy.

David Watson

## You Could Look It Up

### Random Baseball Trivia

In Game 7 of the 1931 World Series, Burleigh Grimes pitched eight innings of shutout ball with a swollen appendix, which he had to have removed after the Cardinals' victory.

# Greenies

Common name for the amphetamine "pep pills" often consumed by major league players. In a typical clubhouse, two coffee pots were used—one labeled "regular" and the other labeled "hot" and spiked with greenies. Players who played the game without stimulants were said to be "playing naked." In 2007, greenies were added to baseball's list of banned substances tested for as part of its **performance-enhancing drugs** policy.

# Gregg, Eric

Morbidly obese major league umpire, often called "Rerun" or "the Plump Ump," who courted controversy due to his unhealthy lifestyle and idiosyncratic approach to calling balls and strikes. Besides his ample girth, Gregg is probably best known as the umpire behind home plate for Game 5 of the 1997 National League Championship Series, a game won by the Florida Marlins in which pitcher Livan Hernandez struck out a career-best

## Baseball by the Numbers | 357

Weight in pounds of umpire **Eric Gregg** at his heaviest

15 batters—a product, some said, of Gregg's galactically wide strike zone. Chronically out of shape, Gregg had a poor reputation within the umpiring community. When 22 umps resigned en masse in a labor action against Major League Baseball in 1999, Gregg was one of 13 whom Commissioner **Bud Selig** elected not to rehire. He died of a massive stroke in 2006.

## Gyroball

Mythical spiraling **trick pitch**, invented in the mid-1990s by two Japanese scientists as part of a supercomputer simulation and popularized by the American baseball writer Will Carroll. Boston Red Sox right-hander Daisuke Matsuzaka, among others, is said to be able to throw a gyroball, whose distinctive bullet-like spin was first described in the Japanese best seller *The Secret of the Miracle Pitch* by Ryutaro Himeno and Kazushi Tezuka. Diagrams and anime cartoons showing how to throw the supposedly unhittable pitch are widely available on the Internet.

## Hahn, Perry

*See* **Robo-Vendor**

## Hairs vs. Squares

Name bestowed by the American media on the 1972 World Series between the free-spirited, bearded, and mustachioed Oakland A's and the conservative, clean-cut Cincinnati Reds. The Hairs took the Series in seven games. See also: **Mustache Gang**

## *Happy Felton's Knothole Gang*

Instructional baseball program for children hosted by ex-Vaudeville comic Francis J. "Happy" Felton that aired before most Brooklyn Dodgers home games on New York's WOR-TV channel 9 from 1950 to 1957. Felton's "gang" consisted of local ragamuffins off the streets of Brooklyn, who would take instruction in rudimentary baseball skills from real-life Dodgers of the era. A workout was conducted, after which the youngster judged to have performed the best in a series of drills was awarded a prize—typically the chance to meet his favorite Dodger.

## Happy Heckler, The

*See* **Szasz, Robert**

## Harmonica Incident

Infamous back-of-the-team-bus confrontation that took place on August 20, 1964, between New York Yankees manager Yogi Berra and middling utility infielder Phil Linz. The Yankees were struggling and had just come off a crushing shutout loss to the Chicago White Sox when the jocular Linz whipped out his harmonica in the middle of a traffic jam and began to play a stark, haunting, country-inflected rendition of "Mary Had a Little Lamb." An enraged Berra, having tried and failed to get Linz to stop the music, ripped the harmonica from his player's hands and threatened to shove it up his ass. Linz was later fined $200 for insubordination but recouped the money in the off-season when the Hohner Company paid him $5,000 to endorse its harmonica. Berra was adjudged to have lost control of the team and was fired following the Yankees' loss to the Cardinals in the World Series.

## Harvey's Wallbangers

Distinctive nickname given to the 1982 American League champion Milwaukee Brewers, a multilayered moniker that riffs on the name of manager Harvey Kuenn, who took over for the fired Buck Rodgers in June and led the club to its first-ever AL pennant; the classic 1970s cocktail made with vodka, Galliano, and orange juice; and the club's proficiency at slugging or "banging" balls off the wall.

## Haskett, Clarence

*See* **Fancy Clancy**

## Heckler

Common term for a fan who mocks, badgers, and distracts players from the stands at baseball games. Notable ballpark hecklers include Ebbets Field's **Hilda Chester**; **Robert Szasz**, "the Happy Heckler" of Tropicana Field; and Miller Park's **Mark "the Doorman" Simons**.

## Hemorrhoids

Painful rectal ailment that irritated Kansas City Royals third baseman George Brett at various points in his career—most famously during the 1980 World Series. Brett begged out of Game 2 of that series in the sixth inning with the Philadelphia Phillies leading 2–1, citing the agony caused by his hemorrhoids. The next day, he underwent surgery to alleviate his discomfort and ended up having a productive series. He had the hemorrhoids permanently removed during spring training in 1981.

## *They Said What?*

"I'd have gone crazy if I'd stayed in teaching. I wasn't too effective as a classroom disciplinarian."

**—Krazy George Henderson**

# Henderson, Krazy George

Mercenary **superfan**, based primarily in Northern California, who calls himself the World's Sexiest Professional Cheerleader and claims to have invented **the Wave**. A former high school shop teacher from Santa Clara, California, Henderson foreswore pedagogy in the mid-1970s for the life of an itinerant crowd-revver-upper. Although he concentrates most of his efforts on football and hockey, his Major League Baseball clients have included the Oakland A's and the Colorado Rockies.

Dave Nelson

AP Images

# Hernandez, Keith

Slick-fielding, mustachioed first baseman of the 1970s, '80s, and '90s who gained celebrity beyond baseball as the celebrity guest star on one of the most popular episodes of the TV sitcom **Seinfeld**. The 1979 National League MVP also courted controversy as one of the **Cocaine Seven** named in the **Pittsburgh Drug Trials** and for indelicate remarks he made about a female massage therapist seen high-fiving players in the San Diego Padres dugout during a New York Mets telecast in 2006.

## They Said What?

"I won't say that women belong in the kitchen, but they don't belong in the dugout."

**—Keith Hernandez**

# Hobbs, Roy

Fictional baseball prodigy who serves as the protagonist of Bernard Malamud's classic baseball novel, **The Natural**, and its film adaptation starring Robert Redford. The term "Roy Hobbs" is often used generically to refer to any young, preternaturally talented prospect.

# Homerdome

*See* **Hubert H. Humphrey Metrodome**

# Homer Hanky

Logo-adorned rally cloth waved by Minnesota Twins fans during the club's postseason games since 1987. The Homer Hanky was the brainchild not of Twins management but of a promotions executive at the *Minneapolis Star Tribune* newspaper, Terrie Robbins, who was looking for a way for the paper to piggyback off the civic goodwill generated by the team's surprising playoff

Jeff Rutherford

run. Inspired by the Pittsburgh Steelers' popular Terrible Towel, Robbins and the paper printed up thousands of Homer Hankies and gave them away to fans. The Twins ended up winning the World Series in seven games, with the decided home-field advantage provided by the boisterous, hanky-waving fans in the **Hubert H. Humphrey Metrodome** playing a significant role in the victory. The phenomenon repeated itself in 1991, and the hankies have since become a fixture at all Twins home playoff games.

# Homer the Beagle

Live dog who served as the official team mascot of the New York Mets in the early 1960s. The sad-eyed hound was sponsored by Rheingold Beer, resided in the Waldorf-Astoria on Park Avenue, and had his own reserved seat on a platform behind home plate at the Polo Grounds. His handler was Rudd Weatherwax, the famed Hollywood animal trainer who once trained Lassie.

# Homer the Brave

Eerie-looking, baseball-headed humanoid who has served as a mascot of the Atlanta Braves since the 1980s. Homer the Brave has largely supplanted **Chief Noc-A-Homa**, the team's well-liked but politically incorrect Native American mascot. He is widely derided by fans as an inferior knockoff of the New York Mets' **Mr. Met**, whom he strongly resembles. (**Mr. Met**, some would say, is just a pale imitation of the Cincinnati Reds' **Mr. Red**.) Compared to **Mr. Met**, Homer the Brave has a much less expressive face. His bulging eyes stare fixedly and his "lips" are drawn

Shawn Latta

back into a not-especially-joyful-looking permanent smile, giving him the somewhat disquieting aspect of an escaped mental patient. For reasons that have never been explained, he is posited as the brother of the Braves' other mascot, **Rally**, a red, furry Muppet-like creature with blue hair.

## *Home Run Derby*

Televised home-run hitting competition that aired in syndication in 1959 and has since become a cult favorite, thanks to late-night airings on classic sports cable networks in the 1990s. "It's a home run or nothing here on *Home Run Derby*," the show's buttoned-down host, Mark Scott, would intone at the start of every telecast—a call to arms that pretty much summed up the contest's rules, which awarded a batter an out for every pitched ball he did not hit fairly over an outfield fence. The series originated from a Los Angeles–area minor league park and featured some of the most prominent major leaguers of the day. Mickey Mantle, Willie Mays, and Eddie Mathews were just some of the sluggers who traded hacks in an attempt to win an ever-escalating sequence of cash prizes. While one player was hitting, his opponent would sit in the broadcast booth with Scott and kibitz about his performance. The show had little drama but today possesses a great deal of nostalgia value. Its prize winnings also provided a sizable supplement to the meager player salaries of the day. *Home Run Derby* lasted only one season before it was canceled, due to the untimely death of host Scott as the result of a heart attack in July of 1960. He was only 45 years old.

## Homosexuality

*See* **Bean, Billy**; **Burke, Glenn**; **Pallone, Dave**; **Priore, Paul**; **"YMCA"**

## GREAT NAMES OF THE GAME

# Honus

One of the first five players inducted to the Hall of Fame, the "Flying Dutchman" Honus Wagner is widely considered one of the finest all-around players the game has ever known. The Pittsburgh Pirates' shortstop hit for average, fielded his position flawlessly, and ran the bases like a jackrabbit. He won eight batting titles and led the league in stolen bases six times. The name Honus is a variant form of Hans, the short form of Johannes, a Middle Latin form of John. In Latin, the word "honos" means "honor."

# House of David

Early 20th century doomsday religious cult that fielded a barnstorming semiprofessional baseball team for several decades as a means of attracting new disciples. Led by broom salesman, baseball enthusiast, and self-styled messiah Benjamin Purnell (who claimed to be the brother of Jesus Christ), House of David adherents lived on a commune in Michigan, cultivated long hair and flowing beards, and abstained from meat, tobacco, alcohol, and sex. They began playing organized ball sometime around 1910 and barnstorming the country around 1920. Mercenary players were eventually brought in to bolster the roster, with the ringers instructed to grow their beards in compliance with the cult's strict facial hair policy. A strategic alliance was forged with one of the most prominent Negro League franchises, the Kansas City Monarchs, and Negro League legend Satchel Paige (wearing a false red beard) took the mound for them on a number of occasions. Although the

Getty Images

House of David split into rival factions following the death of Purnell in 1927, the schism did not put an end to the barnstorming. Various splinter sects were still fielding semipro teams well into the 1950s.

## Hrabosky, Al

Glowering relief pitcher of the 1970s, famed for his mound antics and formidable **Fu Manchu** mustache. (He once told manager Vern Rapp, who ordered him to shave it off, that entering a game without it "felt like a soldier going to war without a rifle.") Dubbed "the Mad Hungarian," Hrabosky was known to stomp behind the mound before each pitch, turn his back to home plate, bow his head, and spew curses in the general direction of the baseball. Then, apparently dissatisfied with the ball's reply, he would slam it angrily into his glove and turn around to face the hitter. Before long, the home crowds began to respond to these gyrations. The organist at Busch Stadium, Hrabosky's home park, chipped in by playing "Hungarian Rhapsody No. 2" every time he walked in from the bullpen. A true artist, Hrabosky regularly

## They Said What?

"A lot of guys question my sanity.
But that's good. I want them to
know I'll do anything it takes to win.
I want them to think I'm crazy."

—Al Hrabosky

added new wrinkles to his act. At one point he took to wearing a Gypsy Rose of Death ring to ward off werewolves.

# Hubert H. Humphrey Metrodome

Enormous domed stadium that served as home park to the Minnesota Twins from 1982 to 2009. Named for former U.S. vice president, Minnesota senator, and Minneapolis mayor Hubert H. Humphrey—and nicknamed "the Homerdome" for its hitter-friendly reputation—the barn-like arena was widely reviled by players and fans for its poor sight lines; slippery, seam-laden **artificial turf**; and a ridiculous white fiberglass roof that made tracking fly balls needlessly arduous. (The roof actually collapsed during the stadium's inaugural season but was successfully re-inflated.) **Billy Martin** once called the Metrodome "the biggest joke in baseball history." In point of fact, it was built for football, and although it has done a serviceable job hosting Vikings games, Final Fours, and other big events over the years, the cavernous building seemed better suited as a setting for cattle auctions, truck and van shows, motocross exhibitions, and religious revivals than playing home to a professional baseball franchise. About the only remotely distinctive features of the Metrodome were the ear-splitting decibel levels sustained when capacity crowds were in attendance—often cited for the

## They Said What?

**"I don't think there are good uses for nuclear weapons, but this place might be one."**

–Kansas City Royals reliever **Dan Quisenberry,** on the **Hubert H. Humphrey Metrodome**

Twins' pronounced home-field advantage during the postseason—and the 16-foot-high plastic wall extension in right field, famously likened by sportswriter Jim Murray to "a bunch of trash bags on hangers" and widely referred to ever since as "the Baggie."

## Hunchbacks
*See* **Bennett, Eddie**; **Van Zelst, Louis**

# I

## Iorg
Unusual family name (pronounced "orge") shared by baseball-playing brothers (and devout Mormons) Garth and Dane Iorg. Dane Iorg is best known today for his game-winning hit in Game 6 of the 1985 World Series, an act of heroics precipitated by umpire **Don Denkinger**'s infamous blown call at first base to start the ninth inning.

## Isotopes, The

Fictional minor league baseball team on TV's ***The Simpsons***. The 'Topes, as they are affectionately known, play at Springfield's Duff Stadium. Homer Simpson briefly served as the team's mascot, Dancin' Homer. The Albuquerque Isotopes, the Triple-A affiliate of the Los Angeles Dodgers, named themselves in honor of the Springfield nine when they relocated to New Mexico from Calgary, Canada, in 2003.

**J**

## JackO

Stage name adopted by John O'Connell, onetime college roommate of wildly popular ESPN "Sports Guy" Bill Simmons, who makes frequent appearances on Simmons' eponymous podcast *The B.S. Report*, providing the Yankees-rooting yin to Simmons' Red Sox–loving yang. An attorney from Hartford, Connecticut (he routinely answers Simmons' phone calls with the catchphrase "Complex Litigation, this is John"), JackO is often used by the host as a barometer of the anxiety level of a typical Yankees fan at any given moment during the baseball season. Over the years, he has become a somewhat unlikely cult figure, with a thriving Facebook fan page, a legion of Twitter followers, and even his own theme song, "The Gregarious Raconteur," written and recorded by Theocracy, a Christian power-metal band comprised of regular Simmons listeners from Athens, Georgia.

## Jacobson, Max

German-born physician, known popularly as Dr. Feelgood, who prescribed amphetamines to baseball players out of his Upper East Side Manhattan office in the 1960s. A close friend of legendary New York Yankees play-by-play man Mel Allen, Jacobson serviced a large and diverse celebrity clientele that included, at one time or another, Truman Capote, Tennessee Williams, Cecil B. DeMille, Nelson Rockefeller, and President John F. Kennedy. His specialty was the so-called miracle shot, a mood-enhancing cocktail of amphetamines, vitamins, painkillers, and human placenta, which he typically injected into a patient's hip. In his tell-all book ***Ball Four***, **Jim Bouton** revealed that Jacobson had administered his miracle brew to Mickey Mantle late in the 1961 season as Mantle was competing with teammate Roger Maris to break Babe Ruth's single-season home-run record. But the contaminated needle he used gave Mantle a painful abscess that slowed his home-run pace and allowed Maris to overtake him. It also nearly caused Mantle to miss the 1961 World Series. In 1972, Dr. Feelgood's reign of ethical error came to an end when he was charged with 48 counts of unprofessional conduct. His medical license was later revoked.

# James, Bill

Onetime night watchman at a pork-and-beans factory who revolutionized the science of statistical analysis in baseball. The longtime baseball fan first began poring through box scores during downtime in his overnight shift at the Stokely Van Camp plant in Lawrence, Kansas, in the mid-1970s. Using mathematical interpretation of recorded data to challenge conventional wisdom and answer questions often left unaddressed by the traditional statistical categories, James began publishing his findings in the form of mimeographed "abstracts" beginning in 1977. The first *Abstract* sold only 75 copies via mail order, but with positive word of mouth (and an influential endorsement from early acolyte Daniel Okrent of *Sports Illustrated*), James soon garnered a loyal following among stat geeks, many of them clustered around the **Society for American Baseball Research**—whose acronym soon gave the movement its nickname, **Sabermetrics**. By the mid-1980s,

James was a veritable messiah among stat-obsessed seamheads, a position he retains to this day despite—or perhaps because of—his propensity for making idiosyncratic, often downright-loopy assertions, such as his roundly criticized contention that closers are overrated or his bizarre insistence that Roy White was a better offensive player than Jim Rice. Although James' unparalleled record of accomplishment as a developer of new statistical tools cannot be denied, teams that have tried to implement his ideas on the field have met with mixed results. The Boston Red Sox's experiment with James' "closer by committee" brainstorm famously flopped in the early 2000s, while general manager **Billy Beane** of the Oakland A's and others have had success applying many of James' Sabermetric principles to the task of constructing solid regular-season teams.

## Jockey
Brand of men's underwear modeled for many years by Baltimore Orioles great **Jim Palmer**.

## Johnny Bench Batter Up
Batting-practice device endorsed by the Hall of Fame catcher and widely used by children growing up in the 1970s. The Johnny Bench Batter Up was a remarkably simple contraption: a baseball was tethered to a tyke-sized pole rising out of a heavy concrete base, allowing the user to whack the ball

*Baseball by the Numbers* | 7

Number of times Johnny Bench's protective cup was shattered by a pitched ball

and then wait for the next "pitch" when the elastic tether swung back in the opposite direction. Former Minnesota Twins and New York Yankees second baseman **Chuck Knoblauch** is one of many major leaguers who claimed to have learned to hit using a Johnny Bench Batter Up.

# Johnstone, Jay

Journeyman major league outfielder of the 1970s and '80s best known for his penchant for playing practical jokes in the clubhouse. In his 1985 memoir *Temporary Insanity*, Johnstone catalogs some of his more inventive pranks, such as: replacing all the autographed photos of celebrities in Dodgers manager Tommy Lasorda's office with signed pictures of Johnstone, Jerry Reuss, and Don Stanhouse; substituting apple juice for a urine specimen during a club-mandated drug test and then drinking

Jay Johnstone
OUTFIELD

it in front of the team nurse; and placing a sun-melted brownie inside **Steve Garvey**'s first baseman's mitt. He famously posed for his 1984 Fleer baseball card wearing a Budweiser umbrella hat. After retiring from the game following the 1985 season, Johnstone worked as a Dodgers broadcaster and hosted the ESPN blooper series *The Lighter Side of Sports*.

# Jones, Chipper

Clean-cut Atlanta Braves third baseman who saw his wholesome reputation besmirched by his admission of an extramarital affair in the late 1990s. The switch-hitting phenom from DeLand, Florida (whose nickname derives from the phrase "chip off the old block" and whose given name, weirdly enough, is Larry), divorced his first wife in 1999 after it was revealed that he had fathered a child out of wedlock with a Hooters waitress. He has since remarried.

# Juiced

Best seller by retired major league outfielder José Canseco, detailing his use of steroids and other **performance-enhancing drugs** and outing several current and former big-league players for their use of the same. Subtitled *Wild Times, Rampant 'Roids, Smash Hits & How Baseball Got Big*, the book was dismissed by many upon its release in 2005 as a collection of vindictive accusations from an unreliable source desperate for publicity. However, with the release of the **Mitchell Report** and the revelations contained in the more journalistically unimpeachable book *Game of Shadows*, many of Canseco's allegations—particularly those concerning former teammate **Roger Clemens**—have been proven accurate. Nevertheless, Canseco—who was widely regarded as a preening showboat during his playing days—remains persona non grata with the big-league establishment, if for no other reason than he continues to argue that steroids, properly administered, pose no health risk and may in fact provide a benefit to athletes looking to bounce back from injury. Canseco's even more self-aggrandizing follow-up, *Vindicated*, earned him additional headlines in 2008.

# Junction Jack

Seven-foot-tall buck-toothed jackrabbit who has been the principal mascot of the Houston Astros since 2000. A train engineer, Junction Jack replaced the Astros' old space-themed mascot, **Orbit**, when the team moved into a new stadium built on the former site of Houston's Union Station in 2000. Junction Jack won the annual Mascot Home Run Derby at the All-Star Game for three years running from 2002 to 2004. He appears in the role of Tony Soprano in "The Mascots," an all-mascot YouTube video parodying the opening credits of *The Sopranos*.

# Kalas, Harry

Longtime Philadelphia Phillies play-by-play man known for his husky baritone voice and old-school, no-nonsense approach to calling a game. "Harry the K," as he was known, assumed Phillies broadcasting duties in 1971 and was paired for the first 27 years of his career with color commentator and former Phillies legend Richie Ashburn, with whom he developed a notable rapport. After Ashburn's death in 1997, Kalas soldiered on, earning iconic status in Philadelphia akin to that possessed by his contemporaries **Harry Caray** in Chicago and **Vin Scully** in Los Angeles. Kalas occasionally supplemented his baseball play-by-play earnings with voice-over work for national advertisers and other clients. He was the primary voice of NFL Films from 1984 until his death in 2009. From 2005 to 2009, he served as the lead announcer for Animal Planet's annual Puppy Bowl, a mock football game featuring a variety of adorable puppies that airs on Super Bowl Sunday. A longtime chain-smoker, Kalas died suddenly of a heart attack in the press box at Nationals Park before a game between the Phillies and the Washington Nationals on April 13, 2009. In addition to wearing memorial "HK" arm patches for the remainder of the 2009, Philadelphia players held a "team smoke" in the clubhouse in Kalas' honor. His distinctive "outta here" home-run call is now played every time a Phillies player hits a ball out of Citizens Bank Park.

*Umpires Gone Wild*

Before he reached the major leagues, longtime American League umpire Ken Kaiser spent several years as a black-hooded, axe-wielding professional wrestler known as "the Hatchet Man."

# Kekich, Mike

*See* **Wife Swapping**

# Kerouac, Jack

Lowell, Massachusetts–born novelist and so-called King of the Beats who had a little-known sideline as one of America's earliest **fantasy baseball** enthusiasts. Long before online fantasy and **Rotisserie** leagues became a national craze, Kerouac was kicking it old school with a set of index cards and multicolored pads of paper. As a child growing up in the mid-1930s, he invented his own league, which he maintained throughout his life. In its use of cards and statistics, Kerouac's game was similar to **Strat-O-Matic**, which became popular in the 1960s. However, Kerouac's version was much more intricate and complex. Composed of six imaginary teams, his league was populated with real-life figures such as Pancho Villa and Lou Gehrig, along with fictitious players such as Homer Landry, Charley Custer, and Luis Tercerero plucked out of the *On the Road* author's fertile imagination. Kerouac made himself the manager of a team known as the Pittsburgh Plymouths. "Games" were played in real time using marbles, toothpicks, and white-rubber erasers, which Kerouac launched at targets some 40 feet away. "Commissioner" Kerouac kept detailed records of each player's performance. He devised scorecards, box scores, and even individual salaries and team financial data. He also put out a newsletter, *Jack Lewis's Baseball Chatter*, and published a broadsheet called the *The Daily Ball*, for which he provided summaries of the day's games, up-to-the-minute standings, and lists of league leaders. Some of these obsessive jottings appear in *Atop an Underwood*, a collection of Kerouac's early writings. Others, sadly, have passed into baseball history.

## *Kiner's Korner*

Beloved postgame recap show, hosted by Hall of Famer Ralph Kiner, which aired regularly after New York Mets home games from 1963 to 1995. On a typical program, Kiner would play highlights from the day's Mets game and then interview a key player from the contest, but occasionally he would welcome in a special celebrity guest as well. Comedian Buddy Hackett was the guest on the very first edition of *Kiner's Korner* on April 30, 1963, and George Carlin made a memorable appearance during a rain delay in 1989. The show was notable for its low-rent, handmade feel (in exchange for their time, Kiner gave his guests complimentary gifts, such as vouchers for free gas) and the host's penchant for verbal miscues (such as referring to Mets third baseman Hubie Brooks as "Mookie" for an entire program).

## Klapisch, Bob

New York–area sportswriter and onetime New York Mets beat reporter who has been a central figure in three notable baseball media controversies. In 1988, Klapisch was the ghostwriter for a playoff diary "penned" by then-Mets ace **David Cone** for the *New York Post*, which enraged and inspired the NL West champion Los Angeles Dodgers with its belittling taunts aimed at reliever Jay Howell. The bulletin board material provided the spark for an unlikely seven-game Dodgers victory in the National League Championship Series. In 1993, Klapisch found himself on the receiving end of Mets slugger Bobby Bonilla's ire after Bonilla objected to Klapisch's chronicle of the team's 1992 campaign, *The Worst Team Money Could Buy*. Confronting Klapisch in the clubhouse early in the 1993 season, Bonilla unleashed a torrent of obscenities before threatening to "show [him] the Bronx" should the two men come to blows. And in 1999, Klapisch returned to ghostwriting, collaborating with faded Mets star Dwight Gooden on his autobiography *Heat*, in which the hurler famously contended that teammate **Kevin**

**Mitchell** had once severed off the head of a live housecat during a domestic quarrel in his Long Island home. Gooden would later deny having written the anecdote in question.

# Knoblauch, Chuck

All-Star second baseman of the 1990s who had his promising career derailed by a grievous case of **the Yips**. The scrappy former Minnesota Twin turned New York Yankee inexplicably lost the ability to throw the ball accurately to first base midway through the 1999 season—coincident with his messy divorce from his wife Lisa and the deterioration in the condition of his father, who suffered from Alzheimer's disease. Knoblauch's problems reached their nadir during the 2000 campaign, when he made 15 errors in only 82 games and brained broadcaster Keith Olbermann's mother Marie with an errant toss during a nationally televised game in June. Knoblauch was eventually relegated to designated hitter duties, partially rehabilitated as a left fielder in 2001, and out of baseball by the close of 2002.

# Knuckleball

Fluttering, agonizingly slow **trick pitch** that has allowed marginally talented pitchers to stay in the major leagues since the turn of the 20th century. Its invention is often attributed to disgraced **Black Sox** hurler Eddie Cicotte, who at the very least popularized the pitch.

# Koch, Kevin

Western Pennsylvania ne'er-do-well turned original **Pirate Parrot** mascot portrayer who was implicated in baseball's mid-1980s cocaine scandal and the ensuing **Pittsburgh Drug Trials**. Specifically, the former Pittsburgh-area high school baseball pitcher, who beat out 125 other aspirants at an open audition to become the Pirates' mascot in 1979, was accused of

## *They Said What?*

"The guilt is so great.
It's hard every day."

**—Kevin Koch**, former **Pirate Parrot** mascot portrayer
implicated in a clubhouse cocaine distribution scheme

introducing members of the Pirates to a local drug dealer and of transporting small amounts of cocaine to and from the clubhouse inside his beak. Koch was stripped of his feathers by team management but successfully avoided prosecution by cooperating with the FBI.

# Koufax, Sandy

Hall of Fame lefty whose retirement in 1966, at the tender age of 31, secured his place as one of the game's most enigmatic legends. Over the course of a 12-year career, Koufax won 165 games, lost only 87, and collected 2,396 strikeouts. He threw four no-hitters, including a perfect game against the Chicago Cubs on September 9, 1965. Teamed in the starting rotation with the hard-throwing right-hander Don Drysdale, Koufax provided one half of a two-headed pitching colossus that led the Los Angeles Dodgers to four National League pennants and three world championships over an eight-year period. After winning his third Cy Young Award in 1966, Koufax stunned the baseball world by announcing his retirement due to an arthritic

AP Images

condition in his left arm. He worked briefly as a commentator on baseball telecasts, but his shy, diffident manner was ill-suited for TV. (Oddly enough, Koufax had appeared as himself on numerous television programs during his playing career, including bizarre guest appearances on the sitcoms *Dennis the Menace* and **Mr. Ed**.) Since the mid-1970s, he has rarely been seen in public, surfacing only to serve as a Dodgers spring training instructor. Koufax is especially beloved in the Jewish American community—both for being inarguably the greatest Jewish player of all time and for refusing to pitch the first game of the 1965 World Series because it took place on the high holy day of Yom Kippur. Yet controversy has dogged him on occasion as well. In 2003, Koufax severed his relationship with the Dodgers for several years after the *New York Post*—owned by then-Dodgers parent company News Corp.—printed a gossip item intimating that Koufax was gay. In 2009, Koufax was among the thousands of investors who found themselves swindled out of large sums by Ponzi scheme operator **Bernie Madoff**.

## LaCock, Pete

Marginally talented first baseman who played nine seasons with the Chicago Cubs and Kansas City Royals between 1972 and 1980 and is regularly cited alongside Dick Pole and Rusty Kuntz as having the smuttiest-sounding name in baseball history. Born Ralph Pierre LaCock Jr. in Burbank, California, LaCock's other claim to fame is the fact that he was the son and namesake of longtime *Hollywood Squares* host Ralph Pierre LaCock, better known by his stage name, Peter Marshall.

## Lady Met

Female consort of longtime New York Mets mascot **Mr. Met**. Often erroneously called "Mrs. Met," Lady Met shares **Mr. Met**'s enormous baseball head, rictus grin, and staring eyes but wears her hair in a shoulder-length orange flip with matching orange lipstick. She is typically attired in a blouse and skirt and projects a fun, ready-for-anything image. Although unofficially retired from active service since the 1970s, Lady Met is presumably still married to **Mr. Met**. A 2003 *SportsCenter* commercial portrayed the couple as the parents of three baseball-headed children.

## Lake Erie Midge

Swarming, mosquito-like chironomid, identifiable by its brush-like antennae, that bedeviled New York Yankees reliever Joba Chamberlain during a critical playoff game at Cleveland's Jacobs Field on October 5, 2007. Popularly known as "muffleheads," the non-biting insects hatch by the millions during the warm weather months in and around Lake Erie. Unseasonably balmy October weather may have tricked the midges into thinking it was time to mate, causing them to descend in droves onto the field in the late innings of a game the Yankees were winning 1–0. Entrusted with protecting the lead, Chamberlain was clearly thrown off his game by the bugs, which carpeted his neck and prompted the team trainer to spray him several times with insecticide. He wound up uncorking two wild pitches as the Indians rallied to tie the game. Cleveland went on to win 2–1 in 11 innings to take a 2–0 lead in the AL Division Series. The Yankees lost the series in four games, with some citing manager Joe Torre's refusal to demand that the **umpires** stop the midge-infested game as Exhibit A in the case for his dismissal.

# La Lob

Slow, high-arcing curveball, a variation on the **Eephus Pitch**, thrown by journeyman left-hander Dave LaRoche as a member of the New York Yankees in the early 1980s. During one memorable game at Yankee Stadium on September 9, 1981, LaRoche struck out Milwaukee Brewers slugger Gorman Thomas with La Lob. The tantalizing **trick pitch** caused Thomas to swing so hard he nearly fell down.

# Landis, Kenesaw Mountain

Stentorian martinet who ruled over the game with an iron fist as baseball's first commissioner from 1921 to 1944. A former federal judge and avowed racist who had personally supervised the politically motivated prosecutions of numerous radicals, socialists, and union agitators during World War I, Landis brought a comparably ruthless efficiency to the task of "cleaning up" baseball in the wake of the 1919 **Black Sox** Scandal. He expelled eight players from the sport for participating in the gambling fix and was widely hailed as the man who restored the integrity of the national pastime. For the next 20 years, "Judge Landis"—as he insisted on being called—never let anyone forget that. Owners so feared the glowering Georgian's wrath that they signed a loyalty oath vowing never to publicly criticize him. They granted him virtually unlimited authority on disciplinary matters, which he wielded

---

## They Said What?

"The colored ballplayers have their own league. Let them stay in their own league."

—**Kenesaw Mountain Landis**

---

with promiscuous glee. At the height of his power, Landis' cojones were so large he had the power to banish even Babe Ruth from the game (for the crime of playing in unauthorized barnstorming exhibitions during the off-season). He also steadfastly safeguarded the unwritten policy keeping blacks and other minorities off of major league rosters. When he died suddenly in 1944 after a brief bout with respiratory illness, he was immediately elected to the Hall of Fame by acclamation. Although it's rarely publicized today, the Most Valuable Player Award in each league is still officially named in his honor. Character actor John Anderson played Landis in the 1988 film *Eight Men Out*.

## Lanzillo, John "Zonk"

Texas Rangers **superfan** who irritates opposing batters by repeatedly beating on a snare drum during their at-bats. A pillar of the local business community, CEO of the eponymous Zonk Group, and longtime season-ticket holder, Lanzillo attended nearly every Rangers home game from 1986 to 2003, at which point he scaled back on his percussive heckling at the age of 70.

## Larry Doby's Cock

Supposedly elephantine penis cited by Hall of Famer Ted Williams as the one thing he would have liked to have if he could live his life over again. As related in David Halberstam's book *The Teammates*, Williams' declaration took place in the 1980s in the dining room of Boston's Ritz-Carlton Hotel, where the retired legend was having lunch with Speaker of the House Thomas P. "Tip" O'Neill. Asked by O'Neill if there was anything in baseball he wished he'd had, the Splendid Splinter bellowed: "Well, I'll tell you one goddamned thing. I would've loved to have had Larry Doby's cock!"

# La Russa, Tony

Highly successful major league manager who ascended to iconic status among pseudointellectual fans after being prominently featured in **George F. Will**'s 1990 best seller *Men at Work: The Craft of Baseball*. A former infielder, La Russa played professionally for 16 seasons but never once spent an entire year in the majors. He began his professional managing career in 1978 and accepted his first major league commission the next year with the Chicago White Sox. Over the course of a 30-plus-year managerial career, he won World Series titles in both leagues, as well as multiple Manager of the Year awards. A notorious control freak, La Russa has developed a reputation as one of the game's most innovative strategists. His promiscuous use of relief pitchers ushered in a new era of specialization in baseball and was widely blamed for lengthening games to almost interminable levels. Other La Russa innovations—such as batting his pitcher eighth and a position player ninth to enhance his third-place hitter's chances of batting with men on base—have been dismissed by detractors as needlessly baroque and hailed by supporters (such as Will and *Three Nights in August* author **Buzz Bissinger**) as evidence of La Russa's Mozart-like strategic genius. Away from the diamond, La Russa has been an outspoken advocate for animal rescue and vegetarianism. He lent his name to one of the most popular baseball video games of the 1990s—Stormfront Studios' **Tony La Russa Baseball**—and he has also courted controversy on

ATHLETICS

TONY LA RUSSA    ss-2b

occasion. Although numerous former La Russa players—including Oakland A's "Bash Brothers" José Canseco and **Mark McGwire**—have been implicated in baseball's ongoing steroids controversy, La Russa has steadfastly denied having any knowledge of illegal drug use in any of the clubhouses under his watch. In March of 2007, he was busted on DUI charges by Jupiter, Florida, police after being found asleep at the wheel of his SUV in the middle of a busy intersection. He later pled guilty. In 2009, La Russa filed—and later dropped—a lawsuit against the social networking site Twitter, claiming that his identity was appropriated by cybersquatters bent on making fun of his DUI arrest.

## Lawrence, Sheryl

Pioneering major league ballgirl who broke baseball's "gender line" for foul ball scooper-uppers in 1971. Oakland Athletics owner **Charles O. Finley** hired the 14-year-old Lawrence, along with future "Mrs. Fields Cookies" magnate **Debbi Sivyer**, as part of an informal initiative "to get the female interested in baseball." With their short white shorts, gold knee socks, and tight kelly-green jerseys, however, the ballgirls appealed more directly to male fans. Together, Lawrence and Sivyer helped usher in the golden era of sexy female stadium employees in the 1970s. See also: **Collins, Marla**; **Sivyer, Debbie**; **Styles, Mary Sue**; **Susie the Sweeper**

*Days of Glory* | **September 22, 2009**

A portrait of former Los Angeles Dodgers manager Tommy Lasorda is unveiled at the National Portrait Gallery in Washington, D.C. It hangs directly across from artist Shepard Fairey's iconic image of Barack Obama.

## They Said What?

"I always understood everything Casey Stengel said. But I knew that all my hours with Casey helped prepare me for **Bill Lee**."

– Rod Dedeaux, **Bill Lee**'s college coach

# Lee, Bill

Free-spirited southpaw reliever known for his long hair, left-wing politics, and (in his later years) bushy mountain man–style beard. "Spaceman" was the apposite nickname bestowed upon Lee, who won 119 games over the course of 14 seasons with the Boston Red Sox and Montreal Expos but invariably garnered more attention for his bizarre off-the-field antics. Lee was once fined $250 by the league for admitting to an interviewer that he sprinkled marijuana on his buckwheat pancakes. He protested Boston management's decision to change the color scheme of the team's caps by affixing a beanie propeller to the top of one and wearing it out onto the field. On other occasions, he entered games wearing a gas mask and a Daniel Boone cap. Lee's most productive years came in the mid-1970s—as was the case with many who shared his countercultural worldview. The junkballing left-hander helped pitch the Red Sox into the World Series in 1975, won 17 games for the club three years in a row, and took part in an infamous brawl with the hated New York Yankees. Boston management was not quite so enamored with the Spaceman, however. Lee's distaste for authority was legendary. He constantly baited manager **Don Zimmer**, whom he dubbed "**the Gerbil**," and walked out on the team after his best friend, Bernie Carbo,

## The Quotable Bill Lee

"Baseball is the belly button of our society. Straighten out baseball, and you straighten out the rest of the world."

"The other day they asked me about mandatory drug testing. I said I believed in drug testing a long time ago. All through the '60s I tested everything."

"The more self-centered and egotistical a guy is, the better ballplayer he's going to be. You take a team with 25 assholes and I'll show you a pennant. I'll show you the New York Yankees."

"People are too hung up on winning. I can get off on a good helmet throw."

"You have two hemispheres in your brain—a left and a right side. The left side controls the right side of your body and right controls the left half. It's a fact. Therefore, left-handers are the only people in their right minds."

was traded. Fed up, the Red Sox traded Lee to the Montreal Expos before the 1979 season. He played his final four seasons in Canada before retiring to Vermont, where he continues to play ball in senior leagues and preach his unique philosophy.

## Lefty and Righty

Anthropomorphized hosiery tandem who have worked intermittently as secondary **mascots** for the Boston Red Sox since 2006. Essentially a pair of socks with arms, Lefty and Righty assist **Wally the Green Monster** in his crowd-revving endeavors.

## Lemonade Shaking Guy

Registered trade name of Marc Rosenberg, Baltimore Orioles **supervendor** who has dispensed lemonade to fans using a proprietary spasmodic full-body shimmy shake for more than a decade. The University of Maryland graduate and onetime Club Med snorkeling instructor developed his shaking routine (described by one fan as resembling "a rooster on acid") in 1997, when a friend who ran concessions at Camden Yards asked him to help out selling lemonade in the upper deck. Rosenberg expected to be put to work behind a counter, but was surprised to learn he would have to walk the stands peddling his wares from a tray. He grew so annoyed at children repeatedly screaming at him for lemonade that he nearly collapsed in a paroxysm of anxiety. The fit earned him laughs—and quite a bit of tip money. (He regularly receives $20 for a $3.50 lemonade.) From that moment on, he made uncontrollable shaking a regular part of his vending routine. He grew so popular that he was soon moved to the best section of the ballpark and began to attract local and national media attention. Often featured on Fox's Saturday *Game of the Week* broadcasts, Lemonade Shaking Guy has also been profiled in *ESPN The Magazine*, *Southern Living*, and the *Washington Post*, among other publications. He started his own business and launched a website, hiring himself out as a motivational speaker, auctioneer, and performer at private parties, Bar Mitzvahs, company picnics, and corporate functions for such big-name clients as the Bose Corporation, the Washington Wizards, and Bacardi.

## Li'l Rastus

Demeaning name given to an African American youth adopted by the 1908 Detroit Tigers as their team mascot. The racially charged term—long used by whites to perpetuate a stereotype of smiling, carefree "Negroes"—was reportedly bestowed personally by Tigers legend **Ty Cobb**, a notorious racist, who insisted that the child sleep under his bed for luck. (Li'l Rastus also worked as Cobb's personal slave during the off-season.) The Tigers batters liked to rub Rastus' head for luck before stepping up to the plate, making him one of the first in a long line of good-luck charm **mascots** that includes the New York Giants' traveling hayseed **Charles "Victory" Faust**, New York Yankees' pet hunchback **Eddie Bennett**, and the Philadelphia Athletics' house dwarf **Louis Van Zelst**.

## Linz, Phil
*See* **Harmonica Incident**

## "Lonborg and Champagne"

Ill-chosen rallying cry of the 1967 American League champion Boston Red Sox, the seeming arrogance of which propelled the St. Louis Cardinals to victory in Game 7 of the World Series. Coined by Red Sox manager Dick Williams after the team's victory in Game 6, "Lonborg and Champagne" referred to Boston ace Jim Lonborg, who would supposedly pitch the Beantown nine to a championship the following day. That morning, the quote filled the front page of the *Boston Herald-American*, enraging the Cardinals, who won the deciding game 7–2 behind Bob Gibson.

## Lou Seal

Orange-clad, fuzz-covered, rump-shaking aquatic creature best described as a kind of hip-hop sea lion who has been the principal mascot of the San Francisco Giants since 1997. Lou Seal is the franchise's first official mascot, not counting the controversial 1980s "anti-mascot" **Crazy Crab**. He was christened Luigi

Rob Corder

## Umpires Gone Wild

Colorful American League ump Ron Luciano (who named his dog after **Billy Martin** and wrote a string of whimsically titled best sellers about life in the majors) committed suicide by carbon monoxide poisoning in 1995 at the age of 57.

Francisco Seal in an homage to Seals Stadium, home of the Pacific Coast League's San Francisco Seals and the park where the Giants played their home games before moving into Candlestick Park in 1960.

## Lyle, Sparky

Jocular, **chewing tobacco**–enthusiast and short reliever of the 1970s and '80s best known for chronicling the rampant dysfunction of the New York Yankees clubhouse in his tell-all book ***The Bronx Zoo***. Lyle was also famous around the majors for dropping his pants and sitting on other players' birthday cakes—and for entering home games to the tune of "Pomp and Circumstance," arranged for stadium organ.

## Mad Hungarian, The

*See* **Hrabosky, Al**

## Madoff, Bernie

Convicted Ponzi schemer whose many high-profile victims included New York Mets owner Fred Wilpon and Hall of Fame pitching legend **Sandy Koufax**.

# Maier, Jeffrey

Twelve-year-old Yankees fan who famously interfered with a fly ball hit by Derek Jeter during Game 1 of the 1996 American League Championship Series. The New Jersey native was loitering behind the right-field fence in the bottom of the eighth inning with the Orioles ahead 4–3 when Jeter hit a long fly ball that Orioles right fielder Tony Tarasco seemed assured of catching. Instead, Maier reached over the wall and tried to snatch the ball away from Tarasco, knocking it back into the stands. Replays confirmed it was a clear case of fan interference, but right-field umpire Rich Garcia ruled the ball a home run and the score was tied at 4–4. The Yankees went on to win the game in extra innings and take the series in five games. Maier briefly became a folk hero in New York, where a newspaper headline branded him the "Angel in the Outfield" and Mayor Rudy Giuliani gave him a key to the city. But he was reviled in Baltimore as the mischievous brat who helped the Yankees steal the pennant. *Washington Post* columnist Tony Kornheiser called Maier "a punk" and "a truant." After laying low for a number of years following the incident, Maier resurfaced as a college baseball star at Wesleyan University in Connecticut. Now styling himself Jeff Maier, he unsuccessfully sought a professional playing career and was last seen trolling for a front office job with various major league clubs. He is the subject of a short film, *I Hate Jeffrey Maier*, shot by one of his Wesleyan classmates, a rabid Orioles fan, in an effort to "exorcise the demons" of his bygone misbehavior.

## *Major League*

Ribald 1989 comedy that vies with the more critically acclaimed ***Bull Durham*** for the title of Best Baseball Movie of the 1980s. Essentially a baseball-themed variation on *The Producers* with some of the lowbrow appeal of the hockey classic *Slap Shot* thrown in, *Major League* follows the exploits of a ragtag Cleveland Indians team as it improbably fights for a division title—foiling the plans of its conniving owner, who wants the club to tank the season so she can move the franchise to Miami. A somewhat unlikely summer box office hit, the film helped make Wesley Snipes a star and reinvigorated the career of ex-catcher turned clownish broadcaster **Bob Uecker**, who played alcoholic play-by-player **Harry Doyle**. His signature call, "Ju-ust a bit outside," entered the lexicon of sports catchphrases.

## "Manny Being Manny"

Catchphrase often used by fans of slugging outfielder Manny Ramirez to explain and/or excuse the eccentric All-Star's bizarre behavior. The first use of the phrase "That's Manny being Manny" is often attributed to Mike Hargrove, Ramirez's manager during his sojourn with the Cleveland Indians. Hargrove reportedly uttered the phrase in response to a sportswriter's inquiry about Ramirez's penchant for leaving uncashed paychecks—often for thousands of dollars—lying around the clubhouse.

## Marcuse, Charley

*See* **Singing Hot Dog Man**

## Marichal Bat Attack

Attempted homicide perpetrated by San Francisco Giants pitcher Juan Marichal on Los Angeles Dodgers catcher Johnny Roseboro during a game at Candlestick Park on August 22, 1965. The shocking assault precipitated a 14-minute bench-clearing brawl and stands out as one of the ugliest incidents of violence in the history of professional sports. The hard-throwing Marichal had already brushed back two Dodgers hitters in the contest, which took place in the midst of a heated pennant race between the two longtime National League rivals. In the bottom of the third, when Marichal came up to bat, Roseboro opted to retaliate by whizzing his return throws to Dodgers ace **Sandy Koufax** uncomfortably close to Marichal's nose. A confrontation

ensued, during which Marichal began to pummel Roseboro upside the head with his Louisville Slugger. Only the intervention of home-plate umpire Shag Crawford prevented the crazed Marichal from counting coup over Roseboro's bloody corpse. As it was, 14 stitches would be needed to close the gash on the catcher's noggin. Marichal was thrown out of the game and eventually suspended for nine days and fined $1,750—an absurdly light sentence. However, his absence from the Giants rotation may have cost the club the National League pennant (they finished the season trailing the Dodgers by two games) and nearly cost him his place in the Hall of Fame. Marichal was unofficially blackballed from induction for four years until Roseboro personally vouched for him. The two combatants eventually became friends, although Marichal weirdly refrained from expressing any remorse about his behavior. "I feel sorry that I used the bat" was about as close as he came to an apology.

# Mariner Moose

Man-sized costumed elk who has served as the official mascot of the Seattle Mariners since 1990. Mariner Moose narrowly edged out a sea monster for the designation and was so named at the suggestion of a Bellingham, Washington, fifth grader who was awarded the $1,000 top prize in a "Name the Mascot" contest. Mariner Moose can often be seen either rollerblading behind or riding on an all-terrain vehicle around the Mariners' home park. This "need for speed" has led to some highly publicized accidents. During the 1995 American League Division Series, the Moose broke his ankle when he crashed into the outfield wall at the Kingdome. In August of 2001, the mascot nearly made roadkill out of Boston Red Sox outfielder Coco Crisp when he clipped him with his ATV between innings. And in August of 2009 the Moose had to slam on the brakes to avoid running over Kansas City Royal David DeJesus as he made his way out to the outfield.

Melissa Shuck

## They Said What?

### "Maybe I'll have some moose jerky."

—Boston Red Sox outfielder Coco Crisp, taking it in stride
after almost getting run over by **Mariner Moose**

# Marshall, Mike

Longtime relief specialist who enjoyed a brief period of dominance in the mid-1970s and is best known for his application of the principles of biomechanics to pitching. Marshall, who holds a PhD in kinesiology, rode his own odd mechanics to the 1974 Cy Young Award and developed a reputation as one of the most durable bullpen workhorses of his era. In retirement, he became a one-man evangelist for a revolutionary pitching motion that he claims could eliminate the risk of arm injury forever.

# Martin, Billy

Second-rate infielder of the 1950s turned successful manager of the 1970s and 1980s—invocations of whose name are invariably accompanied by the adjectives "belligerent," "combative," and "drunk." Martin was the Joey Bishop to Mickey Mantle's Frank Sinatra during the New York Yankees' carousing, Copacabana heyday in the 1950s, but his reputation as a barroom instigator and enabler of Mantle's worst tendencies eventually got him run out of town by Yankee GM George Weiss. He re-emerged on the national scene in the 1970s as a fiery field manager with a reputation for turning around moribund franchises. Hired by the Yankees in 1975, he led the team to two pennants and a World Series title but generated beaucoup bad press with his off-the-field antics, which included public feuds with Yankees owner **George Steinbrenner** and star player Reggie Jackson and drunken brawls with Illinois marshmallow salesman **Joseph Cooper**, Yankees pitcher Ed

Whitson, and others. He was fired and re-hired by the team four times and was thought to be on the verge of a sixth turn in the manager's chair when he was killed in a car crash on Christmas Day, 1989.

# Mascots

*See* **Ace**; **Bernie Brewer**; **Billy the Marlin**; **BJ Birdy**; **Bird, The**; **Bonnie Brewer**; **Buccaneer, The**; **Captain Jolly Roger**; **Charlie-O**; **Chester Charge**; **Chief Noc-A-Homa**; **Chief Wahoo**; **Crazy Crab**; **Dandy**; **D. Baxter the Bobcat**; **Diamond**; **Dinger**; **Fredbird**; **Gapper**; **General Admission**; **Homer the Beagle**; **Homer the Brave**; **Junction Jack**; **Lady Met**; **Lefty and Righty**; **Lou Seal**; **Mariner Moose**; **Mettle the Mule**; **Mr. Met**; **Mr. Red**; **Mr. Redlegs**; **Orbit**; **Paws**; **Philadelphia Phil and Philadelphia Phyllis**; **Phillie Phanatic**; **Pirate Parrot**; **Princess Poc-A-Homa**; **Rally**; **Rangers Captain**; **Raymond**; **Ribbie and Roobarb**; **Rosie Red**; **Screech**; **Slider**; **Sluggerrr**; **Southpaw**; **Stomper**; **Swinging Friar**; **T. C. Bear**; **Waldo the White Sox Wolf**; **Wally the Green Monster**; **Youppi**

# Matsui, Hideki

Japanese slugging sensation turned productive major league outfielder who is known around baseball for his enormous private library of adult movies. A report published in *Sports Illustrated* estimated that Matsui has "55,000 distinct items" in his porn stash.

# Mazzone, Jay

Baltimore Orioles batboy of the late 1960s and early 1970s, known for having metal claws for hands. Mazzone's God-given mitts had to be amputated after they were burned off at the wrists in a kerosene fire when he was two years old. Prosthetic hooks enabled him to pick up bats as easily as one might handle chopsticks, though he could only participate in the "up-or-down" votes in the team's kangaroo court through the use of an enormous cardboard thumb.

# McCarver, Tim

Longtime major league catcher and personal receiver for Hall of Famers Bob Gibson and **Steve Carlton** who since the late 1980s has been the most prominent baseball analyst on television. While not nearly as polarizing a figure as his contemporary **Joe Morgan**, McCarver has annoyed some viewers with his penchant for overexplaining even the simplest rules and elements of strategy. His willingness to criticize players on the air has earned him the enmity of some major leaguers as well. Peeved by comments that McCarver had made about him during a broadcast, outfielder Deion Sanders repeatedly doused McCarver with buckets of ice-cold water during the clubhouse celebrations that followed the Atlanta Braves' victory in the 1992 National League Championship Series.

# McGwire, Mark

Prodigious home-run slugger of the 1980s and '90s whose surefire Hall of Fame candidacy was thrown into question by allegations of steroid use that surfaced in the 2000s. The onetime "Bash Brother" of admitted user José Canseco, McGwire was locked on a commendable, if unspectacular, Dave Kingman–esque career trajectory in 1991 when he suddenly and inexplicably transformed himself into a mulleted, goateed, and pumped-up monster with a pin-sized head and enormous, bulging biceps. By 1998, he was the Caucasian face of baseball's "chicks dig the long ball" era, shattering Roger Maris' single-season home-run record with 70. "Big Mac" was lauded in the press as a good-natured goliath in the mold of Paul Bunyan but was soon caught up in the steroids-fueled media feeding frenzy that attended the 2005 publication of Canseco's tell-all **Juiced**. Although not named in the **Mitchell Report**, McGwire was forced to testify before Congress, where his inane repetition of the presumably attorney-supplied invocation "I'm not here to talk about the past" undermined his reputation as a straight shooter and turned him into a national punch line. In January 2010—after his former manager **Tony La Russa** hired him to serve as the St. Louis Cardinals' hitting coach—McGwire publicly admitted he had used steroids, a mea culpa that was widely seen as an attempt to resuscitate his prospects of one day being elected to Cooperstown.

# McLain, Denny

Talented organist, degenerate gambler, and minor underworld figure who is also the major leagues' last 30-game winner. A high-living right-hander, McLain won the Cy Young and MVP Awards for the world champion Detroit Tigers in 1968, the so-called Year of the Pitcher, in which he went 31–6. He maintained a lucrative sideline as an organist, headlining venues in Las Vegas and other hot spots frequented by professional gamblers and other shady operators, including members of the Syrian Mafia. Those associations finally caught up with McLain in 1970, when he was implicated in a betting scandal and suspended for the first three months of the season. Plagued by arm trouble and financial woes he blamed on "poor business decisions," McLain never regained his former stature as one of the game's top aces. He retired in ignominy in 1973 and became a drug dealer. In 1996, he was found guilty of embezzling more than $2 million from the pension fund of a meatpacking company he owned and spent six years in federal prison. The title of McLain's 2007 autobiography is *I Told You I Wasn't Perfect.*

## They Said What?

**"The rules for Denny just don't seem to be the same as for the rest of us."**

–Teammate Bill Freehan, on **Denny McLain**

# McNeil, Walter

*See* **Wally the Beer Man**

# McSherry, John

Morbidly obese major league umpire who died of a massive heart attack on Opening Day of the 1996 season at Cincinnati's Riverfront Stadium. The 300-plus-pound McSherry collapsed in the top of the first inning, forcing the cancellation of the Reds' traditional first-in-the-majors home opener and prompting Reds owner **Marge Schott**'s famously insensitive remark: "Snow this morning and now this. I don't believe it. I feel cheated."

# "Meet the Mets"

Official song of the New York Mets, whose catchy chorus and delightfully dated lyrics urging a hypothetical male patron to "bring the kiddies, bring the wife" to the team's home games have endeared it to successive generations of fans. Composed in 1961 (before there were any Mets to meet) by veteran songwriters Ruth Roberts and Bill Katz, the peppy sing-along was first recorded in March of 1963 by Glenn Osser and his orchestra and chorus. A 45 rpm vinyl record of the ditty, featuring team mascot **Mr. Met** on its sleeve, was given away to fans at the Polo Grounds that season. The song underwent a substantial rewrite in the 1980s. Sexist references to "the wife" were scrubbed and shout-outs inserted to New York–area locales beyond the east and west side of Manhattan. A new recording was made using modern instrumentation. Further tinkering led to the release of a misbegotten hip-hop version of the tune in 1999. (It was quickly scrapped.) Over the years, a number of artists have covered the song, including the Hoboken, New Jersey–based indie rock band Yo La Tengo and the "Ballgame Trio" composed of comedian Soupy Sales and his two sons, Hunt and Tony, future members of David Bowie's short-lived side band Tin Machine.

## Forgotten Heroes of the Game

### Bebe de Roulet

Pampered daughter of much-despised late-1970s New York Mets owner Lorinda de Roulet, best known for riding grandly around the warning track at Shea Stadium in a carriage pulled by the club's short-lived mascot, **Mettle the Mule**. A notorious cheapskate, Bebe (pronounced Bay-Bay) once suggested that the team extend the lifespan of used baseballs by washing them.

## Mettle the Mule

Onetime live animal mascot of the New York Mets, Mettle the Mule was the brainchild of much-despised New York Mets owner Lorinda de Roulet, who had inherited the club upon the death of her mother, Joan Payson, in 1975. De Roulet knew little about baseball, but by 1979 she could sense that the moribund Mets franchise needed a gimmick to attract fans to half-empty Shea Stadium. Enter the miniature mule in the straw hat, who was stationed near the Mets bullpen in right field and driven along the warning track before every home game. The awkward moniker "Mettle" was chosen by fans as part of a "Name the Mascot" contest. The subject of widespread derision, Mettle the Mule did not return for the 1980 season, by which time de Roulet had completed the sale of the team to businessmen Fred Wilpon and Nelson Doubleday.

## Midget

*See* **Gaedel, Eddie**

## Milano, Alyssa

Television actress and Los Angeles Dodgers season-ticket holder who has parlayed her romantic interest in major league players into a cottage industry as America's foremost female baseball fan. A lifelong follower of the game,

Milano made headlines with her 2009 book *Safe at Home: Confessions of a Baseball Fanatic*, in which she described her exploits as a serial dater of big-league stars including pitchers Carl Pavano, Barry Zito, and Brad Penny (who, she revealed, demanded that she wear his jersey in bed). "Other women dream of papaya facials and mango pedicures," the former *Who's the Boss?* star recorded in her tell-all. "Give me a hot dog, a pitchers' duel, and a late-inning suicide squeeze and I melt like hot **pine tar**." Although she publicly swore off sex with athletes in 2007, Milano has continued to cultivate her fandom. She has covered the baseball playoffs on TV for TBS, contributes a blog to the MLB website, and markets team apparel to women under her signature label, "Touch."

## "Mistake by the Lake"

Derisive term for Cleveland's Municipal Stadium, home to the Indians from 1932 to 1993. A dank, cavernous monstrosity with all the charm of a urinal, the ballpark (later renamed Cleveland Stadium, as if that enhanced its cachet) could accommodate more than 78,000 patrons but rarely attracted even a third that many. The lake in question was nearby Lake Erie, whose frigid winds made playing in the stadium an unbearable ordeal for the Indians and their opponents. The "mistake" was mercifully rectified via demolition in November 1996.

## Mitchell, Kevin

Slugging outfielder of the 1980s and '90s who once beheaded his girlfriend's cat during a domestic dispute, according to a widely circulated anecdote in teammate Dwight Gooden's 1999 autobiography *Heat*. According to Gooden, an enraged, paranoid, and possibly cocaine-addled Mitchell decapitated the helpless animal with a 12-inch kitchen knife during a tense, scary, afternoon-long standoff in Mitchell's Long Island home to back up his contention that it was futile to "fuck with" him when he was angry. Mitchell's girlfriend and

## They Said What?

"I couldn't find one big
enough for my junk."

—**Kevin Mitchell**, explaining why he never wore a protective cup

Mead Chasky, a local card show promoter, were also there to witness the animal slaughter, although neither of them has ever gone on the record to substantiate Gooden's allegation. Mitchell has steadfastly denied that the event depicted in Gooden's book ever took place. Gooden later disavowed his own account, blaming the disputed incident on overzealous ghostwriter **Bob Klapisch**.

# Mitchell Report

Informal name for the report commissioned by MLB commissioner **Bud Selig** documenting the widespread use of **performance-enhancing drugs** in Major League Baseball. So named for former U.S. senator and current Boston Red Sox director George Mitchell, the report relied heavily on already-published accounts and previously circulated documents as well as the compelled testimony of clubhouse employees and trainers with personal knowledge of steroid use among major leaguers. The report implicated 89 players by name, none of whom were prominent members of the Red Sox.

# *Moneyball*

Title of a 2003 best seller by financial journalist Michael M. Lewis that lionized general manager **Billy Beane** and the front office of the early 2000s Oakland A's for their moderately successful track record of using **Sabermetrics** and other newfangled methods of statistical analysis in constructing teams that could make it into the first round of the playoffs, despite mid-market payrolls. The term "Moneyball" has since been applied to describe this team-building philosophy. A feature film based on the book, titled *Moneyball: The Movie* and starring Brad Pitt as Beane, is said to be in development.

# Morgan, Chuck

Longtime Texas Rangers public address announcer and director of in-game entertainment who is credited with inventing the **Dot Race**.

# Morgan, Joe

Hall of Fame second baseman turned ESPN color commentator who has become a lightning rod for criticism among sports media columnists and bloggers. The diminutive infielder was a 10-time All-Star and a mainstay of the Cincinnati Reds' "Big Red Machine" of the 1970s, but started generating controversy after he assumed lead analyst duties for ESPN's *Sunday Night Baseball* telecasts in 1990. The bill of particulars against Morgan, leveled by newspaper writers and websites such as firejoemorgan.com, includes his frequently expressed hostility to **Sabermetrics** and other modern forms of statistical analysis, general windbaggery, and penchant for telling tall tales and embellished anecdotes from his playing days—including repeated instances in which he has claimed to have been present for events he could not possibly have witnessed.

# Morganna

Well-endowed ex-stripper who won international fame for charging the playing field and kissing professional baseball players in the 1970s and '80s. The self-described "Kissing Bandit" (birth name: Morganna Roberts) made her debut appearance in Atlanta in 1969 when she kissed Clete Boyer of the

## *Baseball by the Numbers* | 60-24-39

Measurements claimed by top-heavy ballpark temptress **Morganna** the Kissing Bandit

Braves; two years later, she kissed **Pete Rose** of the Reds at Riverfront Stadium. Her other major league "victims" included Nolan Ryan, Johnny Bench, George Brett (twice), **Steve Garvey**, Don Mattingly, and Cal Ripken Jr. Morganna later branched out to kiss basketball players as well. When apprehended by ballpark security, she would often cite her famed "gravity defense," claiming that her enormous breasts had caused her to topple over the railing and fall onto the field.

# Moskowitz, Harold

*See* **Sterling, John**

# Mossi, Don

Jug-eared, no-necked American League pitcher of the 1950s and '60s who is widely regarded as the ugliest player of all time. The left-handed control artist won 101 games over 12 major league seasons and was named to the All-Star team in 1957, but it was his unusual appearance—marked by a protruding Adam's apple and a permanent five o'clock shadow— that earned him the most attention (along with a pair of derisive nicknames: "Ears" and "the Sphinx"). "Mossi's ears looked like they had been borrowed from a much

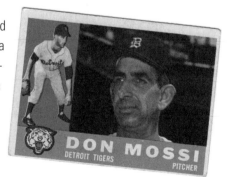

larger species," baseball historian **Bill James** once wrote. "[He] was the complete five-tool ugly player."

# Mr. Baseball
*See* **Uecker, Bob**

# *Mr. Ed*

Classic TV sitcom about a talking horse that featured a memorable guest appearance by **Leo Durocher** and several members of the 1963 Los Angeles Dodgers. In the episode titled "Leo Durocher Meets Mister Ed" from September 1963, the garrulous horse seeks a tryout with the team and gives batting tips to the Dodgers hitters. Moose Skowron, Willie Davis, and Johnny Roseboro all have prominent roles in the episode, which climaxes with Mr. Ed ripping an inside-the-park home run off of **Sandy Koufax**. Durocher, who was out of baseball at the time, also appeared on *The Munsters* and *The Beverly Hillbillies* during this same period.

# Mr. May

Derisive nickname hung on future Hall of Famer Dave Winfield by Yankees owner **George Steinbrenner** during a September 1985 conversation with *New York Times* columnist Murray Chass. Often erroneously dated to the aftermath of the 1981 World Series—during which Winfield went 1-for-21 and curiously called for a souvenir ball to commemorate his lone hit—the remark was actually made in frustration by Steinbrenner nearly four years later, following a September 13, 1985, loss to the first-place Toronto Blue Jays in which Winfield went 1-for-4 with a strikeout. "Where is Reggie Jackson?" Steinbrenner railed to Chass in the press box after the game. "We need a **Mr. October** or a Mr. September. Winfield is Mr. May." The insulting moniker stuck with Winfield for the remainder of his Yankees career. He did not fully live down his reputation as a player who failed to produce in the postseason until he recorded the game-winning hit for the Blue Jays in Game 6 of the 1992 World Series.

## Mr. Met

Grinning, baseball-headed team mascot of the New York Mets. Created for the cover of the 1963 Mets yearbook (and possibly modeled after Cincinnati's **Mr. Red**), Mr. Met broke Major League Baseball's mascot barrier in 1964, becoming the game's first modern live-action mascot. Unlike other team totems who have courted controversy, such as the Cleveland Indians' **Chief Wahoo** or the **San Diego Chicken**, Mr. Met has been content to rev up the Flushing Meadows crowd and fire T-shirts into the stands using an air cannon. In the 1990s, he gained national exposure by appearing with his inamorata **Lady Met** in a series of lighthearted TV promos for ESPN's *SportsCenter*.

Toby Leah Bochan

## Mr. October

Nickname bestowed on Hall of Famer Reggie Jackson for his ability to shine on baseball's annual postseason stage. A slugging outfielder for four big-league teams who helped usher in the era of the high-salaried free agent in

*Days of Glory* | **June 19, 1975**

Pregame ceremonies marking the 200th birthday of the United States Army take a destructive turn when a cannon fired during the National Anthem blows a hole in the center-field fence at Shea Stadium.

the 1970s, Jackson earned Hall of Fame induction based largely on his prodigious World Series play. He also had a candy bar named after him—the execrable **Reggie! Bar**—a powerful indicator of his impact on the popular imagination. "Mr. October" reached his apex during the sixth game of the 1977 World Series, when he clouted home runs on three consecutive pitches, off three different Los Angeles Dodgers pitchers, to lock up the championship for the New York Yankees. In retirement, Jackson served as a coach with several teams and occasionally appeared in films, most notably as a murderous drone assigned to assassinate Queen Elizabeth II in the 1988 comedy *The Naked Gun*. In 1996, he accepted a nebulous front office position with the Yankees but was fired by owner **George Steinbrenner** two years later for running up thousands of dollars in unapproved expenses on his team credit card. The two men later reconciled, and Jackson continues to serve as a roving consigliere for Yankees management to this day.

# Mr. Red

Venerable baseball-headed humanoid—the first of his kind in the majors—who has served as one of the principal **mascots** of the Cincinnati Reds since 1955. The probable inspiration for the New York Mets' **Mr. Met**, Mr. Red began life as a patch on the Reds' uniform and made the transition to full-fledged costumed character in the 1980s. While still listed as an active mascot on the team's website, the current status of Mr. Red is unclear. Beginning in 2002, he was forced to share the stage at home games with a plush red mascot named **Gapper**. And in 2007, Mr. Red appeared to have been supplanted by his mustachioed doppelganger **Mr. Redlegs**. The introduction of a fourth mascot, **Rosie Red**, in 2008, has complicated the club's crowded mascot roster even further.

Paul F. Lori

## Mr. Redlegs

Supposed "best friend" of longtime Cincinnati Reds mascot **Mr. Red** who usurped the latter's position as the club's principal baseball-headed mascot beginning in 2007. Often confused with **Mr. Red** (which is probably just the way he wants it), Mr. Redlegs is distinguished by his impeccably waxed handlebar mustache and old-time pillbox hat. He appears to enjoy a quasi-conjugal relationship with the team's fourth mascot, **Rosie Red**.

Paul Chandler Moulton

## Mr. Splitty

Disquietingly familiar nickname bestowed by legendary right-hander **Roger Clemens** on his split-finger fastball.

## Multipurpose Stadia

Highly practical if aesthetically offensive type of sports facility that proliferated like wildfire throughout North America in the 1960s and '70s. As the name suggests, multipurpose stadia were intended for use by multiple teams in various sports, allowing cash-strapped municipalities to avoid having to build or renovate separate ballparks for their sports franchises. Many multipurpose stadia of the period were situated outside of urban centers and featured **artificial turf**, symmetrical fences, and/or circular design (earning them the epithet "cookie cutters" or "doughnuts"). Examples of multipurpose stadia include the **Astrodome** in Houston, Three Rivers Stadium in Pittsburgh, and **Olympic Stadium** in Montreal. Widely derided by baseball purists, multipurpose facilities began to go out of fashion in the 1980s. Many were demolished and replaced by so-called **retro ballparks** beginning in the 1990s.

## *Time to Make the Doughnuts*

### Five Classic "Cookie Cutter" Stadiums

**Busch Memorial Stadium**
Location: St. Louis
Opened: 1966
Demolished: 2005
Distinctive Features: Massive scoreboard dominated by Anheuser-Busch eagle; electronic flying Cardinal

**Three Rivers Stadium**
Location: Pittsburgh
Opened: 1970
Demolished: 2001
Distinctive Features: Poor sightlines; dank, disgusting concourse

**Riverfront Stadium**
Location: Cincinnati
Opened: 1970
Demolished: 2002
Distinctive Features: Rock-hard **artificial turf**; aesthetically objectionable dirtless infield; airport-like ambience

**Veterans Stadium**
Location: Philadelphia
Opened: 1971
Demolished: 2004
Distinctive Feature: In-house "jail" used as holding pen for rowdy, drunken miscreants

**Shea Stadium**
Location: New York
Opened: 1964
Demolished: 2009
Distinctive Feature: Unidentifiable goo constantly dripping from exposed pipes in drafty mezzanine

## *Days of Glory* | June 9, 1999

After being ejected from a game against the Toronto Blue Jays, New York Mets manager Bobby Valentine returns to the dugout wearing thick-rimmed eyeglasses and a mustache painted on with eye black. He is later fined $5,000 and suspended for the unconvincing ruse.

## Murphy, Arnie

*See* **Arnie the Peanut Dude**

## Mustache Gang

Team nickname given to the Oakland A's of the early 1970s, in recognition of the formidable **mustaches** worn by several of the players.

## Mustaches

*See* **Fingers, Rollie**; **Hrabosky, Al**; **Mustache Gang**

**N**

## "Na Na Hey Hey Kiss Him Goodbye"

No. 1 hit single in 1969 that has become a staple of nearly every ballpark organist's repertoire. Recorded as a lark by three session musicians and released under the imprimatur of a non-existent band called Steam, the meaningless but catchy song had no connection to sports until 1977, when White Sox organist **Nancy Faust** began using it to "play off" opposing pitchers as they were taken out of games at Chicago's Comiskey Park. Fans soon began singing the song's memorable "Na-na-na-na, Na-na-na-na, Hey-hey-hey, Go-od-bye" chorus every time the White Sox closed out a home win. Other arenas in various sports now routinely encourage crowds to sing along with recorded or organ renditions of the tune, which has taken on an all-purpose "Get outta here" connotation, although it remains closely associated with the White Sox.

## Nash, Peter J.
*See* **Nice, Prime Minister Pete**

## *Natural, The*

Lyrical, uplifting 1984 film based on Bernard Malamud's mournful, downbeat 1952 novel that ranks alongside ***Bull Durham*** and *Field of Dreams* as one of the most popular baseball movies of all time. The film introduced the term "**Roy Hobbs**"—the full name of Robert Redford's titular phenom—into the American vernacular as a synonym for "scary gifted athletic prodigy." Composer Randy Newman's majestic main theme, which blares out of the speakers when Redford clouts the movie's

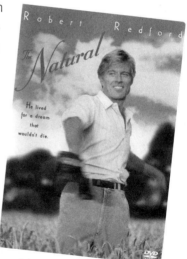

climactic home run—a scene that does not appear in the novel—has become a go-to musical sting for television directors looking to inject added drama into baseball telecasts. See also: **Whammer, The**

## Nice, Prime Minister Pete

Stage name of Long Island–born hip-hop legend Peter J. Nash, who since retiring from the music business in the mid-1990s has become one of America's most respected experts on 19th century baseball. The onetime front man for the pioneering interracial rap trio 3rd Bass, Nice is the author of *Baseball Legends of Brooklyn's Green-Wood Cemetery* and *Boston's Royal Rooters* and the owner of a sports memorabilia shop in Cooperstown, New York.

## Nomomania

Commonly accepted term for the fan frenzy that attended the rookie season of Japanese pitcher Hideo Nomo in 1995. Nicknamed "the Tornado" for his twisting, cyclone-like delivery, Nomo won 13 games and led the league in strikeouts for the Los Angeles Dodgers, snagging Rookie of the Year honors despite the fact that he was 27 years old and had already pitched for five seasons in Japan. His success shattered the myth that all Japanese pitchers were junkballers lacking the stuff to retire American hitters consistently. While it lacked the national profile of **Fernandomania**, Nomomania did inspire at least one popular song: "There's No One Like Nomo," a peppy jazz ditty written for trumpeter/vocalist Jack Sheldon by Academy Award–winning songwriters Marvin Hamlisch and Alan and Marilyn Bergman.

### They Said What?

"There's no one like Nomo! Nomo's pitching today. Nomo, that tornado—he'll blow you away!"

—lyrics to "There's No One Like Nomo"

## "No Pepper"

Mysterious phrase posted on signs at virtually all major league ballparks, often seen in the background during baseball telecasts. The prohibition refers to the turf- (and potentially spectator-) killing pregame fielding drill known as **pepper**.

## Nosemar

Derisive nickname bestowed by fans on infielder Nomar Garciaparra in recognition of his enormous proboscis. Other nicknames for the onetime Red Sox phenom include "Garciaerror" and "Mr. Hamm" (a reference to his status as the husband of women's soccer legend Mia Hamm).

## O'Connell, John

*See* **Jack0**

## Oh, Sadaharu

Sino-Japanese slugger who briefly became an international sensation in the late 1970s when he "broke" Hank Aaron's career home-run record. When Oh retired in 1980, he had compiled 868 home runs, a record recognized in Japan but of no significance anywhere else on the planet. Oh also holds the Japanese single-season record for round-trippers with 55—a mark he has zealously guarded as a manager by ordering his pitchers not to throw strikes to anyone coming close to overtaking it.

AP Images

# Olbermann, Marie

Late mother of onetime ESPN *SportsCenter* anchor turned MSNBC gasbag Keith Olbermann, who briefly became a minor celebrity after she was struck in the head by a ball thrown by New York Yankees second baseman **Chuck Knoblauch** during a game at Yankee Stadium on June 17, 2000. The 71-year-old Yankees season-ticket holder was sitting in her customary seat behind the first-base dugout when Knoblauch unleashed the errant toss after fielding a ground ball off the bat of the Chicago White Sox's Greg Norton. Although Mrs. Olbermann was not injured, her eyeglasses were shattered ("as was her confidence in Knoblauch," quipped her son, then working as a Fox Sports broadcaster) and her photograph was plastered across the front pages of both the *New York Post* and the *New York Daily News*. Replays of the incident brought national attention to Knoblauch's pronounced and ongoing battle with **the Yips**.

# Olympic Stadium

Structurally unsound multipurpose stadium that served as the home facility of the Montreal Expos from 1977 to 2004. Plagued by cost overruns, design flaws, and corruption, construction on the 56,000-seat cookie cutter was only partially completed when the stadium "opened" in time for the 1976 Summer Olympics. The Big O's signature retractable dome never worked properly, while falling concrete and a rock-hard artificial surface made the stadium inhospitable for players and fans alike. Initially estimated to cost no more than $120 million, "Stade Olympique," as it was grandly styled, wound up gouging Québécois taxpayers out of nearly $1.5 billion. Debt on the doughnut-shaped dump was not retired until 2006, well after the Expos had fled the country, earning it the more appropriate nickname "the Big Owe."

## *Days of Glory* | **August 29, 1986**

The retractable roof at Montreal's **Olympic Stadium** catches on fire, forcing the cancellation of that night's game between the Expos and the San Diego Padres.

# Orbit

Lime-green space alien who served as the primary mascot of the Houston Astros from 1990 to 2000. The successor to the club's original mascot, **Chester Charge** (and, for a time, co-mascot with **General Admission**, whom he ritually murdered with a ray gun during the penultimate game of the 1999 season), Orbit was designed by team officials in homage to the city of Houston's long-standing association with the U.S. space program. His antics included riding a bicycle in the outfield between innings and initiating **the Wave**. In 1995, the irascible extraterrestrial joined the Montreal Expos' **Youppi** in the rogue's gallery of professional sports **mascots** who have been thrown out of a game when umpire Gary Darling ejected him for arguing balls and strikes. The Astros replaced Orbit with a new mascot, seven-foot-tall jackrabbit **Junction Jack**, in 2000.

# Owens, Roger

Legendary Dodgers Stadium peanut vendor who has entertained the crowds with his bag-tossing prowess at Dodgers home games since 1962. The oldest of nine children born into a troubled Los Angeles family (his mother was briefly confined to a mental hospital), Owens started out hawking soda at the old Los Angeles Coliseum in 1958 at the age of 15. Four years later, he was elevated to peanut duty. He developed his trademark behind-the-back toss to accommodate a fan in the far back row who insistently cried out for his nuts. The "forward pass" (launched overhand football-style) and "split shot" (thrown between the legs) soon rounded out his repertoire. Owens' genial demeanor and uncanny accuracy quickly turned him into a ballpark folk hero. (He claims he adjusts for wind conditions and the age and gender of the peanut receiver before making every toss.) What started out as a part-time gig became a full-time career, as bemused Angelinos began filling up the seats on the second level of the third-base stands just so they could be on the receiving end of Owens' expertly thrown sacks. By 1976, Owens was so popular he was invited to be a guest on *The Tonight Show* with Johnny Carson, the first of four such appearances he would make over the years. In 1977, he dispersed peanuts to the throngs at Jimmy Carter's presidential inauguration. With fame have come streams of revenue inaccessible to run-of-the-mill vendors. Owens maintains a list of more than a dozen "season peanut holders," Dodger Stadium regulars who mail a check to his home at the start of every season as advance payment for an unending supply of his nuts. He has cultivated a lucrative sideline tossing peanuts at

Steve Neimand

private parties and corporate events—one company even flew him to Japan and back just to rev up an audience—and regularly gives motivational speeches for megadollar fees. Owens' autobiography, *The Perfect Pitch*, was published in 2004.

# Pallone, Dave

Longtime professional umpire whose controversial 10-year career in the majors came to an abrupt end after he was publicly outed and implicated in a teenage sex ring scandal. Baseball's "gay ump" would have been remembered primarily for crossing the picket line during the 1979 **umpires**' strike and secondarily for getting into a well-publicized shoving match with **Pete Rose** had he not had his sexual orientation exposed by the *New York Post* in September of 1988. Pallone was linked to, but never charged in, a case involving an underage sex ring being run out of a friend's house in upstate New York, prompting his firing by Commissioner Bart Giamatti in the off-season. Pallone later wrote about his experiences as a closeted gay ump in his 1990 memoir, *Behind the Mask.*

# Palmer, Jim

Hall of Fame pitcher better known to the general public as a men's underwear model for Jockey brand briefs. A three-time world champion, three-time Cy Young Award winner, and six-time All-Star, Palmer racked up 268 wins for the Baltimore Orioles over the course of a 19-season major league career. Early in his career he was nicknamed "Cakes" for his love of pancakes, which he purportedly ate for breakfast every day he was scheduled to pitch. (An Associated Press news photo shows him digging into a stack of 41 flapjacks prior to Game 2 of the 1966 World Series.) In the 1970s, Palmer parlayed his rugged good looks into a gig providing game analysis for ABC baseball telecasts. That opened the door to a portfolio of local and national endorsements, including mortgage lender The Money Store (formerly the province of ex-Yankees shortstop Phil Rizzuto) and Jockey, which Palmer

helped hawk in person and on advertisements for more than 20 years. The big right-hander made more than 500 in-store appearances on behalf of the underwear purveyor, appeared on numerous talk shows, and emceed fashion events. Most notably, he posed wearing nothing but a smile and a pair of tight white briefs for a Jockey billboard ad that loomed over New York City's Times Square and several other major city centers in the late 1970s.

## Patkin, Max

So-called **Clown Prince of Baseball** who entertained ballpark audiences with his limber-limbed, rubber-faced brand of slapstick comedy for five decades until his death in 1999. Although Patkin gained national exposure through his appearance in the 1988 baseball film ***Bull Durham***, he was at his best in more intimate settings and did not seek a career on the big screen. Barnstorming the country in a baggy baseball uniform festooned with a question mark on its back, Patkin made more than 4,000 consecutive engagements without missing a performance—evidence of a Ripkenesque dedication to his craft. The Philadelphia native grew up dreaming of someday playing major league baseball. He almost made it too, pitching in the minor leagues until World War II put a crimp in his plans. After serving in the U.S. Navy, Patkin turned to clowning, and his antics attracted the attention of Cleveland Indians owner **Bill Veeck**, who hired Patkin to entertain the crowds at Indians games. Gangly, double-jointed, with a bulbous nose and a mouth unencumbered by teeth, Patkin excelled at taking pratfalls and the fine art of the funny face. His regular routines included mimicking the players as they took infield practice and pretending to coach first base. Fans loved Patkin's capering, but some players and many managers did not. Frank Crosetti, the dyspeptic former Yankees shortstop turned third-base coach, once punched Patkin in the mouth for making fun of him on the field. And Patkin himself, like many clowns, had a melancholy side that he kept hidden from the public. "I was never comfortable until I got out there," he said in

Getty Images

1994. "There was always, like, a shadow over me. There was many a day I got into these ballparks and I used to pray for rain." Despite such misgivings, Patkin kept performing right up to the end of his life. Plagued by heart problems for many years, he suffered a ruptured aorta on October 23, 1999, and died eight days later.

# Paws

Costumed tiger who has been the official mascot of the Detroit Tigers since 1995. A product of the mid-1990s trend toward "warm and fuzzy" **mascots**—designed to entice families back to the ballpark in the aftermath of the 1994 players' strike—Paws has on occasion proved himself a little *too* entertaining. During his rookie season, a fan sued the club, demanding monetary damages for neck and jaw injuries suffered when he was hit by a foul ball while distracted by the mascot's capering. A jury ruled in favor of the Tigers and ordered the accuser to pick up the tab for Paws' legal fees.

Shawn Anderson

# PEDs

*See* **Performance-Enhancing Drugs**

# Pepitone, Joe

Beloved New York Yankees first baseman of the late–Mickey Mantle, early–Horace Clarke era, best known for posing nude in the January 1975 issue of the hardcore skin magazine *Foxy Lady*. A high-living playboy with a dandyish streak, Pepitone (or "Pepi" as he was popularly known) reportedly spent part of his $25,000 signing bonus on a sharkskin suit. Pepitone's other

## *Days of Glory* | January 27, 1993

**Joe Pepitone**'s name is dropped for the first time on **Seinfeld**. In the episode titled "The Visa," Kramer relates the story of a bench-clearing melee at a baseball fantasy camp that was touched off by his intentional beaning of Pepitone. It's the first of several Pepitone references on the popular 1990s sitcom.

notable sartorial innovation was his baroque toupee, which he spent countless hours laboriously maintaining with a blow dryer, according to clubhouse legend. The constant air curing may explain why it hasn't changed in color or volume since the mid-1960s. No New York City art opening is greeted with more anticipation by the public than the annual unveiling of Pepitone's wig at Old Timers' Day.

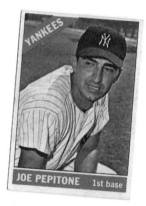

JOE PEPITONE   1st base

## Pepper

Reflex-enhancing warm-up exercise commonly played before games by baseball players of all ages. The fast-paced game requires a batter to bunt balls at a group of fielders standing a short distance away. The fielders then pitch the ball back to the batter as quickly as possible. Pepper is almost universally banned at major league ballparks, both for the damage it does to the grass and the potential for injury to spectators from errantly bunted balls. Hence the ubiquitous **"No Pepper"** signs posted at major league stadiums.

## Performance-Enhancing Drugs

Commonly used term for the various legal and illegal substances ingested by baseball players and other athletes during the steroids craze of the 1980s, 1990s, and 2000s. Examples of PEDs include the hormones testosterone and somatotropin (also known as human growth hormone, or HGH) and the anabolic steroids Androstenedione ("Andro"), Winstrol, and Tetrahydrogestrinone (colloquially known as "the Clear"). Sexual dysfunction and testicular shrinkage are common side effects of many PEDs.

## Peterson, Fritz

*See* **Wife Swapping**

## Petroskey, Dale

Onetime president of the National Baseball Hall of Fame and Museum who generated controversy in 2003 when he disinvited actor Tim Robbins from a Cooperstown event honoring the 15th anniversary of the release of **Bull Durham**. A former Ronald Reagan administration official and outspoken conservative, Petroskey banned the left-leaning thespian from the gala on the grounds that Robbins' public opposition to the Iraq War "helps undermine the U.S. position" and "could put our troops in even more danger." What this all had to do with the screening of a baseball movie was left unexplained. An aggrieved Robbins responded with a letter charging that Petroskey had politicized the Hall of Fame. The ensuing public relations

*Baseball by the Numbers* | **I-285**

Nickname bestowed upon Atlanta Braves pitcher Pascual Perez after he got lost circling the eponymous interstate on his way to the park

debacle nearly cost Petroskey his job. Instead, he lingered in his position for another five years before resigning in disgrace following allegations of financial mismanagement by the Hall of Fame's Board of Directors.

# Philadelphia Phil and Philadelphia Phyllis

Short-lived costumed mascot tandem of the 1970s Philadelphia Phillies. Outfitted in stereotypical colonial garb in celebration of the city of Philadelphia's role in the American Revolution, Phil and Phyllis patrolled the stands at Veterans Stadium from 1971 through 1979 and were included as part of the team logo from 1976 through 1978. They were known for their cumbersome, inexpressive costumes and their prominent role in the Phillies' "Home Run Spectacular." Whenever a Philadelphia player hit a home run, Phil would strike a large replica of the Liberty Bell with a baseball bat, "cracking" it, while Phyllis would fire a cannon aimed toward right field, setting off a loud pyrotechnic display that culminated in the unfurling of a Colonial flag and the playing of "The Star and Stripes Forever" over the P.A. system. Although not as passionately loathed as some **mascots**, Phil and Phyllis were nonetheless shunted aside in favor of the more versatile, fan-friendly **Phillie Phanatic** in 1978.

# Phillie Phanatic

Antic, green-furred beast who has been the official mascot of the Philadelphia Phillies since 1978. Inspired by the success of the **San Diego Chicken**, then–Phillies vice president Bill Giles commissioned the creation of a new mascot (to replace the unpopular tandem of **Philadelphia Phil and Philadelphia Phyllis**) from the husband-and-wife design team of Bonnie Erickson and Wayde Harrison. The resulting character—a plush, Muppet-like creature halfway between a bird and a space alien, with a retractable gecko tongue—was intended to provide general ballpark mischief and be adaptable to merchandising in the form of toys, books, and games. More than 30 years later, he is generally considered one of baseball's best and most beloved mascot ambassadors. The Phanatic made his debut at Veterans Stadium in Philadelphia on April 25, 1978, and instantly became a hit with local fans. Nearly 5,000 rabid Phanatic rooters showed up for one of the character's early public appearances in a Pennsylvania shopping mall; the crowds were so big at an appearance in Delaware that the event had to be scrapped for lack of adequate security. From the beginning, as originally portrayed by former front office intern Dave Raymond, the Phanatic worked from a repertoire of good-natured taunts and silly, sometimes naughty choreographed routines—including goosing **umpires**, cavorting with scantily clad women in the stands, buffing the heads of bald fans, and putting the whammy on opposing players and coaches. "The Phanatic's the guy who actually does the things that the devil inside us puts in our heads," Raymond once explained. That novel approach won the character national attention during an era when the front-running Phillies regularly appeared on NBC's Saturday *Game of the Week*. In fact, it's fair to say that, next to the **San Diego Chicken**, the Phillie Phanatic was at one time the most famous mascot in America. (To illustrate the point: at the height of the disco craze, Raymond showed up one night at Studio 54 and was denied entrance. He went back to his van, put on his Phanatic suit, and was immediately escorted in past the velvet rope.) Although beloved by fans and players (**Tim McCarver** famously dubbed him "baseball's best mascot"), the Phanatic

Serena A. Thaw

did make his share of enemies. Raymond never got along with Ted Giannoulas, creator of the **San Diego Chicken**, and maintained a long-running rivalry with his character. "Ted came off as a Hollywood guy. I couldn't relate to him," Raymond once said. Tommy Lasorda was another longtime nemesis. Lasorda seethed at some of the Phanatic's jokes about his weight, while Raymond considered the Dodgers manager a "phony." "Tommy was really a Philly guy," Raymond once observed, "but he shed his skin to be Mr. Los Angeles. He had pictures with Frank Sinatra on his wall. Everyone hated that. The Phanatic called him out on that stuff." Their feud reached the boiling point during a game in 1988, when the Phanatic began pummeling a grotesquely obese mannequin dressed up in Lasorda's Dodgers uniform. An enraged Lasorda responded by charging out of the visiting dugout and trying to rip the mascot's head off. Raymond repeated and expanded on the routine on subsequent occasions, force-feeding pizza slices to the Lasorda dummy and driving his ATV over several cans of Slim-Fast, a drinkable weight-loss tonic endorsed by the Dodgers skipper. For his part, Lasorda accused the mascot of "demonstrating violence in the ballpark." The confrontations ended after Raymond hung up his green-furred head for good following the 1993 season. But Raymond's replacement by other portrayers did not keep the Phanatic out of the headlines. In 1995, a 72-year-old man won a $128,000 judgment against the Phillies after getting knocked down by the mascot at a

## *They Said What?*

**"I used to be famous as a football coach. Now I'm known as the father of a green transvestite."**

–Tubby Raymond, former University of Delaware head coach and father of Dave Raymond, the original **Phillie Phanatic**

## *Days of Glory* | May 1, 1995

Dodgers catcher Mike Piazza guest stars on *Baywatch*.

church fair in Philadelphia. And in 1998, a jury awarded a $2.5 million verdict to an Exton, Pennsylvania, paint store employee after the Phanatic gave him a bear hug at a grand opening event and ruptured a disc in his back. There have been lighter moments as well. At a dinner welcoming newly installed U.S. Supreme Court Justice Samuel Alito in 2006, Justice Stephen Breyer arranged to have the Phanatic burst into the dining area and give the lifelong Phillies fan a congratulatory hug.

## Pierogie Race

*See* **Great Pierogie Race, The**

**GREAT NAMES OF THE GAME**

# Pie

Harold "Pie" Traynor, a lifelong Pirate, worked as a player, manager, broadcaster, and scout for the Pittsburgh franchise for more than half a century, beginning in 1920. A hitting machine, Traynor finished in the top 10 in batting average in the National League six times. He was also considered the finest defensive third baseman of his era. The origin of his nickname remains murky. Some say he liked pie as a child. Other accounts credit his father, a printer, for claiming the sooty-faced boy resembled pied type.

AP Images

# Piersall, Jimmy

Versatile outfielder of the 1950s and '60s whose chronic mental instability endeared him to fans in five cities. A high school phenom from Waterbury, Connecticut, Piersall is best known as a member of the Boston Red Sox. It was in Boston that he suffered his first major psychotic breakdown in 1952 and where he perfected his "I'm so crazy, I'm entertaining" shtick. Among Piersall's many crowd-pleasing antics: stepping into the batter's box wearing a Beatles wig and strumming his bat like a guitar; running around the bases backward to celebrate his 100th career home run; and swinging from the dugout roof like a monkey. He also beat the stuffing out of New York Yankees infielder **Billy Martin** during a celebrated pregame fistfight. Repeatedly institutionalized over the course of his 17-year career, Piersall was eventually diagnosed with manic depression, or what is today known as bipolar disorder.

## They Said What?

"Probably the best thing that ever happened to me was going nuts."

**—Jimmy Piersall**

His struggles with mental illness are chronicled in the 1957 biopic **Fear Strikes Out**. Democratic Congressman Barney Frank of Massachusetts famously used the phrase "doing a Piersall" during the 2008 U.S. presidential election campaign to describe the seemingly deranged behavior of Republican candidate John McCain during the financial crisis.

## Pine Tar

Thick, sticky wood resin used by ballplayers to improve their grip on bats. Although the substance itself is legal, its overuse was once strictly policed. Hall of Famer George Brett was famously ejected from a 1983 game at Yankee Stadium after hitting a go-ahead home run with too much pine tar on his bat. Pine tar is also occasionally used by pitchers. Los Angeles Dodgers reliever Jay Howell was ejected from Game 3 of the 1988 National League Championship Series for having pine tar on his glove.

## Pine Tar Incident

Infamous altercation between Kansas City Royals third baseman George Brett and home-plate umpire Tim McClelland over Brett's illegal overapplication of **pine tar** to his bat in a game against the New York Yankees at Yankee Stadium on July 24, 1983. Brett had just homered off Yankees closer Rich "Goose" Gossage in the top of the ninth inning to give the Royals the lead when Yankees manager **Billy Martin** demanded that McClelland examine Brett's bat, citing

Getty Images

Rule 1.10(b) of the Major League Baseball rule book, which limits the amount of **pine tar** that may be applied to a bat to no more than 18 inches from the tip of the handle. McClelland ruled in Martin's favor and declared Brett out and the game over, prompting an aggrieved Brett to erupt from the visiting dugout in a frothing rage. American League president Lee MacPhail later reversed McClelland's ruling and ordered the remainder of the game replayed the following month. Fewer than 1,500 fans showed up at Yankee Stadium on August 18 to watch Dan Quisenberry close out the Kansas City victory, with Yankees pitcher Ron Guidry playing center field and lefty Don Mattingly at second at the behest of a peeved **Billy Martin**. Television replays of Brett's near-assault of McClelland were broadcast coast to coast and helped turn the dispute into a national incident celebrated in popular culture. No fewer than two country songs—"The Pine Tarred Bat" by Red River Dave McEnery and "Pine Tar Wars" by C.W. McCall—were hastily written and released to capitalize on the publicity.

## Pirate Parrot

Enormous green Psittaciform bird who has been the ballpark mascot of the Pittsburgh Pirates since 1979. Created to evoke Captain Flint, the talking bird that sits on pirate Long John Silver's shoulder in Robert Louis Stevenson's novel *Treasure Island*, Pirate Parrot has, like its swashbuckling namesake, something of a checkered past. In 1985, the bird found itself tarred by baseball's drug scandal when it was revealed that original Pirate Parrot **Kevin Koch** had helped distribute cocaine to Pittsburgh players by hiding the powder in his beak.

Jonathan Dawson

## Pittsburgh Drug Trials

Widely-used catch-all term for the cocaine and amphetamine scandal that enveloped baseball in the mid-1980s. The trials centered on several Pittsburgh Pirates players and involved the alleged distribution of drugs in and around Three Rivers Stadium in Pittsburgh. A number of prominent players—including **Keith Hernandez**, Dave Parker, and Dale "Son of Yogi" Berra—were called to testify in court under grant of immunity. Testimony implicated baseball legends Willie Mays and Willie Stargell in the clubhouse distribution of amphetamines and prompted stars Hernandez and Parker to cop to out-of-control cocaine habits. Evidence was supplied in part by the Pittsburgh mascot, **Pirate Parrot**, who wore a wire in his headpiece at the request of the FBI. The Parrot also admitted to introducing players to drug dealers and to dispensing cocaine to players using a concealed compartment in his beak. After the trials concluded, MLB commissioner Peter Ueberroth suspended 11 players—the so-called **Cocaine Seven** plus four lesser offenders—for up to a year on the grounds that they had admitted to facilitating the distribution of drugs in major league clubhouses. The suspensions were lifted after the players agreed to perform community service and donate a portion of their 1986 salaries to drug-treatment programs.

# Postema, Pam

Pioneering female umpire whose fast track to the majors was cut short by the untimely death of her principal patron, MLB commissioner Bart Giamatti, in 1989. The first woman to officiate in a professional baseball game, Postema overcame enormous resistance from fellow **umpires** and many players, including Houston Astros hurler Bob Knepper, who famously dismissed her candidacy for a big-league promotion, saying: "I don't think a woman should be an umpire. There are some things that men shouldn't do and some things that a woman shouldn't do. I think umpiring is one of them." After leaving the game, Postema filed a sexual discrimination suit against Major League Baseball, which was eventually settled out of court. She later worked as a truck driver for Federal Express. Her tell-all memoir, *You've Got to Have Balls to Make It in This League*, was published in 1992.

# Powell, Jake

Stalwart American League outfielder of the 1930s and '40s who scandalized the game in 1938 with racist comments made during a pregame radio interview. Broadcaster Bob Elson of WGN in Chicago asked Powell, who was then a member of the New York Yankees, what he liked to do in the off-season. Powell replied that he worked as a policeman in Dayton, Ohio, where he liked to "crack niggers over the head with [his] nightstick." The remark set off a firestorm of protest in New York's African American community. (Oddly enough, in 1936 the Yankees had traded another racist, **Ben Chapman**, to the Washington Senators to obtain Powell.) Powell was eventually suspended for 10 games by Commissioner **Kenesaw Mountain Landis**. For the record, Powell never worked as a police officer and apparently suffered from delusions of grandeur. He committed suicide in a Washington, D.C., police station in 1948 after being arrested for trying to pass several bad checks.

# Price, Jackie

Untalented shortstop of the 1930s and '40s, afforded a cup of coffee by **Bill Veeck**'s Cleveland Indians in 1946, whose pregame antics allowed him to claim the title "**Clown Prince of Baseball**." Price's repertoire of tricks and stunts included hitting pitched balls while hanging upside down; throwing balls simultaneously to the pitcher and the second baseman; and firing baseballs into the air from a spring-loaded "bazooka," which he would then proceed to track down and catch from behind the wheel of a jeep.

# *Pride of the Yankees*

Schmaltzy, hagiographic 1942 biographical film about New York Yankees legend Lou Gehrig that, along with 1948's execrable *The Babe Ruth Story*, set the low standard by which all future baseball biopics would be judged. Aging matinee idol Gary Cooper was hired to play Gehrig, despite the fact that he was at least 10 years too old for the part, right-handed, and spectacularly uncoordinated. (Lefty O'Doul, the crusty former major leaguer hired to coach Cooper for his baseball scenes, commented that the actor threw "like an old woman tossing a hot biscuit.") The film takes serious liberties with Gehrig's inspiring life story, completely rewriting his eloquent farewell speech at Yankee Stadium and depicting the slugger's parents as dimwitted bumpkins fresh off the boat from Germany. Amazingly, *Pride of the Yankees* managed to get nominated for 11 Academy Awards—its enduring popularity no doubt fueled by Babe Ruth's hammy cameo and the repeated use of the Irving Berlin chestnut "Always" as its main love theme.

## Princess Poc-A-Homa

Female consort of Atlanta Braves mascot **Chief Noc-A-Homa** during the mid-1980s. Princess Poc-A-Homa was fired at the request of **Chief Noc-A-Homa** portrayer Levi Walker Jr., who feared she was overshadowing him and had it written into his contract that he be the club's sole mascot.

## Priore, Paul

Onetime New York Yankees clubhouse attendant who briefly made headlines in 1998 when he filed a $50 million lawsuit against the club, alleging sexual harassment at the hands of numerous Yankees, including Mariano Rivera, Derek Jeter, and Jorge Posada. Specifically, Priore claimed that Yankees reliever Bob Wickman had "exposed his penis" and rubbed it on him on numerous occasions, "grabbed and touched" Priore's own privates, and "attempted to insert his penis" into Priore's mouth; that Rivera and fellow reliever Jeff Nelson had subjected him to repeated homophobic taunts and terrorized him with a baseball bat; and that he had once walked in on Jeter and Posada having sex in the Yankee Stadium steam room (at which point they asked him to join them in a three-way). He also claimed that the team officials fired him after they found out he was HIV-positive. The Yankees denied all the allegations and insisted that Priore had been fired for pilfering team equipment. After prevailing at the trial level, Priore saw his case overturned on appeal by the New York State Supreme Court in 2003. In 2007, he unsuccessfully tried to peddle a tell-all book about his experiences, soliciting a ghostwriter through an ad on Craigslist.

## Puckett, Kirby

Genial, glaucoma-afflicted Hall of Famer whose reputation as one of the game's "good guys" was upended by revelations that he had serially cheated on his wife with a string of mistresses, spent an inordinate amount of time urinating in public, and had once sexually assaulted a woman inside the men's room of a suburban Minneapolis casual dining restaurant. Puckett, whose weight had ballooned to more than 350 pounds post-retirement, suffered a massive stroke and died on March 6, 2006, eight days shy of his 46th birthday.

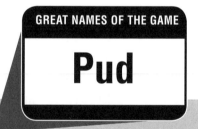

**GREAT NAMES OF THE GAME**

# Pud

Nicknamed "the Little Steam Engine" for his enviable stamina, James F. "Pud" Galvin chugged his way to 360 wins (against 308 losses) in a 15-year career that began in 1875. He was known more familiarly as Pud for his ability to turn opposing batters into pudding, a popular baseball put-down of the 1880s. The premier fireballer of his era, Galvin pitched more innings (5,941) and completed more games (639) than anyone except Cy Young. After brief stints as both a manager and an umpire, Galvin took a job as a bartender in Allegheny, Pennsylvania. He died, penniless, in a Pittsburgh flophouse at age 45.

## Quisenberry, Dan

Mustachioed, submarine-style closer of the 1980s who enjoyed an unusual second career in the 1990s as a published poet. A five-time Rolaids Relief Man of the Year, "Quiz," as he was popularly known, pitched in two World Series for the Kansas City Royals and was so beloved by fans that he was signed to a lifetime contract. Together with catcher Jamie Quirk, he also made up one half of the first Q-to-Q battery in major league history. But he failed to make an impact on the nation's poetic establishment until 1998, when the publication of his debut collection *On Days Like This* revealed a heretofore hidden talent for free verse on topics ranging from baseball to marriage to mortality. Sadly, Quisenberry's burgeoning literary career was cut short by his death from brain cancer later that year.

> *this small man*
>
> *who fought big*
>
> *now looked us in the eyes*
>
> *just a man*
>
> *who no longer talked of winning*
>
> *but hinted at life beyond champagne*
>
> —from "Ode to Dick Howser"
>
> by **Dan Quisenberry**

## Racists

*See* **Chapman, Ben**; **Cobb, Ty**; **Landis, Kenesaw Mountain**; **Powell, Jake**; **Rocker, John**; **Schott, Marge**; **Slaughter, Enos**; **Walker, Dixie**

## Radar Gun Guy

*See* **Brito, Mike**

## Rainbow Uniforms

Colorfully loud double-knit togs worn by the Houston Astros from 1975 to 1986. "It is only too easy to catch people's attention by doing something worse than anyone else has dared to do it before," the art critic Louis Leroy once remarked of Claude Monet. If that was the Astros' intention in donning these garish rainbow threads, they certainly succeeded. But did they have to *keep* wearing them for more than a decade, subjecting national audiences to them on a number of occasions, including the 1978 comedy *The Bad News Bears in Breaking Training* and the thrilling 1986 NLCS against the New York Mets? The sheer repetitiveness of the 'Stros blinding stripes calls to mind a put-down offered by another famous art critic, Cyril Asquith, on the work of Paul Klee: "His pictures seem to resemble not pictures but a sample book of patterns of linoleum."

## Rally

Blue-furred, red-haired, Muppet-like creature who served as an official mascot of the Atlanta Braves from 1986 until 2005. Absurdly positioned as the "brother" of baseball-headed humanoid **Homer the Brave**, Rally was part of the tandem that replaced the politically incorrect **Chief Noc-A-Homa** in the mid-1980s. He was widely reviled by fans, many of whom derided him as "Blood Clot." Atlanta newspaper columnist Lewis Grizzard once called Rally "an absolute embarrassment not only to the Braves, but to the entire city." Rally was quietly mothballed after the 2005 season.

## Rally Caps

Talismanic ritual adopted by players and fans, in which they wear their caps inside-out and/or backward to spark a rally. The invention of the rally cap is often attributed to the 1986 New York Mets, who certainly employed them and helped to popularize them. Other sources date the origin of the practice to the late 1970s or as far back as the early 1940s.

## Rallying Cries

*See* **"Cowboy Up!"**; **"Lonborg and Champagne"**; **"Ya Gotta Believe!"**

## Rally Monkey

White-haired capuchin monkey who since June of 2000 has materialized on the JumboTron screen at Angel Stadium of Anaheim to whip fans into a frenzy every time the home team needs a rally. The Rally Monkey  made his first appearance during a midseason interleague tilt between the Angels and the San Francisco Giants. With the home nine trailing, video board operators Dean Fraulino and Jaysen Humes decided to rev up the comatose Big A crowd by showing a clip of a jittery simian from the film *Ace Ventura: Pet Detective*. The stunt proved so popular that fans demanded a repeat performance the following night. A capuchin monkey named Katie was procured and filmed capering about to the tune "Jump Around" by hip-hop group House of Pain. The words "Believe In the Power of the Rally Monkey" were superimposed and a ballpark ritual was born. The Rally Monkey's national profile was raised during the Angels' drive to a world championship in 2002. Today the monkey appears holding her trademark "Rally Time!" sign whenever the Angels are trailing by three runs or fewer in the late innings, and is often "green screened" into scenes from popular films, including *Borat*, *Shrek*, and *Star Wars*.

# Rangers Captain

Two-legged equine monstrosity who has served as the official mascot of the Texas Rangers since 2003. Described in team literature as having been designed "in the fashion of a palomino style horse" by Street Characters, Inc. of Calgary, Canada (creators of the Houston Texans' Toro the Bull and the Colorado Avalanche's Howler the Yeti, among other characters), the uncomfortably phallic-looking 6'6" man/horse hybrid bears a strong resemblance to longtime cigarette mascot Joe Camel. Rangers Captain wears either stereotypically Western attire or a Rangers uniform festooned with the number 72 in honor of the year the team relocated from Washington, D.C., to Arlington, Texas. Rangers Captain was personally sworn in as mascot by Arlington mayor Elzie Odom.

Karen Matthews

Mark Mauno

## Raymond

Uncategorizable blue-furred creature—officially designated a "sea dog"—who has been the mascot of the Tampa Bay Devil Rays/Rays since 1998. Raymond's signature move is his patented "belly wiggle." For many years, he was also one of the most plugged-in of major league **mascots**, maintaining his own blog, MySpace page, and a YouTube account where videos of his routines were posted. That all ended at the conclusion of the 2008 season, when the then-defending American League champion Rays fired Raymond's longtime portrayer, Kelly Frank, for unknown reasons. Frank was actually the second Raymond to be dismissed since the character's June 1998 debut; original Raymond Shawn Christopherson was let go in 2004 after another team employee complained that he was making too much money.

## Raymond, Dave

*See* **Phillie Phanatic**

# R.B.I. Baseball

Old-school baseball video game, first released in 1988 and widely hailed as the best baseball game ever created for the Nintendo Entertainment System. Developed by Atari subsidiary Tengen and billed in ads as "the one the pros pitch," R.B.I. Baseball was the only video game of its time licensed by the Major League Baseball Players Association. Thus real-life stars of the 1980s such as **Roger Clemens**, Vince Coleman, and Kirk Gibson appeared, although the lack of a license from Major League Baseball meant their team names and logos were not used.

# Redlegs

Alternate name adopted by the Cincinnati Reds whenever they fear that fans will think they're Communists. Originally known as the Red Stockings and then renamed the Redlegs, the National League's Cincinnati franchise has been known as the Reds for most of its 130-plus-year history. But from 1954 to 1959, at the height of the McCarthy Era, the Queen City became home to the Redlegs once more, as nervous owners despaired of a patriotic backlash after "Reds Defeat Yanks" appeared as the headline on a spring training newspaper article. (Curiously, the name "Red Stockings" appears in the club's official logo during this bizarre period.)

# Reggie! Bar

Vile candy bar named after flamboyant New York Yankees superstar Reggie Jackson and offered free to patrons at Yankee Stadium on Opening Day in 1978. While playing for the Oakland A's, Jackson had once boasted, "If I played in New York, they'd name a candy bar after me." Someone at Standard Brands Confectionery was obviously taking notes that day, because in 1978, after signing with the Yankees and winning the World Series MVP, Jackson got his candy bar. An unpalatable mélange of chocolate, peanuts, and corn syrup sculpted to the approximate diameter of a major league baseball, the Reggie! Bar cost a quarter (quite a bargain in the age of inflation) and came packaged in an orange wrapper bearing the slugger's likeness. Sportswriters had a field day with the confection. One wrote that when you opened the wrapper on a Reggie! Bar, it told you how good it was. Another derided it as the only candy bar that tasted like a hot dog. But the ultimate verdict came from Yankees fans, 44,667 of whom were given free samples on April 13, 1978, when the Yankees opened their home campaign against the Chicago White Sox. In typical Jackson fashion, the slugger clouted a home run in his first at-bat, making it four "taters" in four swings at Yankee Stadium dating back to the sixth game of the 1977 Series. The raucous crowd then showered the field with Reggie! Bars as Jackson made his trip around the bases. Ugly orange wrappers quickly carpeted the green field. The only detractor from the prevailing air of absurdist resignation was White Sox manager Bob Lemon, who groused, "People starving all over the world and 30 billion calories are laying on the field."

# Retro Ballparks

Generic term for the faux-classic stadia that proliferated across baseball in the wake of Oriole Park at Camden Yards' opening in 1992. The stampede toward homey, old-timey ballpark designs that ape the "jewel box" aesthetics of ancient "green cathedrals" such as Fenway Park and Wrigley Field actually began in the minor leagues in the 1980s, a reaction to the cookie-cutter **multipurpose stadia** craze that had metastasized since the 1960s. Endless media oohing and aahing over Camden Yards' supposedly endearing idiosyncrasies inspired a wave of imitations in the 1990s and 2000s. Each had its own self-consciously quirky features (an enormous Coke bottle at Pacific Bell Park in San Francisco; a dirt strip between home plate and the pitcher's mound in Detroit's Comerica Park). Many boast precious, self-referential sounding names (The Ballpark at Arlington). All pleased purists by doing away with the symmetrical fences and **artificial turf** that had blighted the "doughnut" ballparks of previous decades.

# Ribbie and Roobarb

Much-despised Day-Glo mascot tandem employed by the Chicago White Sox organization from 1981 to 1988. Commissioned by incoming White Sox owners Jerry Reinsdorf and Eddie Einhorn as part of an initiative to "class up" the atmosphere at decrepit Comiskey Park, the ill-defined Muppet-like characters were designed by Harrison/Erickson of New York City, the same firm that had created the **Phillie Phanatic** four years earlier. Their names derive from the acronym for RBI and a commonly used slang term for an argument with an umpire. As for their appearance, *Chicago Tribune* columnist Bruce Buursma once described Ribbie and Roobarb as looking like "the dim-witted son of Oscar the Grouch" and "a chartreuse anteater with a genetic flaw." Patrons at Comiskey Park took an immediate and intense dislike to the colorful pair, in part because they were seen as part of a club-led effort

Richard Lindberg

to muscle out the stadium's homegrown buffoon, **Andy the Clown**. In a 1992 interview with the *Chicago Tribune*, the performer who played Roobarb admitted that fan antipathy occasionally turned violent. "We took some shots from people," he charged. "Even little kids thought it was hilarious. They'd ask for an autograph and the next thing you knew you'd get a fist in the back or a kick in the leg." Dismayed by the public response, the White Sox front office mothballed Ribbie and Roobarb after the 1988 season. So mortified was the organization that the team went without a costumed mascot for the next 13 seasons, until the advent of the more well-received **Southpaw** in 2003.

# Richardson, Bill

Onetime U.S. Secretary of Energy, ambassador to the United Nations, and governor of New Mexico who for more than 20 years bamboozled the public with the false assertion that he had once been drafted by the Kansas City A's. In the mid-1960s, Richardson *was* a pitcher on the Tufts University baseball team and for the Cape Cod League's Cotuit Kettleers, but he was never drafted, as he repeatedly claimed in official biographies beginning with his election to Congress in 1982. Disclosure of the false claim precipitated a political mini-scandal for Richardson in 2005, when he was running for a second term as New Mexico governor.

# Ripken, Billy
*See* **Fuck Face Card**

# Rivera, Bombo
Strong-armed Puerto Rican outfielder and novelty song inspiration of the 1970s. Jesus "Bombo" Rivera played for three teams over the course of a six-year major league career before finishing up in Japan in 1986. Best known as a Minnesota Twin, the happy-go-lucky Rivera became something of a cult figure in the Twin Cities thanks in large part to his distinctive nickname. (A bombo is a cylindrical bass drum used in Latin American music.) In 1978, the novelty ditty "Fare Thee Well, Bombo" was written in his honor.

# Road Beef
Term used by baseball players and other athletes to refer to the women they consort with sexually during road trips. See also: **Baseball Annie**

# Robo-Vendor
Nickname bestowed upon Baltimore Orioles beer vendor Perry Hahn, a onetime mechanical engineering student from Riverdale, Maryland, who invented a device that could peel the tabs off two aluminum beer cans simultaneously, allowing for a quick, easy, and relatively spill-free pour. Hahn was a 21-year veteran of the vending game by the time he hit upon his idea in the early 1990s. He spent $4,500 of his own money to develop and patent the device, which the U.S. Patent and Trademark Office calls a "Tandem High

Speed Can Opener." The battery-operated contraption can open and pour two beers in six seconds, or one case of 24 12-ounce cans in one minute. Hahn began wearing it on his wrist while he worked the stands at Orioles games, prompting fans at Camden Yards to dub him Robo-Vendor. The gizmo once helped him sell 25 cases of suds during a single

Eric London

game. Local and national press attention followed, earning Hahn **supervendor** status. Later in the decade, after ballparks started to transition to plastic beer bottles, Hahn designed another machine that twists the caps off of two bottles at a time.

# Rocker, John

Hard-throwing left-handed reliever of the late 1990s and early 2000s whose racist, homophobic rants—typically directed at New York City residents—earned him national villain status while a member of the Atlanta Braves. The Macon, Georgia, native was already reviled in the Big Apple for his propensity for trash-talking Mets fans, but he upped the ante during a December 1999 interview with *Sports Illustrated* in which he railed against single mothers, immigrants, and people with AIDS. He also referred to an African American teammate, **Randall Simon**, as a "fat monkey." Derided in the press as "John Cracker" and repeatedly lampooned on late-night TV, Rocker became a PR nightmare for the Braves—and a security risk every time he pitched at Shea Stadium, even after he issued a half-hearted, obviously club-compelled apology. His on-field performance also declined. Widely loathed in the Atlanta clubhouse, Rocker was eventually traded to the Cleveland Indians, spent parts of several seasons as a journeyman, and retired following the 2003 season.

# Ronnie Woo Woo

*See* **Wickers, Ronnie "Woo Woo"**

# Rose, Pete

Hard-nosed, headfirst-sliding hit machine whose Hall of Fame–quality career spanned almost four decades but who was deemed permanently ineligible for enshrinement in the wake of gambling revelations in the late 1980s. The feisty sparkplug of the Cincinnati Reds so-called Big Red Machine, Rose attracted national attention in the 1970s for his belligerent style of play and gargantuan bowl-cut hairdo. Long known for his penchant for buckraking (he reportedly sold the bat he used to shatter **Ty Cobb**'s all-time hit record for $129,000) and his inveterate womanizing (he attributed his success with the ladies to his willingness to "go in headfirst"), "Charlie Hustle," as he was nicknamed, was also a degenerate horseplayer and big-time sports bettor whose numerous wagers on baseball games were documented in a stinging 225-page report prepared for Commissioner Bart Giamatti in 1989 by prominent attorney John M. Dowd. For many years, Rose denied ever having bet on baseball, for or against the Reds, despite ample evidence to the contrary. Nevertheless, he accepted Giamatti's offer of voluntary instatement on baseball's permanently ineligible list in August of 1989—a designation no subsequent commissioner has seen fit to reverse.

---

*They Said What?*

**"Playing baseball for a living is like having a license to steal."**

—Pete Rose

---

# Rosenberg, Marc

*See* **Lemonade Shaking Guy**

# Rosie Red

Baseball-headed female who has been a mascot of the Cincinnati Reds since 2008. Outfitted in a skirt and heavily made up with red lipstick, Rosie is named after the acronym for the team's women's booster club, Rooters Organized to Stimulate

Leonard McGurr

Interest and Enthusiasm in the Cincinnati Reds. She presumably maintains some sort of conjugal relationship with **Mr. Redlegs**, the team's other baseball-headed mascot, or perhaps to **Gapper**, the red-furred muppet who helped push **Mr. Red** off the stage in the mid-2000s. Rosie Red was unleashed on the Great American Ball Park faithful on Ladies' Night in 2008, to the tune of "Sisters Are Doin' It for Themselves."

# Rothstein, Arnold

New York City gambling parlor proprietor who facilitated the fixing of the 1919 World Series in the so-called **Black Sox** Scandal. A dapper underworld *macher* nicknamed "the Brain" for his shrewd business sense, Rothstein made his first million by the age of 30, running speakeasies and fixing horse races. He branched out into baseball when the opportunity to make a killing on the World Series presented itself, allegedly fronting the money to eight crooked White Sox players through one of his lackeys, onetime featherweight boxing champion Abe Attell. When the White Sox lost the series in an astounding upset, Rothstein cleaned up by betting on the Cincinnati Reds. Called before a grand jury investigating the affair, he denied all involvement and was never indicted. Character actor Michael Lerner played Rothstein in the 1988 film *Eight Men Out*.

# Rotisserie

Commonly used name for one of the earliest forms of **fantasy baseball**, invented by sportswriter Daniel Okrent and a group of friends over dinner at the restaurant La Rotisserie Française in New York City one evening in 1980. Rules for Rotisserie Baseball were initially written out on the back of a cocktail napkin.

## They Said What?

"I feel the way J. Robert Oppenheimer felt after having invented the atomic bomb: if I'd only known this plague that I've visited upon the world."

–Daniel Okrent, on his invention of **fantasy baseball**, otherwise known as **Rotisserie**

# Routh, John

*See* **Billy the Marlin**

# Rozdilsky, Andrew Jr.

*See* **Andy the Clown**

# Rusty the Mechanical Man

Widely reviled giant robot who menaced fans from a brick redoubt beyond the right-field wall in San Francisco's Pacific Bell Park during the 2000 season. Sponsored by Old Navy, the 14-foot-high, 11,000-pound tin simulacrum of a baseball player was meant to be a permanent fixture of what is

## *They Said What?*

"If you're drinking a beer right now, the can might have been part of Rusty."

−San Francisco Giants marketing director Pat Gallagher, on the afterlife of **Rusty the Mechanical Man**

now known as AT&T Park. As originally designed by the Technifex special effects company, Rusty resided in a shed along the arcade wall in right field and appeared after important plays to lead cheers and gesticulate at fans. The mechanical monstrosity, which some observers said resembled a young Felipe Alou, consisted of 18 moving parts, including hands that could be transformed into baseball gloves and back again. Technifex had programmed Rusty to give signs, tip his cap, and wave his arms and legs about in a parody of human locomotion. Sadly, he seemed to possess no facility for winning over people's hearts. Booed from the first moment he came out, Rusty was routinely pelted with food and refuse—to the point where Old Navy suits insisted that he be banished to his enclosure for good. After several years had passed, the Giants quietly removed the robot—written off by one team official as a "multimillion-dollar mistake"—and had him disassembled for recycling. In 2008, his brick house was condemned to make way for a new luxury suite.

# S

## Sabermetrics

School of statistical analysis of baseball popularized by historian **Bill James**, the influential website Baseball Prospectus, and others, that attempts to provide quantitative answers to what were long considered qualitative questions regarding the relative value of players. The name Sabermetrics derives from the acronym for the **Society for American Baseball Research**, which since 1971 has served as an ad hoc think tank for Sabermetric research. Sabermetric principles are widely used in **fantasy baseball** and have increasingly been adopted by major league general managers, most famously by **Billy Beane** of the Oakland A's and **Theo Epstein** of the Boston Red Sox. Sabermetrics adherents specialize in developing buzzword-worthy acronyms for the invariably arcane, not-often-entirely-useful metrics they devise to measure player performance. Among the less confounding of these are WHIP (walks plus hits per inning pitched), OPS (on-base plus slugging percentages), and VORP (value over replacement player). Sometimes the metric is proprietary and so excruciatingly esoteric as to merit its own book, as in the case of **Bill James'** *Win Shares*.

*Days of Glory* | July 27, 1993

Squirt gun–wielding New York Mets pitcher Bret Saberhagen sprays bleach on reporters in the clubhouse, earning himself a $15,000 fine and a new nickname: the Clorox Kid.

# San Diego Chicken

Pioneering costumed mascot, long associated with the San Diego Padres although he never had any official connection to the team. Variously called the San Diego Chicken, the Famous Chicken, or simply "the Chicken," the brightly colored fowl began life as the KGB Chicken, the featured player in a promotional stunt run by San Diego's rock radio station, KGB-FM, in 1974. Hired to don the chicken suit—for the princely sum of $2 per hour—was area college student Ted Giannoulas. "There was no application, no interview or audition," the San Diego State journalism major would later recall. "There was only a handshake." Despite his lack of formal training, the 5'3" Giannoulas proved himself a born showman, and the Chicken so wowed the crowds during his appearance at the San Diego Zoo (where he handed out Easter eggs, appropriately enough) that he was soon hired to repeat his performance at Padres home games. For the next three years, Giannoulas' between-innings clowning delighted sparse San Diego Stadium crowds for whom the mediocre brand of baseball practiced by the hometown nine (and the mediocre brand of entertainment supplied by the club's official mascot, the **Swinging Friar**) was insufficiently diverting. He became a local icon, beloved by fans of all ages and wizened journalists alike. Legendary San Diego sportswriter Jack Murphy once observed that the Chicken "has the soul of a poet. He is an embryonic Charles Chaplin in chicken feathers." But his bond with the city of San Diego would be tested. In 1977, a dispute with sponsor KGB-FM led to Giannoulas' ouster. He was briefly replaced by a replacement portrayer, but the firing went public and San Diego fans lustily booed the usurper Chicken.

After two years away from the arena, Giannoulas sued the radio station to reclaim the right to play the character. Giannoulas prevailed after a lengthy court battle and, on June 29, 1979, staged his triumphant return as the Chicken in an elaborate pregame ceremony known as **the Grand Hatching**. He went on to appear at 520 consecutive Padres home games and build the mascot into a national brand. Later in 1979, the Chicken went into the studio to record a cover version of Rod Stewart's disco-era smash "Do Ya Think I'm Sexy?" From 1980 to 1985, the Chicken co-starred with perennial All-Star Johnny Bench on a syndicated instructional television series for children, *The Baseball Bunch*. The character spawned literally hundreds of imitators, as sports teams across the country rushed to develop costumed **mascots** of their own. *The Sporting News* named the Chicken one of the 100 most important sports figures of the 20th century. But there was controversy as well. In 1993, a Chicago Bulls cheerleader was awarded $317,000 in damages for injuries she sustained when the overexcited fowl rolled her around on the hardwood floor at a basketball game. And in 1997, the creators of Barney the Dinosaur unsuccessfully sued the Chicken for pummeling a Barney lookalike during a pregame routine. A court ruled the Chicken's actions were Constitutionally protected. Now retired from the major league game, the Chicken currently confines his capering to minor league ballparks.

## They Said What?

"If you can't stand the heat,
stay out of the chicken."

—**San Diego Chicken** Ted Giannoulas, remarking
on the occupational hazard of working inside
a chicken suit during a heat wave

# Sasser, Mackey

Journeyman backup catcher of the 1980s and '90s, best known for developing an especially debilitating case of **the Yips** that prevented him from throwing the ball back to the pitcher. The affable backstop found himself mentally blocked from completing the routine task following a collision at home plate with Jim Presley of the Atlanta Braves on July 8, 1990. He was soon double-pumping on almost every toss back to the mound, to the point where Brett Butler once stole second while the infielders waited for Sasser to get his act together. Even the hometown fans began to taunt him, derisively counting out the hesitations each time he tried to return the ball to the pitcher. It got so bad Sasser started to experience panic attacks the night before games he was scheduled to catch. After trying unsuccessfully to correct the problem with psychotherapy and yoga, Sasser saw his once-promising career hit the skids. He caught just 86 games from 1991 until the end of his career in 1995.

# Sausage Race

Footrace among costumed sausage **mascots** that has taken place at Milwaukee Brewers home games since 1994. The exhibition—officially known as the Klement's Racing Sausages, after the Milwaukee deli meats purveyor that sponsors the competition—traces its roots back to the early 1990s, when a cartoon race featuring three popular types of sausage began airing on the County Stadium scoreboard. Real runners wearing full-body sausage suits replaced the animated racers for select games beginning in 1994. By 2000—the final year the Brewers played at County Stadium—the live race was being run before the bottom of the sixth inning at all Milwaukee home games. Originally, the Sausage Race involved contestants Brett Wurst the Bratwurst, Stosh Jonjak the Polish Sausage, and Guido the Italian Sausage. The race was later expanded to include Frankie Furter the Hot Dog and Paco the Chorizo. Celebrity guests and baseball players occasionally run

Kelly Hafermann

with the sausages as well. On July 9, 2003, the lighthearted exhibition took a dark turn when Pittsburgh Pirates first baseman **Randall Simon** viciously clubbed the Italian Sausage with a baseball bat—knocking its portrayer, **Mandy Block**, off her feet and nearly causing serious injury. Major League Baseball fined and suspended Simon for the incident, which was replayed endlessly on ESPN's *SportsCenter* and other highlight programs. The popularity of the Sausage Race among fans of all ages inspired the Pittsburgh Pirates to develop their own version of the promotion, known as the **Great Pierogie Race**.

# Sax, Steve

Promising Los Angeles Dodgers second baseman who came down with a severe case of **the Yips** during the 1983 season. A year after a stellar debut campaign in which he was named the 1982 National League Rookie of the

Year, Sax inexplicably lost the ability to throw the ball accurately to first base. He was charged with 30 errors and made numerous other errant tosses, prompting fans in the seats behind first base to start wearing helmets to protect themselves from the barrage. Over the course of several years, the problems abated and Sax's accuracy returned. By 1989, as a member of the New York Yankees, he had the highest fielding percentage in the American League.

# Schacht, Al

World War I–era major league pitcher turned Depression-era third-base coach whose uproarious comedy routines earned him the nickname "**Clown Prince of Baseball**." An Orthodox Jew, Schacht first perfected his *tummler* act while manning the third-base lines for the Washington Senators as one half of the coaching comedy team of Schacht and Altrock. During World War II, he lit out on his own, barnstorming Europe, Africa, and the Pacific on USO tours in his trademark top hat and frock coat. He is considered a forerunner of baseball's postwar "Clown Prince," **Max Patkin**.

# Schott, Marge

Racist, homophobic Nazi sympathizer who was inexplicably allowed to own and run the Cincinnati Reds from 1984 to 1999, even as players and owners with much less odious rap sheets were being banned from the game. At one time or another during her 15-year reign on the national scene, the crotchety, chain-smoking lumber heiress and widow of a prominent Cincinnati auto dealer managed to insult or demean African Americans (she called two of her star players "million-dollar niggers"), Jews (she labeled them "sneaky"), gays ("Only fruits wear earrings," she once said), and tragically deceased **umpires** (she famously sent regifted flowers to the grieving colleagues of man in blue **John McSherry** after he died of a heart attack on Opening Day at Riverfront Stadium). She also enjoyed taunting Asians in a mock-Japanese

## *They Said What?*

"Hitler was good in the beginning,
but he went too far."

−Marge Schott

accent and reportedly had Christmas ornaments with swastikas on them. About the only living creature for whom she showed any regard was her incontinent St. Bernard, **Schottzie**. Schott's propensity for making racially insensitive statements earned her repeated temporary suspensions at the hands of her fellow owners, although none of them seemed inclined to demand she sell the team. She did that on her own in 1999. Schott died of respiratory failure in 2004.

## Schottzie

Beloved St. Bernard of onetime Cincinnati Reds owner **Marge Schott**, famous for using the artificial surface at Riverfront Stadium as her personal toilet. At the height of her fame, the drooling, 180-pound bitch had her own baseball card and was featured on the Meaty Bone dog biscuit box. There were actually two Schottzies. Schottzie 01 died in 1991, shortly after meeting First Lady Barbara Bush at the 1990 World Series. Schottzie 02 then enjoyed a 10-year reign of terror, repeatedly "going" on the Riverfront carpet until she followed her predecessor into doggie heaven in 2001. (She was buried in a Reds cap.) So taken was **Marge Schott** with the canine that she often rubbed Schottzie's fur on her managers and players for good luck.

## Schuman, Freddy

One-eyed, toothless **superfan** who has prowled the stands at Yankee Stadium banging on a frying pan with a metal spoon since 1988. Known to

Stadium regulars simply as Freddy "Sez" or Freddy, Schuman exhorts fans with his cacophonous clanking and his colorful hand-painted signs, each one bearing a message for the team underneath the header "Freddy 'Sez'…" (Example: "Freddy 'Sez': Yanks quit? Hell no!!! Fight on!!!") A Bronx native and onetime candy store proprietor, Schuman lost his right eye in a childhood stickball accident. He was inspired to pick up his pan and spoon by an eccentric uncle who used to celebrate the Fourth of July by riding through town on horseback carrying a flaming broomstick. He has attended virtually every Yankees home game since 1988 and is considered something of a good-luck charm by the team and its fans. All the pounding and cheerleading has not come without a price, however. In 2006, the *New York Times* reported that Schuman is almost totally deaf as a consequence of his pan-banging.

Eric Hetzel

# Screech

Pot-bellied bald eagle who has served as the official mascot of the Washington Nationals since 2005. The 6'2" costumed bird's design was based on a sketch submitted by Washington, D.C., nine-year-old Glenda Gutierrez, who also named the creature and supplied its defining characteristic: a ravenous appetite. Screech was hatched from an enormous eggshell at Robert F. Kennedy Memorial Stadium on April 17, 2005. Beset with complaints that the mascot was too fat, Major League Baseball designers gave the obese eaglet a slimming makeover in 2009.

Adam Fagen

# Scully, Vin

Honey-voiced Hall of Fame broadcaster, known primarily as the longtime play-by-play man for the Los Angeles Dodgers, whose work on national telecasts, including NBC's *Game of the Week* from 1983 to 1989, exposed his mellifluous vocal stylings to viewers from coast to coast. Scully joined the Brooklyn Dodgers' broadcast team in 1950, just a year after graduating from Fordham University in the Bronx. Under the tutelage of Red Barber, he developed a warm, personable on-air style that perfectly suited the game's slow, wheeling pace. His vivid descriptions of such events as **Sandy Koufax**'s 1965 perfect game ("Two and two to Harvey Kuenn…") and Kirk Gibson's dramatic home run in Game 1 of the 1988 World Series ("In a year that has been so improbable, the impossible has happened!") remain iconic moments in baseball play-by-play history. On rare occasions, Scully's calls have teetered on the brink of self-parody: "If you have a sombrero, throw it to the sky!" he famously gushed at the conclusion of Mexican native Fernando Valenzuela's no-hitter in 1990. After the 1997 season, Scully retired from national broadcasting to concentrate solely on his local responsibilities with the Dodgers. Alone among baseball play-by-play men, he works without a color commentator and reportedly refuses to attend or watch a game he is not broadcasting.

## *Seinfeld*

Screamingly popular television sitcom that is revered by baseball fans for its knowing references to New York sports icons of the 1980s and '90s. Especially beloved by Mets fans is a two-part 1992 episode, "The Boyfriend," guest-starring former major leaguer **Keith Hernandez** as himself. The episode is highlighted by a scene referencing an apocryphal Mets-Phillies game at Shea Stadium on June 14, 1987, during which Hernandez was said to have made a key error. (Series star Jerry Seinfeld is a lifelong Mets fan.) For Yankees partisans, the show offered recurring scenes set in and around the club's front office suites, including a partially obscured actor portrayal of Yankees principal owner **George Steinbrenner**—voiced by *Seinfeld* co-creator Larry David—in which "Big Stein" is depicted as a logorheic despot obsessed with calzones.

## Selig, Allan "Bud"

Small-time used-car dealer who was crowned commissioner of baseball at the behest of his fellow club owners in 1992. The scion of a Milwaukee auto leasing empire, Selig first entered the national consciousness as the cigarillo-puffing owner of the Milwaukee Brewers in the 1970s. He was one of the architects of the owners' **collusion** scheme in the 1980s and an outspoken critic of strong, independent commissioners Bart Giamatti and Fay Vincent. This made him the logical candidate to succeed Vincent when Vincent was ousted in an owner-led coup d'état in 1992. Selig became acting commissioner and then permanent commissioner in 1998. He presided over the 1994 players' strike and cancellation of the World Series, the institution of the wild card playoff format in 1995, and baseball's return following the September 11 attacks in 2001. Detractors have criticized Selig for being little more than a tool of his fellow owners, for doing nothing about the mushrooming steroids scandal in the 1990s, and for diluting the game's talent pool through promiscuous expansion.

## Sergio, Michael

Emmy Award–winning actor, director, and producer who famously skydived onto the playing field at Shea Stadium during Game 6 of the 1986 World Series. Clad in a white jumpsuit and carrying a sign that bore the legend "Go Mets," the 36-year-old parachuting aficionado and semi-regular on the ABC soap opera *Loving* descended from the skies above Flushing with one on, one out, and soon-to-be World Series goat **Bill Buckner** at bat in the top of the first inning for the Red Sox. Sergio was arrested and spent 21 days in jail for the stunt, which electrified the crowd and made him a minor folk hero in New York for several weeks afterward. The Mets even hired another jumper to re-create Sergio's glide at a ceremony marking the 20th anniversary of the World Series team in 2006.

## Short Pants

Unconventional sartorial choice made by the Chicago White Sox during the first game of a doubleheader against the Kansas City Royals on August 8, 1976. The idea to outfit the team in dark navy-blue shorts and striped knee socks came from Sox owner **Bill Veeck** himself. In fact, Veeck, who had a wooden leg, personally modeled the shorts for the press before the game. The gimmick seemed to have its intended effect, as the meaningless game between the visiting AL West leaders and the homestanding also-rans generated more publicity than it was worth. Wolf whistles rained down from the stands as soon as the Chicago players took the field for the opener of the twin bill, which was played before a half-empty Comiskey Park. The Royals players mercilessly taunted the Sox throughout the game. "You guys are the sweetest team we've seen yet," cackled Kansas City's John Mayberry, promising to give Sox outfielders a kiss if he reached first base. Even the Chicago players had trouble keeping straight faces. Sox pitcher Dave Hamilton joked that his fellow reliever Clay Carroll looked "like a pilgrim going out to shoot wild turkey." Undaunted by their inability to slide without skinning themselves alive, the Sox beat the Royals 5–2. They switched back to conventional long pants for the nightcap and lost 7–1. The club would

Richard Lindberg

wear their shorts once more that season and then wisely consign them to the big hamper in the sky.

## Sianis, William "Billy Goat"

Publicity-seeking Chicago tavern owner who purportedly placed a curse on the Chicago Cubs after the team kicked his smelly goat **Sonovia** out of Wrigley Field during a World Series game. For more details, see: **Billy Goat Curse**.

## Sign Man

Commonly used sobriquet for German-born commercial artist Karl Ehrhardt, a Queens, New York, resident and New York Mets **superfan** who held up handmade cardboard signs at Shea Stadium from 1964 to 1981. A former Brooklyn Dodgers rooter who switched his allegiance to the Mets after the club moved to Los Angeles, Sign Man typically wore a black derby emblazoned with the Mets logo and alternately exhorted and lampooned the team and its players. "There Are No Words," screamed his most famous sign, which he displayed before the jubilant crowd after the underdog Mets upset the Baltimore Orioles in the 1969 World Series. "Jose Can You See" would be flashed at journeyman Jose Cardenal each time he struck out. Ehrhardt made each of his block-lettered 20-by-26-inch signs personally, took about 60 signs to each game, and at one point owned as many as 1,200. He was a fixture at team functions and was friendly with several of the players during the franchise's heyday in the early 1970s. But as the club's fortunes declined, management grew weary of Sign Man's penchant for calling out examples of poor play. (Whenever one of the weak-hitting Mets of the late 1970s managed to reach base, Ehrhardt held up a sign reading "It's Alive!"—accompanied by a drawing of Frankenstein's monster.) Sensing that he was no longer welcome at Shea, Ehrhardt packed up his signs and left the park for good in 1981. He made a rousing cameo appearance at the club's 40th anniversary celebration in 2002 (holding up a placard that declared "The Sign Man Lives") and died in 2008 at the age of 83.

## Simon, Randall

Journeyman first baseman of the 1990s and 2000s, best known for bludgeoning Miller Park's Italian Sausage, Guido, with his bat during a well-publicized **Sausage Race** incident on July 9, 2003. See also: **Block, Mandy**

## Simons, Mark "the Doorman"

Longtime Milwaukee Brewers season-ticket holder who has heckled opposing players from his seat behind the visitors' dugout at Miller Park since 2001. Simons is often caught on TV cameras celebrating Brewers home runs or showing opposing players "the door" after they strike out.

## *Simpsons, The*

Unexpectedly long-lived animated comedy series known for its arcane pop cultural allusions, including numerous knowing references to baseball players and lore. In *The Simpsons*' most famous baseball episode, 1992's "Homer at the Bat," nuclear power plant mogul Montgomery Burns assembles a company softball team of ringers consisting of then–major league stars José Canseco, Ken Griffey Jr., Daryl Strawberry, **Roger Clemens**, Don Mattingly, **Steve Sax**, Ozzie Smith, **Wade Boggs**, and Mike Scioscia— each of whom lent his vocal talents to the episode. Other *Simpsons* installments name-drop **Bill Buckner**, Ron Santo, and Carl **Yastrzemski's muttonchops**, while storylines occasionally feature the town of Springfield's minor league baseball team, **the Isotopes**. Series creator Matt Groening has credited the prevalence of baseball references to the writing staff's obsession with **Rotisserie** baseball.

## Singing Hot Dog Man

Detroit Tigers **supervendor** who annoys some and delights others by belting out the words "Hot dogs!" over and over again in an operatic baritone. A onetime buying manager for a high-end Detroit-area men's clothier, Charley Marcuse got the idea for his unique frankfurter pitch while vending at a

David Scaramucci

Three Tenors concert at Tiger Stadium in 1999. His booming hot dog come-on sometimes lasts as long as 15 seconds and can often be heard above the crowd noise on Tigers TV broadcasts. While many fans became enamored with the Singing Hot Dog Man's act—he claimed at one point to be selling 200 wieners and raking in $400 per game—others complained that his incessant braying got in the way of the game and severely degraded the ballpark experience. The complaints reached a fever pitch in 2004, when the vending company that employed Marcuse opted to put a muzzle on his Opera Man act. A pro-Marcuse backlash, dubbed the "Let Charley Sing" campaign, culminated in the creation of a "Free Charley" website. Eventually a compromise was reached wherein Marcuse was allowed to sing once per game and have it broadcast on the Comerica Park JumboTron. In 2008, Singing Hot Dog Man tried to extend his brand, starting his own company, Charley's Food Inc., and marketing his preferred hot dog condiment under the name Charley's Ballpark Mustard. (Tagline: "It will make you sing.")

# Sivyer, Debbi

Pioneering major league ballgirl who used the proceeds from her job with the Oakland Athletics to transform herself into the international snack foods magnate Mrs. Fields. The younger sister of A's owner **Charles O. Finley**'s secretary, Sivyer was hired by in 1969, at the age of 13, to field foul balls and provide companionship for the team's other ballgirl, **Sheryl Lawrence**. Sivyer distinguished herself by serving chocolate chip cookies and lemonade to the **umpires** between innings. She also plowed most of her $5-per-hour salary into baking ingredients. She left baseball after two years and started her own business—originally called Mrs. Fields Chocolate Chippery—in 1977 after marrying investment banker Randy Fields. She is one of two former teenaged Oakland Athletics employees to become millionaires. See also: **Burrell, Stanley "Hammer"**

*They Said What?*

"I was never really gifted at throwing or catching, but it was a wonderful experience."

—**Debbi** "Mrs. Fields" **Sivyer**, on her experience as an Oakland A's ballgirl in the early 1970s

## Slaughter, Enos

Belligerent, hard-nosed outfielder of the 1940s and '50s whose well-earned reputation for hustle is overshadowed by allegations that he led his fellow St. Louis Cardinals in an abortive boycott against Jackie Robinson's breaking of the major league color line in 1947. Although he never copped to charges that he circulated an anti-integration petition, Slaughter certainly let his feelings for Robinson be known when he viciously and intentionally spiked him in the leg during a game that August.

*They Said What?*

"A guy got in my way, I ran over him."

—**Enos Slaughter**

## Slider

Magenta-colored, carpet-like creature that has served as the principal ballpark mascot of the Cleveland Indians since 1990. Portrayed by the same performer, Dan Kilday, since his debut, Slider presents a more fan-friendly public face than the controversial **Chief Wahoo**, the Tribe's official mascot.

The character's only brush with notoriety came during the American League Championship Series in 1995, when Kilday fell off the center-field wall at Jacobs Field while attempting to execute a somersault and tore his medial collateral ligament. In 2009, Slider became the fourth baseball mascot to be inducted into the Mascot Hall of Fame, following in the footsteps of the **Phillie Phanatic**, the **San Diego Chicken**, and **Mr. Met**.

Cary Whitt

## Sluggerrr

Giant costumed lion who has been the official mascot of the Kansas City Royals since 1996. The mustard-colored King of the Jungle sports a crown where his head should be and shoots hot dogs at the crowd from a frankfurter-shaped air cannon.

## Society for American Baseball Research

Respected affinity organization for baseball geeks, especially stats geeks. Its acronym (SABR) inspired the name of the method of statistical analysis called **Sabermetrics**.

## Sockalexis, Louis

New England–born Penobscot Indian whom most historians credit with being the first Native American to play in the major leagues. Variously known as "the Abanaki Adonis," "the Chief of Sockem," and "the Deerfoot of the Diamond," Sockalexis was one of the emerging stars of the late 19<sup>th</sup> century

National League, celebrated in song and serenaded with war whoops every time he took the field. But his three-year big-league career was cut short by alcoholism and womanizing—he once seriously sprained his ankle jumping off the roof of a whorehouse on the Fourth of July. Historians continue to debate whether the Cleveland Indians were named in his honor.

# Sonovia

Malodorous billy goat who attended Game 4 of the 1945 World Series at Wrigley Field as a guest of Chicago saloon keeper **William Sianis**. Sonovia's ejection by ballpark ushers inspired Sianis to invoke the so-called **Billy Goat Curse,** jinxing the franchise from ever again winning a World Series game in its home park.

# Soriano, Louis

Disabled Brooklyn Dodgers fan and leader of the club's beloved Sym-Phony Band, a five-man musical combo that heckled **umpires** and Dodgers opponents from 1938 until 1957. The group of self-taught musicians was known for parading up and down the aisles at Ebbets Field playing ragtime standards and banging on snare drums.

# Southpaw

Rachel M. Campbell

Fuzzy green Snuffleupagus-like creature who has held the position of official Chicago White Sox mascot since 2004. He succeeded **Waldo the White Sox Wolf**, the club's short-lived cartoon character mascot of the early 1990s. In January of 2009, Southpaw became the first baseball mascot to appear in a presidential inaugural parade, when he rode on the Illinois float at the ceremonial parade marking the inauguration of President Barack Obama.

# Spaceman

*See* **Lee, Bill**

# Spira, Howard

Degenerate gambler who played a key role in the bitter feud between New York Yankees owner **George Steinbrenner** and superstar outfielder Dave Winfield in the early 1990s. Steinbrenner paid Spira $40,000 to dig up dirt on Winfield, whom he was trying to discredit in an effort to avoid making previously pledged payments to the slugger's charitable foundation. A college dropout turned small-time hustler with a mountain of gambling debts and no prospects for employment, Spira not only failed to deliver the goods but went on to demand an additional $110,000 in exchange for keeping his mouth shut about the scheme. Steinbrenner was forced to admit the details of his plan to federal authorities, and Spira was arrested, tried, and convicted of extortion. ("My father really should have worn a condom," he admitted at his sentencing hearing.) He served 26 months in federal prison.

# Spitball

Catch-all term for a variety of **trick pitches** in which the ball is slathered with saliva, tobacco juice, **Vaseline**, or some other foreign substance. Invention of the spitter dates back to the turn of the 20th century and is often attributed to Elmer Stricklett of the Chicago White Sox. Although the pitch was officially banned in 1920, pitchers continued to throw it surreptitiously, though most latter-day hurlers prefer to cheat using the more sanitary method of scuffing the ball with sandpaper, hidden emery boards, or nail files. Gaylord Perry, a proponent of petroleum jelly, is considered the modern master of the spitter.

## They Said What?

"I reckon I tried everything on the old apple but salt and pepper and chocolate sauce topping."

–Gaylord Perry

# Steinbrenner, George

Imperious Ohio shipbuilding magnate who has owned the New York Yankees since 1973, building an enviable track record of success while redrawing the archetype of the mercurial, demanding boss from hell. A onetime graduate assistant under Ohio State Buckeyes martinet Woody Hayes, Steinbrenner brought some of the rah-rah ethos of Big Ten college football to the task of running a professional baseball team. Although this despotic style was not always conducive to the game's unique culture—early on, Steinbrenner cycled through managers on an almost yearly basis, instituted a strict personal grooming policy, and routinely demeaned his employees in public in an effort to motivate them—few could argue that his hard-charging approach (and willingness to spend freely on free-agent talent) did not succeed at turning around the losing culture that had permeated the club like a bad odor since the late-1960s. Naturally, when the team stopped winning pennants, the New York media turned on "the Boss" with a vengeance. Chants of "Steinbrenner sucks!" were commonplace in Yankee Stadium throughout the 1980s and early '90s. Steinbrenner himself became something of a national joke and an occasional embarrassment to baseball. In 1990, he reached his nadir when he was suspended from the game a second time— the first was for making illegal campaign contributions to Richard Nixon's

## They Said What?

**"I clocked them. There are two guys in this town looking for their teeth."**

—**George Steinbrenner**, on his confrontation with two Dodgers fans in a Los Angeles elevator during the 1981 World Series

1972 presidential campaign—for hiring a lowlife gambler, **Howard Spira**, to dig up dirt on star player Dave Winfield. Public sentiment toward the Yankees owner did not turn around until the club started winning World Series again in the mid-1990s—the groundwork for which had been laid by others while Steinbrenner was sweating out his three-year exile. Restored to architect-of-champions status, a somewhat less volcanic Steinbrenner lived out his dotage as a more sympathetic figure—caricatured on the popular sitcom **Seinfeld** as "Big Stein," a calzone-obsessed motormouth— and publicly reconciled with former enemies such as Winfield, Reggie Jackson, and Yogi Berra. His influence on his team and the game was curtailed by the onset of dementia in the mid-2000s.

## Umpires Gone Wild

Dick Stello, a popular National League umpire of the 1960s and '70s, was a former nightclub comic. He was married to stripper Chesty Morgan—she of the 73FF breasts—from 1974 to 1979. Interestingly enough, Stello was crushed to death—not by Chesty's breasts, but by two cars—in a gruesome auto accident in Lakeland, Florida, in November of 1987.

# Stengelese

Proprietary brand of doubletalk spoken by legendary major league manager Casey Stengel, best exemplified by the quotation that appears on his tombstone: "There comes a time in every man's life, and I've had plenty of them." Unlike Yogi Berra's celebrated "Yogi-isms"—many of which were apocryphal and most of which actually made a strange kind of sense—Stengel's utterances were invariably devoid of logic, syntax, or meaning. Here, for example is a portion of his "testimony" before the U.S. Senate Anti-Trust and Monopoly Subcommittee in July of 1958:

> There are 16 men in baseball who own ballclubs. We will say that an individual can hardly make it anymore unless he is wealthy. That is how it has grown. I would say the biggest thing in baseball at the present time now, and with the money that is coming in, and so forth, and with the annuity fund for the players, you can't allow the commissioner to just take everything sitting there, and take everything insofar as money is concerned, but I think he should have full jurisdiction over the player and player's habits, and the way the **umpires** and ballclubs should conduct their business in the daytime and right on up tight up here.

# Sterling, John

Stage name used by Harold Moskowitz (b. 1938), bombastic New York Yankees radio play-by-play man whose contrived calls irritate purists. Traditionalist media critics routinely cite Sterling's reliance on overwrought, inaccurate home-run calls ("It is high, it is far, it is gooooone!" he will bellow—often when the medium-deep line drive in question is none of those things) and showy, **Chris Berman**—like habit of bestowing nicknames on favored players (such as "the Giambino" for lumbering first baseman

Peter Kreder

Jason Giambi). For years, Sterling has also indulged a bizarre affectation for deliberately mispronouncing the home players' names, calling infielder Randy Velarde "Velarday" despite plain evidence that this was erroneous. Somewhat less polarizing is Sterling's signature end-of-game victory call: "Ballgame over! Yankees win! Theeeeeeeee Yankees win!"

## Steroids
*See* **Performance-Enhancing Drugs**

## Steve Blass Disease

Puzzling mental condition, named after onetime Pittsburgh Pirates pitcher Steve Blass, in which a formerly effective pitcher inexplicably loses the ability to throw strikes. The right-handed Blass was a consistent double-digit winner for the Pirates in the late 1960s and early '70s, issuing a walk every three innings during a 19-win 1972 campaign that saw him named to the National League All-Star team. In 1973, that walk total ballooned to one every inning, as his ERA soared to 9.85 and he simply could not locate the strike zone. Blass threw in only one major league game in the 1974 season and was out of baseball the following year. Other pitchers who have struggled with Steve Blass Disease over the years include Mark Wohlers of the Atlanta Braves and **Rick Ankiel** of the St. Louis Cardinals. Position players suffering from a similar disorder are said to have a case of **the Yips**.

# Stomper

Dancing costumed elephant who has served as the official mascot of the Oakland Athletics since 1997. The use of an anthropomorphic pachyderm as team mascot reflects the long-standing association between the Athletics franchise and elephants, which dates back to the club's inception at the turn of the 20th century. New York Giants manager

Kimberly Nguyen

John McGraw reportedly joked that the then-Philadelphia Athletics were a "white elephant" for owner Benjamin Shibe—incapable of competing with the city's existing National League franchise, the Phillies. Athletics manager Connie Mack defiantly adopted the elephant as the team symbol, and the animal appeared intermittently on the club's uniforms through the 1920s. Stomper (whose full name, according to his official team bio, is Stomper Ele Phant) was created in the 1990s as part of an initiative to restore the elephant to its former place of prominence on team insignia. He is known for his break-dancing and for riding around the park in a tiny red car to the beat of "Jungle Boogie" by Kool and the Gang. A popular YouTube clip shows Stomper being bodyslammed by several members of the Kansas City Royals.

# Strat-O-Matic

Legendary baseball board game introduced in 1961, the very name of which is catnip to stats geeks and tabletop enthusiasts of a certain age. **Rotisserie** inventor Daniel Okrent, filmmaker Spike Lee, and video game designer Richard Garfield are just a few of Strat-O-Matic's prominent adherents. A precursor to **fantasy baseball** (and a direct competitor to the decidedly less complex **All-Star Baseball**), classic Strat-O-Matic is played with cards and dice and uses statistical data compiled from past seasons to simulate game play. Initially, two versions of the game were marketed: basic and advanced. Later, the Strat-O-Matic game company expanded into computer-based and online versions of the game that utilized sophisticated statistical algorithms.

# Styles, Mary Sue

Nubile blonde ballgirl for the 1970s Philadelphia Phillies and one of baseball's first ballpark sex symbols. The twentysomething Philadelphia native with the well-formed posterior worked from a stool down the left-field line at Veterans Stadium during the team's NL East–leading heyday from 1976 through 1980. She is remembered for playing a part in two unusual incidents. During a series between the Phillies and the San Diego Padres in 1978, Styles was mock-ravished by the **San Diego Chicken**, who was in town for a "Battle of the Mascots" face-off with his archrival the **Phillie Phanatic**. The routine called for the Chicken to surprise Styles from behind and carry her kicking and screaming off the field and into the tunnel behind home plate. A few seconds later, the Chicken emerged from the tunnel and comically zipped up his "fly" as if he had just finished having sex with the ballgirl. To the delight of the crowd, a visibly disheveled Styles then resumed her place along the left-field line, affecting a pronounced limp as she trudged out to her stool. The following season, Styles' bodacious body nearly cost the Pittsburgh Pirates the National League East title. The Pirates were in a dogfight with the Expos for the division crown when they visited Philadelphia for a crucial series. On September 20, 1979, with the game tied at 1–1 in the bottom of the sixth, Phillies catcher Keith Moreland hit what was ruled a two-run home run just inside the left-field foul pole at the Vet. When Pirates manager Chuck Tanner argued that the ball was foul, third-base umpire **Eric Gregg** was forced to admit he was too busy watching Styles' bouncing, jiggling reaction to the shot to tell whether it was a home run or not. "I believe Mary Sue," Gregg would later admit. "She's a fox." Gregg eventually conferred with home-plate umpire Doug Harvey, who reversed the call. Moreland went on to strike out, keeping Pirate hopes alive—at least temporarily. The Pirates lost the game 2–1, but wound up winning the division and their third world championship.

# Superfan

Name for an obsessive rooter who shows up at all his or her team's home games to lead cheers, urge on rallies, or otherwise make a public spectacle of themselves in a noisy, clownish, or ritualized display of fervor. Examples of superfans include **John Adams**, the data systems analyst who pounds on a bass drum during Cleveland Indians home games, and **Freddy "Sez" Schuman**, the one-eyed former candy store proprietor who leads the cheers at Yankee Stadium by banging on a frying pan with a metal spoon. See also: **Chester, Hilda**; **Henderson, Krazy George**; **Lanzillo, John "Zonk"**; **Sign Man**; **Soriano, Louis**; **Wickers, Ronnie "Woo Woo"**

# Superjew

Politically incorrect nickname bestowed on first baseman Mike Epstein, one of the most prominent Jewish big leaguers of the 1970s. Epstein earned his moniker during his minor league days in the Baltimore Orioles system, where he was famous for carving the Star of David into his mitt. The devout lefty slugger hit 130 homers in 907 games over the course of a nine-year major league career spent with five different American League teams. He earned a World Series ring with the 1972 Oakland A's and once hit four homers in consecutive at-bats—all with 20/35 vision. He led a contingent of A's players wearing black armbands in the wake of the massacre of 11 Israeli athletes at the 1972 Summer Olympics in Munich.

# Supervendor

*See* **Arnie the Peanut Dude**; **Captain Earthman**; **Fancy Clancy**; **Gomez, Chuy**; **Lemonade Shaking Guy**; **Owens, Roger**; **Robo-Vendor**; **Singing Hot Dog Man**; **Wally the Beer Man**

## Susie the Sweeper

Curvaceous woman who used to entertain fans at Atlanta Braves games in the early 1970s by appearing mid-game to dust off the bases with a broom. A club-authorized precursor to **Morganna** the Kissing Bandit, Susie dressed in then-stylish hot pants and occasionally tarried to kiss an umpire or player (or swat them with her broom) before departing the field of play. Johnny Bench once memorably spoofed Susie before a Braves-Reds game in 1972. Donning white hot pants (and dubbing himself "Bench the Basepath Beauty"), he entertained the crowd during a pregame Husbands vs. Wives softball exhibition by planting a kiss on the cheek of the game's honorary umpire, boxer Jerry Quarry.

## "Sweet Caroline"

Hit song by pop tunesmith Neil Diamond that has been played at Boston Red Sox home games since 1998 and regularly during the eighth inning at every game played at Fenway Park since 2002. Written by Diamond in homage to presidential daughter Caroline Kennedy, the 1969 chart-topper has nothing to do with baseball or the Red Sox and was initially selected by club officials to honor a Red Sox employee who had just had a baby named Caroline.

## Swinging Friar

Merry mendicant who has been the official mascot of the San Diego Padres since 1958. A pudgy, tonsured monk in sandals and a shit-brown cloak, the Swinging Friar shares the same appalling fashion sense as the franchise he represents, which year in and year out retires the prize for the dreariest uniforms in the major leagues. Concocted to represent the Spanish missions established by Franciscan

Jeremy Taylor

friars along the California coast (whose "mission" was to convert Native Americans to Christianity), the Friar is one of baseball's oldest **mascots**. His debut predates the Padres' entry into the majors by 11 years. The adjective "Swinging" refers to the cenobite's penchant for wielding a baseball bat and not to any profligate sexual practices, which presumably would be frowned upon by his order. Over the decades, the Swinging Friar has occasionally been featured on Padres uniform patches and team logos. In the 1970s, he was overshadowed by the regular appearance at Padres games by the **San Diego Chicken**, who, it should be pointed out, has never been the club's official mascot.

## Szasz, Robert

Central Florida real estate developer and Tampa Bay Rays season-ticket holder who has become one of baseball's most celebrated **heckler**s, thanks in part to a clear, loud voice that is often picked up by television microphones. From his seat behind home plate at Tropicana Field, Szasz has called out one opposing player per series and relentlessly ragged on him with a stream of PG-rated insults since 2003. Personal appearance and off-the-field activities are considered off-limits by the resolutely ethical taunter, who keeps his vocal cords in top shape by swigging from a bottle of Robitussin between innings. Szasz's pitiless efficiency in heckling Rays opponents has led to several personal confrontations with players, including Cincinnati Reds outfielder Jose Guillen, who tried to bribe Szasz into refraining from zinging him with the promise of an autographed bat. In 2005, Szasz tried to capitalize on the notoriety generated by his occasional *SportsCenter* appearances by releasing a book, *The Happy Heckler*. In 2009, he was sued by several banks for allegedly defaulting on more than $9 million in loans.

THE UNDERGROUND BASEBALL ENCYCLOPEDIA

## "Talkin' Baseball"

Popular baseball-themed ditty composed and recorded by songwriter **Terry Cashman** in 1981. Originally titled "Willie, Mickey & The Duke" as a tribute to the three great New York City outfielders of the 1950s—Willie Mays, Mickey Mantle, and Duke Snider—the song quickly became a ballpark sing-along favorite, prompting Cashman to write new versions featuring customized lyrics for every team in baseball. A parody version of the song, titled "Talkin' Softball" and also written by Cashman, appears in the popular baseball episode of **The Simpsons** titled "Homer at the Bat."

## T.C. Bear

Fuzzy 6'4" brown bear who has served as the official mascot of the Minnesota Twins since 2000. (The T.C. stands for "Twin Cities.") T.C. was inspired by the Hamm's Beer Bear, the longtime corporate mascot of Minnesota-based Hamm's Brewery, an early sponsor of the Twins. When not engaged in the customary ballpark clowning, T.C. has occasionally taken part in skills competitions. He won the mascot home-run derby at All-Star Week three years in a row in the mid-2000s, capping off his run with a

### Umpires Gone Wild

In June of 1993, umpire Terry Tata was drugged and robbed by a female con artist in his room at the Hyatt Regency Hotel in Burlingame, California. The thief, who plied the man in blue with a bottle of red wine before slipping him a tranquilizer, made off with Tata's Rolex watch, a gold bracelet, two World Series rings, and $500 in cash.

dominant performance in San Francisco in 2007, during which he clubbed nine homers and fended off a stiff challenge from Milwaukee's **Bernie Brewer** and the Houston Astros' **Junction Jack**.

# Ten-Cent Beer Night

Spectacularly ill-conceived ballpark promotion, rivaled only by **Disco Demolition Night** as the dumbest theme night in baseball history. The date was June 4, 1974, and the Cleveland Indians' marketing and promotions department had decided to drum up fan interest in the dismal 24–25 Indians—who were drawing fewer than 10,000 people to a typical game in cavernous Municipal Stadium—by pricing beer at 10¢ per cup. (Stroh's Beer, to be precise.) The cheap swill proved to be just the tonic for bedraggled Clevelanders in the midst of a crushing recession. Some 25,000 turned out to the park that night to watch their Tribe take on the Texas Rangers. But the promotion soon took an ugly turn. The game was barely an inning old before inebriated fans started setting off fireworks in their seats. Streakers descended onto the field at regular intervals—including one naked man who slid into second base and a woman who strode out to the on-deck circle and flashed the crowd. A pair of father-and-son exhibitionists mooned the stands. People pelted the players with hot dogs, beer, batteries, smoke bombs, and an empty gallon jug of Thunderbird. By the seventh inning, the Rangers—who had brawled with the Indians in a game the previous week—chose to evacuate their bullpen out of concern for their players' safety. The chaos came to a head in the bottom of the ninth, when an Indians fan rushed the field and swiped Rangers right fielder Jeff Burroughs' glove. A near-riot ensued, as both dugouts emptied and fans took to the field en masse. Some of the players wielded bats. Umpire Nester Chylak was hit on the head with a folding chair during the melee. "They were uncontrollable beasts," Chylak later recalled. "I've never seen anything like it, except in a zoo." The bloodied man in blue ordered the game called and forfeited the victory to the Rangers. After an investigation, American League president Lee MacPhail put the kibosh on Cleveland's plans for additional 10-cent beer promotions. "There was no question that beer played a part in the riot," MacPhail concluded. "America may need a good five-cent cigar, but it doesn't need 10-cent beer."

## "Thank God I'm a Country Boy"

John Denver song that has been played during the seventh-inning stretch at Baltimore Orioles home games since 1975. Orioles shortstop Mark Belanger, a personal friend of Denver's, first suggested to club officials that they add the up-tempo country-and-western hit to the ballpark repertoire. It quickly caught on with fans and players and today is played by several other major sports franchises, including the Atlanta Braves and the Calgary Flames. Indeed, Baltimore fans have grown quite protective of the "Country Boy" tradition, resisting attempts by the team to replace it with other songs— including "Take Me Out to the Ballgame" in 1994 and the proprietary club jingle "Oriole Magic" in 1980.

## *This Week in Baseball*

Weekly baseball highlight show that has aired nationally since 1977, often as the lead-in to the Saturday national baseball telecast. Created at the behest of Commissioner Bowie Kuhn, *TWIB* was conceived as baseball's version of the popular *NFL Films Game of the Week*. Highlights from the previous week's game action are interwoven with instructional segments, bloopers, and feel-good profiles of players, managers, and others in and around the game. From 1977 to 1996, the program was hosted by legendary New York Yankees play-by-play man Mel Allen, whose honeyed Southern drawl and repeated use of his "How about that?" catchphrase endeared him to a whole new generation of fans. The show was also notable for its memorable opening and closing themes—especially the end theme, "Gathering Crowds," which built to a majestic crescendo over a slow-motion clip of Dave Parker throwing out Brian Downing at the plate in the 1979 All-Star Game.

## Throneberry, Marv

Mediocre major league outfielder/first baseman who parlayed his brief association with the 1962 New York Mets into a lucrative second career as a light beer pitchman and icon of baseball ineptitude. "Marvelous Marv," as he came to be known, spent less than one full season with the Mets (he actually came up as a Yankee and was once thought to be the heir to Mickey Mantle), but his leadership role on their slapstick '62 squad ensured him a certain comic immortality. In the 1970s, after more than a decade in retired obscurity, he resurfaced in a series of TV commercials for Lite Beer from Miller, using the catchphrase "I still don't know why they asked me to do this commercial."

## Tomahawk Chop

Widely used term for the Native American war chant performed by crowds at Atlanta Braves home games, beginning with the 1991 season. The Tomahawk Chop was adapted from the war chant performed at Florida State Seminoles football games. It was appropriated by Braves fans and the Atlanta Fulton County Stadium organist as an homage to newly arrived Brave Deion Sanders, who had played college football at FSU. Repeated footage of Braves owner **Ted Turner**, his then-inamorata Jane Fonda, and ex-President Jimmy Carter "doing the chop" during network telecasts of the 1991 World Series helped popularize the chant nationwide.

# Tony La Russa Baseball

Popular baseball video game of the 1990s, which utilized the artificial intelligence of Oakland A's manager **Tony La Russa** and built on the innovations developed for EA Sports' **Earl Weaver Baseball**, while adding a **Sabermetrics**-inspired stats component that was revolutionary for its time.

# Toppsy Curvey

Stage name used by Laurie Stathopoulos, a grotesquely endowed stripper/porn star from Boston, Massachusetts, who briefly attempted to launch a **Morganna**-like career of rushing onto baseball diamonds and kissing players in the summer of 1991. According to published accounts of her kissing spree, Toppsy Curvey claimed only two "victims": **Roger Clemens**, whom she smooched during a game between the Boston Red Sox and the Chicago White Sox on July 27, 1991, at Fenway Park; and Scott Kamieniecki of the New York Yankees, on whom she planted a wet lipstick kiss a day later in the second inning of a tilt between the Yankees and the California Angels at Yankee Stadium. Security guards stormed the field and led Toppsy Curvey away in both instances. Arrested and charged with trespassing, the top-heavy entertainer claimed the stunts were part of a campaign to promote her exotic dance revue at the Fantasy Island strip club in Nyack, New York. The buxom ballpark nuisance later became the proprietor of Crow Haven Corner, a witchcraft supply shop in Salem, Massachusetts. According to the online "Boobpedia," which bills itself as America's authoritative "encyclopedia of big boobs," she has retired from adult films but still dances occasionally at a strip club in Billerica, Massachusetts.

# Torres, Rusty

Mediocre former major league outfielder who qualifies as the Forrest Gump of baseball riots. Torres was the only man who was on the field for all three of the great melees of the 1970s: the final home game of the Washington

## You Could Look It Up

**Random Baseball Trivia**

Legendary Pittsburgh Pirates third baseman Pie Traynor, who never learned how to drive a car, once walked more than 100 city blocks on his way to a World Series game.

Senators on September 30, 1971 (oddly enough, Torres' 23rd birthday), during which enraged patrons rushed the field in the top of the ninth, forcing the Senators to forfeit; **Ten-Cent Beer Night** in Cleveland on June 4, 1974, where overserved Indians fans throwing batteries and other debris sparked a violent brawl; and **Disco Demolition Night** at Comiskey Park in Chicago on July 12, 1979, an ill-conceived pyrotechnic promotion that culminated in an orgy of mayhem.

## Trick Pitches

*See* **Eephus Pitch**; **Folly Floater**; **Forkball**; **Foshball**; **Gyroball**; **Knuckleball**; **La Lob**; **Spitball**

## Turner, Ted

Accomplished yachtsman and broadcasting mogul who owned the Atlanta Braves from 1976 to 1996, helping to turn them from a National League laughingstock into a pennant-winning powerhouse that he grandly proclaimed "America's Team." An America's Cup winner and four-time Yachtsman of the Year, Turner acquired the Braves along with the NBA's Atlanta Hawks in 1976, principally to provide programming fodder for his TBS Superstation. His eccentric stewardship of the club was lowlighted by a short-lived stint as his own self-appointed manager in May of 1977. National League president

## They Said What?

"If I'm smart enough to save $11 million to buy the team, I ought to be smart enough to manage it."

—**Ted Turner**, on his one-game managerial stint with the Atlanta Braves

Chub Feeney banished him from the dugout after one game, citing rules prohibiting field managers from having an ownership stake in their teams. Turner would later take a more hands-off role in running the franchise, only occasionally surfacing in public to make the odd embarrassing comment (as when he derided Christianity as a "religion for losers") or appear on camera in his owner's box during playoff games to do the **Tomahawk Chop** alongside his celebrity consort Jane Fonda. Turner relinquished his controlling interest in the Braves in 1996, as part of his empire's merger deal with Time Warner. The team's home stadium is named after him.

## Tyler, Ernie

Longtime umpires' attendant at Baltimore Orioles home games, known informally as the world's oldest ballboy. The onetime Memorial Stadium usher worked every single Orioles home game from Opening Day in 1960 until July 27, 2007, curtailing his streak only so he could attend the Hall of Fame induction ceremony for fellow Iron Man Cal Ripken Jr.

# Uecker, Bob

Light-hitting former major league catcher who parlayed his goofball persona into a new role as the clown prince of baseball sportscasters. Uecker hit .200 over the course of a six-year major league career with the Braves, Cardinals, and Phillies. He undoubtedly would have vanished into obscurity after his retirement in 1967 had he not started making regular appearances on Johnny Carson's *Tonight Show*. Uecker's self-deprecating humor (he once joked that he had won Comeback Player of the Year Award five years in a row) earned him laughs and a shot at network color commentary gigs on ABC's *Monday Night Baseball* and the NBC *Game of the Week*. He was a regular fixture on postseason baseball coverage as well, usually alongside fellow yuckmeister Joe Garagiola. In the 1980s, Uecker cemented his cult status in a series of humorous TV commercials for Miller Lite. "I must be in the front row!" he boasted in one of them, introducing a line that would become his trademark. Uecker also scored success as an actor, portraying clownish baseball play-by-play man **Harry Doyle**—a thinly disguised version of himself—in the 1989 comedy ***Major League***. From 1985 to 1990, Uecker played George Owens, a genial sportswriter who can inexplicably afford his own live-in valet, on the ABC sitcom *Mr. Belvedere*. Since 1971, Uecker's primary gig has been as play-by-play man for the Milwaukee Brewers, though he has occasionally branched out to cover other sports as well. He was famously choked by WWF legend Andre the Giant at a 1988 Wrestlemania event in Atlantic City, New Jersey.

# Uecker Seats

Term used by fans to describe the highest, most remote seats in a baseball stadium (also known as "nosebleed seats"). The term derives from a popular 1980s TV commercial for Miller Lite, in which a blustery everyfan played by **Bob Uecker** is shown being escorted from his presumably purloined seat to a new one far away from the action.

# Umpires

*See* **Denkinger, Don**; **Gregg, Eric**; **McSherry, John**; **Pallone, Dave**; **Postema, Pam**; **West, Country Joe**

# Urine Therapy

Controversial skin conditioning technique practiced over the years by several big-league players—most notably outfielders Moises Alou and Vladimir Guerrero and catcher Jorge Posada. Although many scientists dispute the contention that urinating on one's hands "toughens them up"—it may actually make them softer—Alou, who for years was one of the only major leaguers to eschew batting gloves while hitting, liked to pee all over his paws before digging in at the plate. "You don't want to shake my hand during spring training," Posada once informed the *New York Post*, copping to his long-standing urine therapy regimen. "A lot of guys like my father, who worked on the land, always used to do it. It keeps your hands from getting callused and cracking." Pitchers have been known to try the technique as well. Right-hander Kerry Wood once told a Chicago radio host that he used urine to remedy blisters on his pitching hand.

# Van Zelst, Louis

Hunchbacked dwarf who served as batboy and unofficial mascot for the Philadelphia Athletics from 1910 to 1914. Crippled by a childhood fall, "Little Van," as he was called, routinely and with good humor offered his gnarled hump to A's hitters to be rubbed for good luck. It must have worked. The club won the pennant in 1911 and defeated the New York Giants (who had their own luck-bringing disabled mascot, **Charles "Victory" Faust**) in the World Series 4–2. Always frail and sickly, Van Zelst contracted Bright's Disease in 1915 and died after a brief illness.

# Vaseline

Brand of petroleum jelly favored by **spitball** master Gaylord Perry. In his autobiography *Me and the Spitter*, Perry revealed that he liked to smear the lubricant on his uniform fly because that was the one place **umpires** would never check for a foreign substance.

# Veeck, Bill

Peg-legged former Wrigley Field ivy-planter and self-styled "hustler" who rose through baseball's front office ranks to become majority owner of three different major league franchises, fashioning a well-earned reputation as the game's most flamboyant showman. The son of a former Chicago Cubs executive, Veeck returned from service in World War II with a leg wound that would eventually require amputation and a hankering to acquire his own baseball team. He would eventually own three: the Cleveland Indians from 1946 to 1949; the St. Louis Browns from 1951 to 1953; and the Chicago White Sox from 1959 to 1961 and then again from 1976 to 1980. Veeck specialized in devising outrageous publicity stunts, which delighted fans enervated by his almost unfailingly terrible teams and enraged his fellow owners, who thought they made a mockery of the game. Among his many brainstorms: hiring a midget, **Eddie Gaedel**, to make a single plate appearance during a meaningless late-summer game; instituting "Grandstand Managers' Day," where fans voted on managerial decisions by holding up large signs marked "YES" and "NO"; installing baseball's first **exploding scoreboard**; outfitting his players in **short pants**; and staging the infamous **Disco Demolition Night** promotion, during which a pyrotechnic protest against the then-popular form of dance music devolved into a riot. Some of Veeck's less rococo innovations, like his plan for revenue sharing among owners and putting player names on the back of road uniforms, were ahead of their time and would eventually be widely adopted. But he forever remained on the outs with his fellow Lords of Baseball and struggled to adapt his medicine-show marketing style to the new era of free agency. Fed up with the way money was corrupting the game, he sold the White Sox in 1981 and died in retirement five years later.

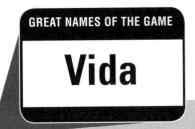

**GREAT NAMES OF THE GAME**

# Vida

Vida Rochelle Blue was one of the most dominating American League pitchers of the 1970s. A hard-throwing left-hander, Blue won 121 games for the Oakland A's between 1971 and 1977. He also resisted A's owner **Charles O. Finley**'s suggestion that he change his first name to "True" for promotional purposes. The more distinctive name Vida derives from the Latin word "vita," meaning "life."

# Waddell, Rube

Left-handed strikeout artist of the early 20ᵗʰ century whose bizarre, child-like behavior has befuddled armchair psychologists for more than a century. Tales—some of them undoubtedly apocryphal—of Waddell leaving the mound in the middle of games to chase fire trucks, leaping from roofs to prove he could fly, or losing count of how many wives he'd had have led diagnostic-minded historians to speculate the Hall of Famer may have been mentally retarded, developmentally disabled, or a high-functioning autistic. Others claim he was merely a semi-literate hayseed with a serious drinking problem. Whatever the cause of his psychological distress, Waddell died of tuberculosis in a San Antonio sanitarium on April Fool's Day, 1914.

## You Could Look It Up

### Random Baseball Trivia

**Rube Waddell** was once discovered standing in the window of Wanamker's Department Store in Philadelphia, posing as a mannequin.

# Waldo the White Sox Wolf

Short-lived lupine mascot of the Chicago White Sox. Waldo appeared in cartoons that aired on the U.S. Cellular Field JumboTron in the early 1990s. His appearance was clearly modeled on the character designs in the cult classic animated series *Ren and Stimpy*.

## Walker, Dixie

All-Star outfielder of the 1930s and '40s who spearheaded the opposition to Jackie Robinson's integration of the major leagues as a member of the 1947 Brooklyn Dodgers. An unlikely fan favorite in Brooklyn—where he was christened "the People's Cherce"—the Alabaman claimed fear of retribution from his neighbors back home, not racism, motivated him to request a trade rather than take the field behind Robinson during the second baseman's rookie season. Though his request was denied, Walker went on to serve as ringleader of an anti-Robinson petition campaign. He was dealt to the Pittsburgh Pirates in the off-season.

## Wally the Beer Man

Popular, publicity-seeking **Hubert H. Humphrey Metrodome** beer vendor who has hawked suds at Minnesota Twins home games since 1982. Born Walter McNeil, the onetime operations manager for a Twin Cities pharmaceutical firm leveraged his distinctive cry of "Beer here!" into the cultivation of his own mini-brand

Kati Berwald

during the 1980s. In only his second season on the job, he began handing out his business card to fans in the stands. He soon branched out to more lucrative areas of self-promotion, peddling his own line of "Wally the Beer Man" branded matchbooks, T-shirts, and autographed baseball cards featuring his trade name and likeness. Acclaimed as one of the most famous vendors in America, he was featured on the *NBC Nightly News* and profiled in *Sports Illustrated*. Away from the park, he appeared in commercials for local liquor stores and filmed PSAs about the dangers of drunk driving. Even his sneakers were sponsored by an area brewery.

# Wally the Green Monster

Green-furred Muppet-like creature, named for the 37-foot-high left-field wall in Fenway Park, who has been the official mascot of the Boston Red Sox since 1997. Wally was unveiled to the public on April 13, 1997, during a special "Kid's Opening Day" ceremony celebrating the 50th anniversary of the Green Monster. (According to the official club-sanctioned back story, Wally had been living a hermit-like existence inside the wall since 1947.) Greeted with a deafening chorus of boos, Wally was quietly phased out after several weeks of abuse from Fenway Park fans enraged at the idea of a focus group–tested mascot who had no organic connection to the franchise's rich history. After a few months of exile spent cutting ribbons at auto dealerships throughout New England, Wally was eased back into the ballpark entertainment rotation. His endorsement by popular Red Sox television analyst Jerry Remy, who kept a small stuffed Wally close at hand during game telecasts, helped overcome the resistance of the more traditionalist precincts of Red Sox Nation.

Serena A. Thaw

# Wave, The

Spectator-generated phenomenon, performed by large crowds at baseball games and other mass events, in which fans in each successive section rise and sit in unison like a human swell coursing around an orbicular bathtub. The consensus view holds that the Wave was invented by **superfan Krazy George Henderson** during an American League Championship Series game between the New York Yankees and the Oakland A's at the Oakland Coliseum on October 15, 1981, although Henderson has admitted he adapted the concept from Waves he had seen performed at hockey games and high school pep rallies. After two abortive attempts to choreograph the standing and sitting of the crowd—during which his efforts were loudly booed— Henderson finally succeeded in getting a Wave to travel all the way around the stadium bowl. On the fourth attempt, all four decks participated and baseball saw its first successful Wave. In the broadcast booth, NBC play-by-play man Joe Garagiola and producer Don Ohlmeyer frantically tried to get cameramen to train their lenses on the phenomenon, but they were always caught one section behind. The Wave eventually migrated to other parks and other sports, where it continues to entertain bored spectators—and irk purists, who consider it an idiotic distraction from the game at hand—to this day. It should also be noted that the above-related Wave origin story is the subject of some dispute. Many college football fans claim the Wave actually originated two weeks later, at a game between the University of Washington and Stanford at Husky Stadium in Seattle and was led in part by future *Entertainment Tonight* co-host Robb Weller.

## They Said What?

**"It was a great feeling. It's so powerful."**

–**Krazy George Henderson**, on what it felt like to lead the first **Wave** in baseball history

# "We Are Family"

Infectious, sisterhood-celebrating disco hit that became the unlikely anthem of the 1979 World Series champion Pittsburgh Pirates. Written by the Chic songwriting team of Bernard Edwards and Nile Rodgers and recorded by four female siblings from Philadelphia calling themselves Sister Sledge, the song reached No. 2 on the *Billboard* singles chart during the summer of 1979. It blared so often out of the Three Rivers Stadium loudspeakers and in the Pirates clubhouse that the players adopted it as their unofficial song for the second half of the season. Players later credited the get-happy tune with inspiring their come-from-behind victory over the Orioles in the World Series.

# Wells, David

Lardaceous, gouty left-handed pitcher who brought the hardcore ethos of an outlaw biker club to several pennant-winning teams in the 1990s and 2000s. Nicknamed "Boomer," Wells is best known as a mainstay of the Joe Torre–era New York Yankees, for whom he pitched an unlikely perfect game on May 17, 1998. In his autobiography—titled, appropriately enough, *Perfect I'm Not*—Wells confessed to being hungover from a drinking binge the night before. He attracted national headlines in 2002 when he was assaulted inside a New York City diner by Yonkers bartender **Rocco Graziosa**.

# West, Country Joe

Uncommonly well-rounded major league umpire, also known as Cowboy Joe West, whose range of outside interests include country music, which he has performed with the like of Merle Haggard, Mickey Gilley, and Boxcar Willie. West also holds the patent on one of the game's most popular chest protectors, the so-called West Vest, and markets a line of umpiring equipment endorsed by Major League Baseball. He was elected president of the World Umpires Association in 2009.

# Whambold, Walter

*See* **Whammer, The**

# Whammer, The

Nickname of fictional slugger Walter Whambold, a character loosely based on Babe Ruth, who appears in Bernard Malamud's classic baseball novel *The Natural*. In one of the book's more memorable scenes, teenage prodigy **Roy Hobbs** strikes out the Whammer on three pitches during an impromptu showdown at a county fair. Actor Joe Don Baker played the Whammer in the 1984 movie version.

# Wheeze Kids

Whimsical nickname bestowed by the media on the 1983 National League champion Philadelphia Phillies in recognition of the advanced age of many of the club's star players. The 90-win squad, which lost the World Series in five games to the younger Baltimore Orioles, featured six players over the age of 38: **Pete Rose** (42), Tony Perez (41), Ron Reed (40), **Joe Morgan** (39), Tug McGraw (38), and **Steve Carlton** (38). The term Wheeze Kids was a play on Whiz Kids, the team nickname for the pennant-winning 1950 Phillies, the youngest club ever to make the World Series to that point.

# "Who Let the Dogs Out?"

Catchy, canine-themed novelty rap song that briefly became a ballpark sing-along anthem in the summer of 2000. A cover version of an obscure Trinidadian dance club hit, originally recorded by composer Anslem Douglas and re-recorded by the nine-member Bahamian combo The Baha Men, the song relied on nonsensical lyrics and an infectious woof-and-response chorus to ascend to No. 40 on the *Billboard* Hot 100 chart. It made the leap to baseball stadiums largely through the efforts of Seattle Mariners promotions director Gregg Greene, who first played the song to herald the arrival at home plate of backup catcher Joe Oliver in June of 2000. Then-Mariners shortstop Alex Rodriguez was so taken with the tune that he asked that it be played before every one of his at-bats as well. Sensing a commercial opportunity, Virginia-based sports marketing company Pro Sports Music Marketing soon began aggressively promoting the song for use in stadiums and arenas nationwide.

## "Who's on First?"

Iconic baseball-themed comedy routine perfected and made famous by the popular Vaudeville, radio, and movie team of Bud Abbott and Lou Costello. Derived from an old burlesque routine known as "The Baker Scene" (and claimed over the decades by various writers), "Who's on First?" mines humor out of straight man Abbott's fast-paced wordplay and "dumb kid" Costello's attendant confusion—in this case the semantic hall of mirrors Abbott erects out of a baseball team composed of players whose names are various interrogative pronouns. The skit first drew national attention after the comedy team performed it on the *Kate Smith Radio Hour* on February 3, 1938. (Smith's manager reportedly detested the routine and implored the comics not to do it; they convinced him to change his mind only by claiming they had no other material.) They repeated it in their debut feature *One Night in the Tropics* in 1940 and delivered what is considered the definitive interpretation in 1945's *The Naughty Nineties*. It is this version that plays in an endless loop near the entrance to the National Baseball Hall of Fame at Cooperstown, New York. All in all, Abbott and Costello performed the routine more than 10,000 times over the course of their career. It was adapted for the stage by James L. Seay in 1975 and turned into a board game in 1978. In 1999, *Time* magazine named "Who's on First?" the best comedy sketch of the 20th century—which is odd, considering it's a routine and not a sketch.

# Wickers, Ronnie "Woo Woo"

Semi-employed window washer and Chicago Cubs **superfan** who revs up the Wrigley Field faithful with his incredibly odd, distinctive-sounding cheers. A premature baby who spent the first few months of his life in an incubator, Wickers was physically abused by his mother and raised by his grandmother on Chicago's South Side. He began attending Cubs games as a child in the 1940s and began emitting his ear-splitting "Cubs, Woo! Cubs, Woo!" chant

John Tolva

in his late teens. Nicknamed "Leather Lungs" by longtime Cubs announcer **Harry Caray**, Wickers is known for his indefatigable cheering ability, which some find endearing and others deem unbelievably irritating. Unlike other **superfan**s, he does not receive free tickets from club management. In fact, the Cubs once considered banning him from the ballpark and demanded that he tone down his "woos" when they invited him to sing "Take Me Out to the Ballgame" in 2001. Wickers has also endured his share of personal trauma. He worked as a night custodian at Northwestern University for many years before a series of reversals of fortune left him homeless for much of the 1980s. During this time, he lived out of a cardboard box and could not afford to buy his own bleacher tickets. In 2000, a public campaign was launched to raise the money to buy Wickers a set of dentures. In April 2005, he was struck by a car outside Wrigley Field and taken to the hospital for treatment. That same year, Wickers was the subject of the documentary film *WooLife*, an adulatory chronicle of his nearly half a century of "wooing."

# Wife Swapping

Unconventional marital practice engaged in by New York Yankees pitchers Fritz Peterson and Mike Kekich before the start of the 1973 season. The two left-handers and their wives had been friends for some time when the subject of switching partners first came up over a round of beers following a night out at the movies in the spring of 1972. In the off-season, after each man had enjoyed a romp in the hay with the other man's spouse, the foursome decided to formalize the arrangement. In one of the most unusual

Land ho! The Kekiches-Petersons enjoy an afternoon sail in the early 1970s.

trades in baseball history, Peterson's wife Marilyn, his two children, and the family poodle were sent to live with Kekich in exchange for Susanne Kekich, the two Kekich children, and a Bedlington terrier. "We didn't trade wives; we traded lives," Kekich would later declare by way of an explanation. When word of the swap leaked out during spring training of 1973, the Yankees organization was scandalized. "We may have to call off Family Day this season," quipped Yankees general manager Lee MacPhail. Commissioner Bowie Kuhn issued a statement deploring the situation, although there was little he could do about it. At first, all parties seemed happy with the trade—including the children and the two dogs. But like all such transactions there were winners and losers. Fritz Peterson ended up getting the better of the deal. He married Susanne Kekich in 1974. Marilyn Peterson was overcome by guilt and broke off her relationship with Mike Kekich a few weeks after the wife exchange became public. He later remarried.

# Will, George F.

Orotund, bow tie–wearing right-wing political columnist who cultivated a lucrative sideline as the polemicist laureate of baseball purists following the publication of his 1990 best seller *Men at Work: The Craft of Baseball*. A collection of windy, self-consciously erudite observations on game strategy, the book appealed to pseudointellectuals and other literary-minded traditionalists who required an ennobling fig leaf to justify their fandom. Of special note was Will's Renfield-like treatment of manager **Tony La Russa**, whose media cult of personality was largely erected on the basis of his *Men at Work* portrayal. Will himself became a go-to pundit for **Ken Burns** and others looking for pretentious commentary on the glory of the game. For a time, Will was even considered a possible successor to Fay Vincent as commissioner of baseball. The author's pompous affect was famously lampooned on a 1990 *Saturday Night Live* sketch, "George Will's Sports Machine," which depicted him as an effete loser ashamed by his own lack of athletic prowess.

# Williams, John Henry

Only son of Hall of Famer Ted Williams who sickened and outraged fans of the famed slugger when he had his father's mortal remains placed in cryonic suspension after his death. A failed sports card entrepreneur and owner of a porno web hosting company, John Henry Williams lived in the shadow of his legendary father. In 2002, shortly before Ted Williams' death, he even tried to follow in the old man's footsteps by embarking on a professional baseball career—at the absurdly old age of 33. Although Ted Williams was able to pull enough strings to secure him a place on a Boston Red Sox rookie league team, John Henry proved woefully inept at the game and soon quit to devote himself full-time

to cashing in on his father's legacy. When Ted Williams died of cardiac arrest in July of 2002, John Henry had his corpse flown with indecent haste to the Scottsdale, Arizona, facilities of the **Alcor** Life Extension Foundation, there to be beheaded and suspended frozen inside a stainless steel tank for all eternity (or at least until medical science had advanced to the point where it could revive him). Denying claims by his half-sister that the Splendid Splinter wished to be cremated, John Henry produced a tattered, oil-stained document, purportedly signed by his father, stating his wish that the entire family undergo cryonic biostasis in the hopes of being reunited in a glorious, disease-free future. Critics charged that John Henry planned to auction off Ted's DNA, using the promise of breeding an advanced race of superhitters as the come-on. Whether this was the son's ultimate intention may never be known. In October of 2003, John Henry Williams disclosed that he had terminal leukemia. He died less than five months later. In keeping with his wishes, his body was placed in cryonic freeze beside his father's.

## *Days of Glory* | **February 3, 1955**

Cleveland Indians hurler Early Wynn appears in costume as the Lone Ranger at a minstrel show in Venice, Florida.

## Winfield Seagull Incident

Notorious birdslaughter perpetrated by New York Yankees outfielder Dave Winfield on August 4, 1983, during a game at Exhibition Stadium in Toronto. Winfield was making warm-up throws in center field before the home half of the fifth inning when one of his tosses struck and killed a seagull. ("It's the first time he's hit the cutoff man all season," Yankees manager **Billy Martin** would later quip.) Fans who witnessed the killing began showering Winfield with obscenities and garbage—and at least one outraged bird lover must have called the police. When the game ended, Winfield was arrested and charged with "willfully causing unnecessary cruelty to animals." He faced up to six months in jail and a $500 fine. Charges were dropped the next day after Winfield issued a half-hearted apology: "It is quite unfortunate," he said, "that a fowl of Canada is no longer with us."

## "Woo Woo"

Nickname of Chicago Cubs **superfan Ronnie Wickers**.

# X

## Xenophobia

*See* **Rocker, John**

# "Ya Gotta Believe!"

Rallying cry of the 1973 NL champion New York Mets, who came from last place at the end of August to capture their division and nearly steal the World Series from the heavily favored Oakland A's. Popularized by the club's eccentric relief ace Tug McGraw, the motto was interpreted in the media as an inspirational exhortation along the lines of Barack Obama's "Yes We Can," but it actually represented McGraw's mocking response to Mets chairman M. Donald Grant's awkward attempt at a clubhouse pep talk.

# Yastrzemski's Muttonchops

Funky sideburns grown by straitlaced Boston Red Sox icon Carl Yastrzemski prior to the 1973 season. A turning point in America's long cultural war between "hairs" and "squares," Yaz's decision to grow muttonchops gave thousands of clean-cut kids all over New England permission to let their freak flags fly. By the end of the year, long hair, sideburns, wide collars, and bell bottoms had become the de rigueur off-the-field look for players across baseball. Decades later, Yaz's righteous white boy 'chops were still being name checked by popular culture. In a May 1991 episode of **The Simpsons**, Bart's friend Milhouse wants to spend $30 on a Carl Yastrzemski baseball card from 1973 "when he had big sideburns," but Bart and Martin convince him to go in with them on a copy of *Radioactive Man* No. 1 instead.

## You Could Look It Up

### Random Baseball Trivia

Original plans for Yankee Stadium did not include its legendary 15-foot-high copper façade. Instead, stadium architects at the Osborne Engineering Company called for a triple-decked stadium, with a roof all the way around, designed so that events on the field would be "impenetrable to all human eyes, save those of aviators."

# Year of the Balk

Derisive term for the 1988 baseball season during which an absurd number of balks were called by major league **umpires** as a consequence of a rule change instituted in the off-season. Cardinals manager Whitey Herzog and National League president A. Bartlett Giamatti were the prime movers in the "Balkmania" fiasco. Herzog lobbied for the change after discerning what he said were 19 uncalled balks in the 1987 World Series, which his Cardinals lost in seven games. At Herzog's insistence, Giamatti—who was on Major League Baseball's rules committee—pushed through a change in the wording of the balk rule so that pitchers had to come to a "complete and discernible stop, with both feet on the ground," rather than a mere "complete stop," before delivering the ball to home plate. The tiny change gave **umpires** the liberty they had long sought to gleefully enforce the balk rule. As a result, a total of 924 balk violations were called during the 1988 season—up from 356 the previous season. **Umpires** called 73 balks in the first week of April alone. Seven different pitchers—including one reliever—finished the year with at least 11 balks. Dave Stewart of the Oakland A's established a new single-season balk record of 16. The ridiculous overenforcement of one of the game's most obscure ordinances, which some likened to a municipal police force crackdown on jaywalking, seeped into the wider popular culture and threatened to make a mockery of the game. During a late July appearance at Shea Stadium to take part in ceremonies honoring Mets great Tom Seaver, Giamatti was roundly booed by fans. When the season ended, an embarrassed rules committee quietly reverted the balk rule to its original wording.

## Yips, The

Name for a mysterious mental disorder in which a position player loses the ability to throw, or throw accurately, on the baseball diamond. Famous victims of the Yips include second basemen **Steve Sax** and **Chuck Knoblauch** and catcher **Mackey Sasser**. The pitcher's version of the Yips is known as **Steve Blass Disease**.

## "YMCA"

Gay-themed disco anthem, recorded in 1978 by The Village People, which became an unlikely ballpark sing-along in the 1990s. An irresistibly catchy song that extols the joys of trolling the Young Men's Christian Association for anonymous gay sex, the record peaked at No. 2 on the U.S. singles chart in January of 1979, but lived on in the form of an exuberant group dance wherein participants spell out the letters "YMCA" with their arms. On Opening Day of 1996, the New York Yankees introduced the YMCA dance as part of their between-innings ballpark entertainment—reportedly at the behest of owner **George Steinbrenner**'s son-in-law, Joe Molloy. In the

Jonathan Sacks

bottom of the fifth inning, a five-man groundskeeping crew performed a tightly choreographed rendition of the dance as they raked the infield at Yankee Stadium. Dubbed "the Dragsters," the dirt-dredging troupe became an instant sensation and has executed the routine at every subsequent Yankees home game (save for the occasional substitution of the Macarena in 1996). Other ballparks now routinely include "YMCA" in their repertoire of sing-along favorites.

## Yoo-hoo

Vile-tasting, cramp-inducing milk chocolate beverage that improbably became one of the fastest-growing soft drink brands in America due to the promotional efforts of Hall of Fame catcher Yogi Berra. The Yankees star began publicly endorsing Yoo-hoo in the 1950s, after meeting company president Albert Olivieri at a golf outing in New Jersey. In return for a 15-year personal services contract and the use of his likeness in ads for the product (the most famous of which featured a grinning Berra in a business suit, holding up a bottle of the stuff, and the tagline "It's Me-He for Yoo-hoo!"), the business-savvy backstop asked for and received a minority stake in the company. He retained it well into the 1970s, appearing occasionally in person at New York–area supermarkets to promote the drink and periodically inspecting the Yoo-hoo processing plant in Carlstadt, New Jersey.

## Youppi

Inexplicable orange-furred official mascot of the now-defunct Montreal Expos. The product of a mascot-creation firm, Youppi (whose name means "Hooray" in French) was commissioned by the team's marketing department to replace Souki, the Expos' original space-creature mascot,

Kirk Anderson

in 1979. ("The kids were afraid of him," a club official admitted to the *Washington Post* in 2005.) By contrast, Youppi was engineered to project a teddy bear–like cuddliness akin to Jim Henson's Muppets. (In fact, one of Henson's own designers worked on the Youppi Project.) An orange goliath of indeterminate parentage, Youppi capered on top of the **Olympic Stadium** dugouts in the manner of the **Phillie Phanatic**, to whom he is often compared. Where the Phanatic was universally loved, however, Youppi routinely got under the skin of opposing players and managers—most famously during a 1989 altercation with Dodgers manager Tommy Lasorda which saw Youppi "ejected" from the game by the home-plate umpire. With the dissolution of the Expos following the 2004 season, Youppi switched allegiance to hockey and became the official mascot of the NHL's Montreal Canadiens.

## Z

# Zimmer, Don

Incredibly odd-looking ex–major league infielder who overcame a horrific beaning and a spotty managerial career to become the endearing, Uncle Fester–like public face of the late-1990s New York Yankees. Zimmer's playing career was undistinguished but for a beanball incident that nearly killed him on July 7, 1953. Hit in the head by a pitch thrown by minor leaguer Jim Kirk, Zimmer might never have recovered had surgeons not drilled four holes in his skull to relieve the pressure. (There is an urban myth that Zimmer has a "steel plate" in his head; in fact, his head holes were plugged up with "buttons" made of tantalum, a metal used to make light bulb filaments.) After many years spent beating the bushes as a minor league coach, Zimmer re-emerged in the mid-1970s as the coach and then manager of the Boston Red Sox. Mocked in the press as "Popeye" and "**the Gerbil**," after the

## GREAT NAMES OF THE GAME

# Zoilo

Cuban-born Zoilo Versalles enjoyed a dream season in 1965. He led the league in doubles, triples, and runs scored and propelled the Minnesota Twins to the World Series for the first time in franchise history. The slick-fielding shortstop also earned the second Gold Glove of his career and beat out teammate Tony Oliva for AL MVP. Back problems curtailed Versalles' promising career in 1971 at the age of 31. Zoilo is a variant form of Zola, a name derived from the German word "zoll," meaning "toll" or "cost."

cartoon character and the household rodent whom he strongly resembles, he was routinely undermined by his own players—especially pitcher **Bill Lee**. Run out of town after five mostly disappointing seasons, Zimmer might have been remembered primarily as the ungainly dunce who presided over the Red Sox's epic collapse in the 1978 AL East race against the Yankees had he not re-invented himself yet again as Joe Torre's kindly bench coach during New York's dynastic run from 1996 to 2003. This final, sympathetic image of Zimmer was solidified by two events: Zimmer's accidental beaning in 1999 by a ball off the bat of Yankees second baseman **Chuck Knoblauch** (after which he emerged wearing an army helmet with "Zim" painted on the side) and a celebrated brawl with the Boston Red Sox at an ALCS game in 2003, during which Red Sox ace Pedro Martinez threw the 72-year-old grandfather to the ground in a fit of rage.

# Zonk

Nickname for longtime Texas Rangers **superfan John Lanzillo**.

# Acknowledgements

The author would like to thank Tom Bast, Adam Motin, Paul Petrowsky, and everyone at Triumph Books for their valuable contributions to this book. Also, thanks to all the fans who generously contributed their photos to this project.

# Selected Bibliography

Alexander, Charles C. *Ty Cobb*. New York, NY: Oxford University Press, 1984.

Bouton, Jim. *Ball Four*. New York, NY: Dell, 1970.

Bowman, John, and Joel Zoss. *Diamonds in the Rough: The Untold History of Baseball*. New York, NY: Macmillan, 1989.

Burns, Ken. *Baseball: An Illustrated History*. New York, NY: Alfred A. Knopf, Inc. 1994.

Colbert, David, editor. *Baseball: The National Pastime in Art and Literature*. New York: Time Life Books, 2001.

Dark, Alvin and John Underwood. *When in Doubt, Fire the Manager*. New York, NY: Dutton, 1980.

Dickson, Paul. *Baseball's Greatest Quotations*. New York, NY: HarperCollins, 1991.

Dickson, Paul. *New Dickson Baseball Dictionary, The*. New York, NY: Harcourt, Brace and Co., 1999.

Enders, Eric. *Ballparks: Then and Now*. San Diego, CA: Thunder Bay Press, 2002.

Garagiola, Joe. *Baseball Is a Funny Game*. New York, NY: Bantam Doubleday Dell, 1974.

Golenbock, Peter. *Wrigleyville: A Magical History Tour of the Chicago Cubs*. New York, NY: St. Martin's Press. 1996.

Gutman, Dan. *Baseball Babylon: From the Black Sox to Pete Rose, the Real Stories Behind the Scandals that Rocked the Game*. New York, NY: Penguin, 1992.

Hall, Donald. *Dock Ellis in the Country of Baseball*. New York, NY: Simon & Schuster, 1976.

James, Bill. *The Bill James Historical Baseball Abstract*. New York: Villard Books, 1985.

Lee, Bill with Jim Prime. *Baseball Eccentrics: The Most Entertaining, Outrageous, and Unforgettable Characters in the Game*. Chicago, IL: Triumph Books, 2007.

Leventhal, Josh and MacMurray, Jessica. *Take Me Out to the Ballpark: An Illustrated Tour of Baseball Parks Past and Present* (Revised Edition). New York, NY: Black Dog & Leventhal Publishers, 2003.

Martin, Billy and Peter Golenbock. *Number 1*. New York, NY: Delacorte, 1980.

Martinez, David H. *The Book of Baseball Literacy*. New York, NY: Plume, 1996.

McBride, Joseph. *High and Inside: An A-to-Z Guide to the Language of Baseball*. Lincolnwood, IL: Contemporary Books, 1997.

National Geographic Society. *Baseball as America: Seeing Ourselves Through Our National Game*. Washington, D.C.: National Geographic Society, 2002.

Neyer, Rob. *Rob Neyer's Big Book of Baseball Legends: The Truth, the Lies, and Everything Else*. New York, NY: Fireside, 2008.

Peary, Danny. *Cult Baseball Players*. New York, NY: Simon & Schuster, 1990.

Pepe, Phil. *Talkin' Baseball: An Oral History of Baseball in the 1970s*. New York, NY: Ballantine Books, 1998.

Pietrusza, David. *Baseball, The Biographical Encyclopedia*. New York, NY: Total Sports, 2000.

Porter, David. *Biographical Dictionary of American Sports: Baseball*. Westport, CT: Greenwood Press, 1987.

Purdy, Dennis. *The Team by Team Encyclopedia of Major League Baseball*. New York, NY: Workman Publishing, 2006.

Rielly, Edward J. *Baseball: An Encyclopedia of Popular Culture*. Santa Barbara, CA: ABC-CLIO, 2000.

Ritter, Lawrence S. *The Glory of Their Times: The Story of the Early Days of Baseball by the Men Who Played It*. New York, NY: Vintage Books, 1985.

Scheinin, Richard. *Field of Screams: The Dark Underside of America's National Pastime*. New York, NY: W. W. Norton & Company, 1994.

Shalin, Bruce. *Oddballs*. New York, NY: Penguin, 1990.

Shannon, Bill and Kalinsky, George. *The Ballparks*. New York, NY: Hawthorn Books, 1975.

Skipper, James. *Baseball Nicknames: A Dictionary of Origins and Meanings*. Jefferson, NC: McFarland, 1992.

Stone, Steve and Barry Rozner. *Where's Harry?* Dallas, TX: Taylor Publishing, 1999.

Thorn, John., Palmer, Pete., Gershman, Michael.,and Pietrusza, David. *Total Baseball: The Official Encyclopedia of Major League Baseball*. New York, NY: Viking Press., 1997.

Vrusho, Spike. *Benchclearing: Baseball's Greatest Fights and Riots*. Guilford, CT: The Lyons Press, 2008.

Ward, Geoffrey. *Baseball: An Illustrated History*. New York, NY: Knopf, 1994.

Watts, Robert G. and A. Terry Bahill. *Keep Your Eye on the Ball: The Science and Folklore of Baseball*. New York, NY: W. H. Freeman and Co., 1990.

Will, George F. *Men At Work: The Craft of Baseball*. New York, NY: Harper & Row Perennial Library, 1990.

Zumsteg, Derek. *The Cheater's Guide to Baseball*. New York, NY: Houghton Mifflin Company, 2007.

# About the Author

Robert Schnakenberg is a member of the Society for American Baseball Research. He is the author of numerous books of irreverent nonfiction, including *Distory: A Treasury of Historical Insults*, *The Encyclopedia Shatnerica*, and *Secret Lives of Great Filmmakers*. Visit him online at www.robertschnakenberg.com.